Postcolonial Life-

Postcolonial Life-Writing offers a sustained critique of this increasingly visible and influential field on cultural production.

Bart Moore-Gilbert considers the relationship between postcolonial life-writing and its western analogues, identifying the key characteristics that differentiate the genre in the postcolonial context. Focusing particularly on writing styles and narrative conceptions of the Self, this book uncovers a distinctive parallel tradition of auto/biographical writing and analyses its cultural and political significance.

Original and provocative, this book brings together the two distinct fields of Postcolonial Studies and Auto/biography Studies in a fruitful and much-needed dialogue.

Bart Moore-Gilbert is Professor of Postcolonial Studies at Goldsmiths, University of London. His publications include *Kipling and 'Orientalism'*; *Postcolonial Theory: Contexts, Practicesp; Politics, Writing India: British Representations of India 1757–1990*; and *Hanif Kureishi*.

POSTCOLONIAL LITERATURES

Edited in collaboration with the Centre for Colonial and Postcolonial Studies, University of Kent at Canterbury, this series presents a wide range of research into postcolonial literatures by specialists in the field. Volumes will concentrate on writers and writing originating in previously (or presently) colonized areas, and will include material from non-Anglophone as well as Anglophone colonies and literatures. The series will also include collections of important essays from older journals, and re-issues of classic texts on postcolonial subjects. Routledge is pleased to invite proposals for new books in the series. Interested authors should contact Caroline Rooney or Donna Landry at the Centre for Colonial and Postcolonial Studies, University of Kent at Canterbury, or Routledge's Commissioning Editor for Literature.

The series comprises three strands:

Routledge Research in Postcolonial Literatures is a forum for innovative new research intended for a specialist readership. Published in hardback, titles include:

Postcolonial Literatures makes available in paperback important work in the field. Hardback editions of these titles are also available, some published earlier in the *Routledge Research* strand of the series. Titles in paperback include:

Readings in Postcolonial Literatures offers collections of important essays from journals or classic texts in the field. Titles include:

Postcolonial Life-Writing

Culture, politics and self-representation

Bart Moore-Gilbert

 Routledge
Taylor & Francis Group

LONDON AND NEW YORK

First edition published 2009 by Routledge
2 Park Square, Milton Park, Abingdon, Oxon OX14 4RN

Simultaneously published in the USA and Canada
by Routledge
270 Madison Ave, New York, NY 10016

Routledge is an imprint of the Taylor & Francis Group, an informa business

© 2009 Bart Moore-Gilbert

Typeset in Baskerville by
Taylor & Francis Books
Printed and bound in Great Britain by
CPI Antony Rowe, Chippenham, Wiltshire

British Library Cataloguing in Publication Data
A catalogue record for this book is available from the British Library

Library of Congress Cataloging in Publication Data
Moore-Gilbert, B. J., 1952-
    Postcolonial life-writing : culture, politics, and self-representation /
Bart Moore-Gilbert. – 1st ed.
        p. cm. – (Routledge research in postcolonial literatures)
    Includes bibliographical references and index.
    1. Autobiography. 2. Commonwealth literature (English)–History and
criticism. 3. Authors, Commonwealth–Biography–History and criticism. 4. Self
in literature. 5. Identity (Psychology) in literature. 6. Commonwealth countries–
In literature. 7. Postcolonialism in literature. 8. Biography as a literary form.
I.   Title.
    PR9080.5.M66 2009
    820.9'35–dc22
                        2008052260

ISBN10: 0-415-44299-0 (hbk)
ISBN10: 0-415-44300-8 (pbk)
ISBN10: 0-203-87624-5 (ebk)

ISBN13: 978-0-415-44299-2 (hbk)
ISBN13: 978-0-415-44300-5 (pbk)
ISBN13: 978-0-203-87624-4 (ebk)

In memoriam Edward W. Said, 1935–2003

'Speak Truth to Power'

Contents

Acknowledgements

Many people have aided me in this project. I'd particularly like to thank Nadje el-Ali, Suad Amiry, Santiago Borja, Sophia Brown, Anthony Carrigan, Assia Djebar, Alan Downie, Peter Dunwoodie, Nelida Fuccaro, Sara Suleri Goodyear, Anna Hartnell, Jane Hiddleston, Philip Holden, Stephanie Jones, Debra Kelly, Javed Majeed, Mairi Neeves, Sarah O'Mahoney, Brett St Louis, Julia Watson, Gillian Whitlock and Amina Yaqin. Caroline Rooney has proved an exceptionally supportive and informed series editor. Without Beth Jackson's editorial assistance with the footnotes, the text would have been unconscionably delayed. Belinda Moore-Gilbert also helped with checking references at a crucial stage. I'm extremely grateful to both Sally Knyvette and Bernadette Buckley for checking the index with me, and to the latter for devoting holiday time to getting her hands dirty in 'the filthy workshop of creation'.

Successive cadres of MA students at Goldsmiths have sharpened my thinking by vigorously debating the issues addressed here on my 'Postcolonial Life-Writing' module. I would also like to thank the College for granting me a sabbatical between October–December, 2007; the AHRC for a matching term's leave, January–March, 2008; the Department of English and Comparative Literature for providing additional financial support; and a final massive thanks to Maria MacDonald for abundant help with the boring bits.

Introduction

This text aims to provide the first detailed investigation of the distinctive properties of postcolonial life-writing as a branch of auto/biographical[1] literatures. In doing so, it also seeks to promote closer connections between two sub-fields of cultural criticism, Postcolonial and Auto/biography Studies, which have hitherto insufficiently engaged with each other. This lack of sustained dialogue is surprising given how much postcolonial life-writing has flourished since the decolonisation of European empires. As far back as 1973, the eminent Auto/biography critic James Olney described African examples as already 'plentiful'[2] and demand for such work shows no sign of diminishing. To cite just one recent instance, Ishmael Beah's *A Long Way Gone: Memoirs of a Boy Soldier* (2007) sold 700,000 copies within months of publication.[3] However, there has long been a market for such texts. One precursor form of postcolonial life-writing, the slave narratives of figures like Ukawsaw Gronniosaw, John Marrant and Olaudah Equiano (whose *Interesting Narrative* (1789), discussed in Chapter 1, went through nine editions in its author's lifetime alone), began to circulate from as early as 1770. This is roughly the same moment as Rousseau's *Confessions*, widely regarded as the inaugural instance of western autobiography in a recognisably modern form. Life-writing became an increasingly popular genre in the Indian sub-continent in the nineteenth century and by the end of the Second World War, a considerable number of auto/biographies had been written by colonised subjects across many other regions of the European empires.[4]

Auto/biography Studies has thus far paid little detailed attention to this rich body of work. Adopting Sidonie Smith and Julia Watson's division of the critical formation into three periods,[5] one can detect some interest in non-western autobiography in the first phase, which lasts roughly from the late nineteenth century to the Second World War. Georg Misch's *A History of Autobiography in Antiquity* (1907), notably, discussed a range of examples in the classical period, concluding as follows: 'In the literature of various races, not only European ... there appear at a certain stage of development writings of the autobiographical type, and the tendency to self-portrayal.'[6] Yet Misch is adamant that 'a history of autobiography, since it has to deal with the more complicated phenomena of mental life, cannot reach back to the primitive peoples'.[7] This judgement rests not, as one might expect, on questions of 'literacy' or the transmissibility of cultural artefacts, but on the issue of sophistication of consciousness which, Misch implies, belongs only to the 'advanced' peoples. In any case, his work did little to redirect fellow-critics in the West away from their customarily parochial geo-cultural focus. Indeed, in the second phase of Auto/biography Studies, which lasts until approximately 1980 and is dominated by figures like Georges Gusdorf and Roy Pascal, there is something of a disavowal of Misch's catholic tastes and comparative cultural relativism. Gusdorf's seminal essay, 'Conditions and Limits of Autobiography' (1956), insists that the genre 'expresses a concern peculiar to Western man' and that it is 'the late product of a specific civilisation'.[8] The 'unconsciousness of personality' allegedly characteristic of 'primitive' societies and their lack of a proper sense of historical temporality, within which the development of self-reflecting individuals can be charted, are Gusdorf's primary explanations of why autobiography emerged in the West rather than elsewhere. Pascal's *Design and Truth in Autobiography* (1960) operates within similarly ethnocentric conceptual parameters:

> It is beyond my scope to suggest why autobiography does not come into being outside Europe, and the existence of a work such as Bàbur's memoirs of the sixteenth century, which would occupy a significant place in the history of autobiography had it belonged to Europe, makes one hesitate to generalise. But there remains no doubt that autobiography is essentially European.[9]

While this argument is transparently circular, it is equally clear that only the non-European provenance of the Moghul Emperor's text disqualifies it from belonging in the genre.

One might infer from such readings that autobiography in the non-western world is a secondary and belated practice, which seeks merely to replicate the norms and conventions of the genre as it has developed in the West. As such, Gusdorf claims that its emergence elsewhere attests to the success of the West's imperial project. Indeed, he somewhat ominously suggests that the genre has 'been of good use in [the West's] systematic conquest of the universe'; in the course of this process,

> [it] has communicated to men [*sic*] of other cultures; but those men will thereby have been annexed by a sort of intellectual colonizing to a mentality that was not their own. When Gandhi tells his own story, he is using Western means to defend the East.[10]

This blatantly ignores Gandhi's explicit disavowal that – despite his title, *An Autobiography* (1927–29) – he is deploying the genre as conventionally understood in the West,[11] a position embraced by many other postcolonial life-writers, as will be seen.

The third phase of Auto/biography Studies begins with texts such as Philippe Lejeune's 'Autobiographical Pact' of 1975 (but not translated into English until 1982), Paul de Man's 'Autobiography as De-Facement' (1979), William

Spengemann's *The Forms of Autobiography* (1980) and Olney's landmark edited collection, *Autobiography: Essays Theoretical and Critical* (1980). For much of this period, too, postcolonial life-writing remained largely invisible within the sub-field. Lejeune, de Man and Spengemann address the western canon exclusively. By contrast, Olney's volume includes discussion of contemporary African American writing (while only cursorily acknowledging slave narratives), thus making ethnicity an issue in mainstream Auto/biography Studies. However, it offers no engagement with more recent postcolonial life-writing, a surprising omission given Olney's own ground-breaking work on African autobiography. Indeed, his introductory essay rather sneers at Misch's misdirected interest in non-western analogues of the genre.[12] The continuing influence of Gusdorfian perspectives on the early part, at least, of this most recent phase of Auto/biography Studies is evident in Richard Coe's *When the Grass Was Taller* (1984), an examination of childhood autobiography, which asserts that

> the Childhood [*sic*] is a genre which presupposes a sophisticated culture. It is inconceivable among primitives; even in the contemporary Third World, it emerges only in imitation of culturally more advanced models. It demands a sense of form, and the intellectual ability to adapt the ill-balanced and misshapen material of experience to the harmony of literary expression without overmuch distortion of the original truth … It demands self-knowledge; it demands also the most delicately graded sense of values relating the individual to the community.[13]

It is perhaps redundant to detail how much of this account is structured by the language of stereotype and ideas of cultural/racial hierarchy which are alike anathema to Postcolonial Studies.

In that field, engagement with auto/biographical forms has been both more long-standing than in Auto/biography Studies and, as one might expect, more serious and sympathetic. These genres play no role in Edward Said's analysis of the discourses shaping imperial relations in *Orientalism* (1978), widely acknowledged as the founding text of modern Postcolonial Studies. However, they were already being studied in one precursor formation, Commonwealth Literary Studies,[14] culminating in the ambitious preliminary attempt by Doireann MacDermott to survey the varieties of 'Commonwealth' auto/biography.[15] Since then, there have been further regional studies of the genre as it has developed in, for example, Australia, the Caribbean and North Africa.[16] Cross-regional comparative work has also flourished. For example, Alfred Hornung and Ernstpeter Ruhe analyse Anglophone and Francophone autobiographical writings, predominantly fictional in kind, from the Caribbean and *Maghreb*.[17] Drawing on feminism and 'Black Studies', by contrast, Françoise Lionnet has investigated correlations between African American and postcolonial women's life-writing, again predominantly of fictional kinds.[18] Gillian Whitlock, in turn, has provided a substantial feminist-inflected comparison of non-fictional life-writing by colonial and postcolonial women.[19] Equally notable are the emerging explorations of more specific aspects of the field. For example, both Javed Majeed and Philip Holden examine nationalist autobiography in the (former) British Empire, which they see as structurally linked to larger questions of political self-representation.[20] More recently, Whitlock addresses autobiographical representation in non-traditional forms and media in a framework which extends from the postcolonial context to the contemporary non-West more widely.[21] Also worthy of mention, though his strategic aims are tangential to both my project and much of the work surveyed above, is the work of David Huddart, who argues that autobiography is a central explanatory category for postcolonial theory.[22]

Despite these considerable achievements, much remains to be done to provide a convincing general account of postcolonial life-writing as well as to effect a satisfactory dialogue between the sub-fields of Postcolonial and Auto/biography Studies. A number of obstacles to achieving these aims present themselves in the work of postcolonial colleagues described above. One is that the focus of much of the material discussed in the previous paragraph has been on *fictional* auto/biography (see Chapter 5 for a discussion of this apparently oxymoronic conjunction of genres). Where this is not the case, the critics concerned have tended to limit themselves *either* to men's *or* women's writing, rarely considering them together. Finally, the geo-cultural and historical range of many of my predecessors is often too limited both geographically (especially in the case of work confined to one or two regions) and historically (the emphasis is overwhelmingly on the period since 1960) to support convincing generalisation about the distinctive attributes of postcolonial life-writing as a specific sub-genre of auto/biographical writing. These are all problems which I will address in the course of this monograph.

Nor has there been an adequately rigorous theorisation either of postcolonial life-writing or of its relation to auto/biographical writing in the West. The reluctance to theorise the specific properties of the former field is understandable. The difficulty of defining the larger generic field to which it belongs is evident from the beginnings of modern Auto/biography Studies. Thus, in 1907, Misch complained that the genre 'defies classification'.[23] Seven decades of institutional criticism later, Olney despaired that: 'There is no way to bring autobiography to heel as a literary genre with its own proper form, terminology, and observances.'[24] The problem has been exacerbated by the advent of post-structuralism, which not only threatens 'the end of autobiography',[25] but of genre itself as an analytical category.[26] The key question these debates raise for my strategic project is this: without a stable set of definitions of autobiography as practised in the West, how can its postcolonial analogues be distinguished generically? The task is further complicated by the heterogeneity of contexts and cultures from which postcolonial life-writing has emerged, not to mention the range of sub-forms it operates within – from autobiography as conventionally understood, through memoir, to *testimonio*, diary, email and blogging. (This poses the further danger of flattening such sub-generic diversity to fit a single totalising model.)

However, similar problems have attended efforts to define 'the postcolonial novel' or 'postcolonial poetry' – without preventing some convincing taxonomies of these equally elastic and fissile genres.[27] Moreover, considerable work has in fact been done in the past two decades within Auto/biography Studies itself towards addressing the challenge identified by Misch and Olney, on the one hand, and post-structuralism, on the other. Gender perspectives have perhaps proved most productive in renewed attempts to elaborate a poetics of auto-biography. Following Estelle Jelinek's edited collection, *Women's Autobiography: Essays in Criticism* (1980) – another landmark in the emergence of the third phase of Auto/biography Studies and widely cited as the inaugural text of its kind[28] – a large body of feminist work has sought to anatomise the specificities of women's life-writing and to demonstrate how those properties led to its critical margin-alisation relative to the male tradition. This project has proved enormously suc-cessful, making women's life-writing far more visible than was the case in the first two phases of Auto/biography Studies and rendering the third much more sen-sitive to the relationship between gender and genre. Thus, as Debra Kelly sug-gests in her recent study of North African autobiographical discourse, there may be considerable mileage for postcolonial colleagues in adapting some of the insights and techniques of feminist inflections of Auto/biography Studies to our own purposes. 'Of particular relevance,' Kelly argues, 'is the analysis of the alternative and diverse practices of women writers that call into question the assumptions made by Western male autobiography and by histories of the development of the genre written by male critics.'[29]

Nonetheless, while I'm grateful for such leads and intend to follow them up (and extend them), such a methodological template poses potential problems for my project. Kelly ultimately rationalises its advantages by claiming that: 'Women share many of the characteristics of the colonized subject ... to the extent that some commentators have spoken of the need for a "self-decolonization" of the female subject.'[30] However, leaving aside the vexed issue of the comparability of these two social constituencies – and, indeed, the compatibility of feminist and postcolonial critical practices[31] – western feminist inflections of Auto/biography Studies have often proved no more open to postcolonial life-writing than the male critical tradition. Thus, whereas contemporary African American women's life-writing is addressed by Jelinek's volume, its postcolonial analogues are not. And while subsequent collections like Domna Stanton's *The Female Autograph* (1984) and Bella Brodzki and Celeste Schenck's *Life-Lines* (1988) each include a single chapter on postcolonial women life-writers, Janet Gunn's *Autobiography* (1982), Sidonie Smith's *A Poetics of Women's Autobiography* (1987) and Shari Benstock's anthology, *The Private Self* (1988), ignore them. It was not until Smith and Watson's landmark collection, *De/Colonizing the Subject: The Politics of Gender in Women's Autobiography* (1992) that western feminist auto/biographical criticism began to acknowledge postcolonial women's life-writing in any sustained way. However, the volume's scope is much wider than its main title might suggest, including considerable and sympathetic attention to autobiographical work by western women *colonisers*.[32] And in its treatment of issues relating to the Self-representation of non-dominant ethnicities, the focus is as much on writing from US-based minorities (Chicano, Native American and African American) as postcolonial constituencies. Moreover,

some of the conclusions drawn about the latter field are debatable, if not damagingly essentialising. For example, in an otherwise acute piece on Leila Khaled,
which remedies her earlier monograph's oversights, Janet Gunn argued that
'Third World autobiography'

> differs in two respects from mainstream Western autobiography, both male
> and female. First it involves an unmasking or what I have called a denos-
> talgizing of the past; second, it orients itself toward a liberated society in the
> future. In the first respect, it is a form of resistance literature; in the second, it
> is a form of utopian literature.[33]

While there are suggestive ideas here, to which I will return (see Chapter 7
especially), Gunn's generalisation rests on a single text by a Palestinian revolutionary. Certainly, Khaled's predicament, her motive for telling her story, her
choice of form and conception of audience, are not necessarily representative of a
good deal of postcolonial life-writing, let alone of 'Third World autobiography',
as will be demonstrated.

The limited impact made by this strand of Smith and Watson's volume on
subsequent feminist work in Auto/biography Studies is evident in more recent
critical overviews of the genre. Despite the many invaluable functions it performs – and recognition of the theoretical importance of greater attention to
issues of ethnicity – Laura Marcus's *Auto/biographical Discourses* (1994), for example,
finds minimal space for analysis of examples of postcolonial life-writing or the
discourses surrounding it. Linda Anderson's *Autobiography* (2001) discusses only two
postcolonial texts in a sub-section towards the end of her book. Perhaps more
surprisingly, in view of the lead given both by *De/Colonizing the Subject* and the
similar emphasis on postcolonial women's experience in their subsequent edited
collection, *Women, Autobiography, Theory: A Reader* (1998), Smith and Watson's latest
survey of the field, *Reading Autobiography* (2001), is barely more forthcoming than
Marcus and Anderson. By its own admission, it offers only 'a glimpse at practices
of life narration outside the West'.[34]

One might consider this minimal attention to postcolonial life-writing justifiable
in view of the vast range of other work which each of these three texts has to
cover in considering auto/biographical genres across their historical range. On
the other hand, feminist interventions within Auto/biography Studies might be
deemed to contribute to the problem of the continuing relative critical invisibility
of postcolonial life-writing. This is particularly true in relation to writing by men.
Of the work cited in the last two paragraphs, only Anderson offers any engagement with male writers, albeit that her discussion of Ondaatje and Naipaul is
extremely compressed. Yet there is no theoretical justification for this omission,
especially insofar as part of the feminist project is to critique patriarchal discourse,
particularly its representations of women. The lacuna is especially surprising given
that, like Buchi Emecheta's *Head Above Water* (1986), much postcolonial women's
life-writing is animated not so much by a wish to escape the oppressions of (neo)
colonialism as those of an indigenous patriarchy which seeks to (re)position

gender identities within coercive discourses of tradition and authenticity, whether or not as part of the struggle against foreign domination.[35] (As will be seen, these and more 'modernist'[36] forms of patriarchy are consistently reproduced, as well as contested, in life-writing by postcolonial men.) Seen alongside its relative neglect of postcolonial women life-writers, then, one might even be tempted to argue in Spivakian terms that the consolidation of the feminist Subject of a revised Auto/biography Studies, which the critics I've mentioned have laudably done so much to accomplish, has been achieved partly at the expense of the widespread occlusion of contributions made to the genres of life-writing by the (formerly) colonised.[37] Thus, there is considerable justification in Linda Warley's complaint, made long after the feminist reconstitution of Auto/biography Studies was underway, that 'theoretical formulations of the poetics of autobiography by and large continue to ignore post-colonial writings ... Displaying an all too familiar geographic and ethnocentric bias, [auto/biographical] theory is made in the West and it speaks of the West.'[38] Drawing on Warley's argument, I will attempt in particular to demonstrate that greater attention to male postcolonial life-writing might have provided some feminist critics with pause for thought before claiming certain attributes of western women's life-writing as specific to that sub-genre.

However, with these cautions in mind, the interventions within Auto/biography Studies described above have, as Kelly suggests, much to offer the critic interested in the strategic issues addressed by this volume. If feminism challenges the conflation of male subjectivity with 'the human',[39] postcolonialists question the equally common, if often only implicit, historical equation of the (theoretically ungendered) western Self with 'the human'. Equally, if feminist critics critique the traditional supposition that autobiographical writing is a male (as well as middle-class and heterosexual) preserve, so postcolonial frameworks can interrogate the idea that it is also a distinctively western cultural practice.[40] Above all, in seeking to identify those aspects of women's life-writing which have traditionally precluded such work from serious critical attention within the traditionally male-dominated formation of Auto/biography Studies, feminist critics provide templates for defining what is *sui generis* about its postcolonial equivalents. The difference of women's life-writing from canonical western male autobiography has been asserted in three distinct areas, which I will consider in turn in relation to the postcolonial field. These are: first, thematics of subjectivity; second, issues of form; and third, questions surrounding the social function/cultural politics of life-writing.

In terms of the thematics of subjectivity, I am guided by Marcus's argument that 'the gender [im]balance of autobiographical history cannot be corrected simply by adding more women to the list; basic suppositions about subjectivity and identity underlying autobiographical theories have to be shifted.'[41] In seeking to avoid a reinscription of patriarchal ideas about women's difference grounded in essentialist ideas about the 'nature' of gender, feminist auto/biography critics have tended to assert the distinctiveness of women's 'subjectivity and identity' on the basis of the specific modes of socialisation and cultural insertion of each sex. Work as varied as Nancy Chodorow on the social reproduction of gender, Judith

Butler's on its performativity and the psychoanalytically-inflected French philosophy of Hélène Cixous, Luce Irigaray and Julia Kristeva has all proved influential
in critiques of the assumptions governing the 'nature' of personhood in traditional
Auto/biography Studies.[42] As a result, three aspects of women's subjectivity in
particular have been identified as the source of important differences of emphasis
between auto/biographical writing by western men and women.

First, it is regularly argued that women's life-writing is characterised by a
rejection of the model of sovereign, centred, unified Selfhood allegedly constructed in western male autobiography. From its first phase until well into the
third, Auto/biography Studies has represented the Subject of canonical autobiography 'as the whole and coherent human being who underwrites ... the
possibility of knowledge about the self'.[43] By contrast, women's life-writing is
widely deemed to promote models of dispersed and decentred subjectivity. Thus,
Sidonie Smith proposes that women writers look 'to the politics of fragmentation'
as a means to counter masculinist notions of Selfhood.[44] Second, feminist critics
repeatedly claim of canonical autobiographers that a primary concern is the
establishment of an autonomous personhood which is clearly marked off from the
author's circumscribing social world. By contrast, women's life-writing is often
presumed to offer a more dialogical conception of Selfhood as something which is
essentially social and relational. Leigh Gilmore usefully summarises this line of
argument as follows (while also warning against the dangers of reification):

> men are autonomous individuals with inflexible ego boundaries who write
> autobiographies that ... place the self at the center of the drama. Women, by
> contrast, have flexible ego boundaries, develop a view of the world char-
> acterized by relationships ... and therefore represent the self in relation to
> 'others'.[45]

Third, critics like Shirley Neuman suggest that: 'Bodies rarely feature in [cano-
nical male] autobiography.'[46] By contrast, while recognising the dangers of confirming patriarchal stereotypes which equate Woman with Body, many women
life-writers – and their critical advocates – have insisted on the constitutive role of
a (reconceptualised) discourse of embodiment to women's subjectivity. As Hélène
Cixous, for example, argues: 'By writing her self, woman will return to the body
which has been more than confiscated from her, which has been turned into the
uncanny stranger on display ... Inscribe the breath of the whole woman.'[47]

Such strategic claims invite the question of whether there exist conceptions of
Selfhood within the postcolonial domain which are specific to the cultures
involved, such that what Smith and Watson, following Paul Smith, call the
'ideological "I"'[48] of postcolonial life-writing might be deemed to differ in significant ways from its western counterparts. To find answers, it is necessary to
return to a line of inquiry which has been theoretically available to Auto/bio-
graphy Studies since Misch alerted his readers to 'potentialities of human nature
that are in strange contrast with our European attitudes toward the individual
self'.[49] In the first instance, such differences might be understood to originate in

material and historical particularities of social arrangements in non-western cultures which subtend the socialisation and cultural insertion of its subjects. Thus, the formation of selfhood in a culture with an enlarged and more plastic conception of (extended) family is, in principle, likely to differ in terms of its patterns of individuation and psychic development to what characterises the western bourgeois nuclear (or single-parent) family. Conversely, in a context like the Caribbean, where the plantation economy fatally undermined the institution of family among the enslaved, one might anticipate a more radical deviation from the normative conceptions of Selfhood and identity-formation in the West. Indeed, such factors lead Sandra Pouchet Paquet, for example, to argue for the existence of a specifically 'Caribbean architecture of consciousness'.[50]

Some non-western cultures clearly articulate ideologies, epistemologies and cosmogonies which are often strikingly at odds with the norms of, notably, the secular post-Enlightenment West. This is the thrust of the critique by Wole Soyinka (see Chapter 4) of George Thomson's writing on Greek drama, in the course of which the Nigerian writer insists that his colleague's conception of tragic interiority 'betrays a Eurocentric conditioning or alienation':

> To describe a *collective* inner world as a fantasy is not intelligible [in the West African context], for the nature of an inner world in a cohesive society is the essentialisation of a rational world-view, one which is elicited from the reality of social and natural experience and from the integrated reality of racial myths into a living morality.[51]

There is much one might want to question here; for example, whether West African society was ever as cohesive as Soyinka implies; whether men and women experience that 'collective reality' in the same way; how the collective inner world is accessed or mediated; and what Soyinka means by 'racial myths'. However, the essential theoretical point is that any auto/biographical writer working within an epistemology of 'collective inner worlds', partly derived from specific 'racial myths', is likely to have a different conception of psyche and Selfhood to what usually obtains in the West, which one might also expect to be reflected in his/her life-writing.

It is therefore no surprise, perhaps, that a variety of postcolonial commentators have attempted to 'provincialise'[52] western paradigms of Selfhood and psychic development – and thereby, by inference, of western auto/biographical subjectivity. While one might assume that Soyinka would be at least somewhat sympathetic to a figure like Jung, given the latter's interest in ideas of the 'collective unconscious', this is not the case. For the Nigerian writer, Jung's model of psychic economy is compromised disastrously by being predicated on a racial schema which is the product of colonial histories.[53] Freud's work has been subjected to similar critique by Frantz Fanon. *Black Skin, White Masks* (1952) famously claimed that the conditions of Antillean society meant that 'the Oedipus complex' had no writ there.[54] Ashis Nandy, meanwhile, has described Freud's work as 'the West's major *ethno*psychology', clearly relativising its applicability to the Indian context which is the focus of his voluminous work.[55] More recently, Gayatri Spivak has argued that the 'regulative psychobiographies' elaborated in both western psychoanalysis *and* feminist revisions of that body of work cannot be applied unthinkingly to subaltern women in the (former) colonies.[56]

To this extent, one might assume that postcolonial auto/biographical subjectivity can be relatively easily distinguished from its western analogues. Throughout its history, indeed, postcolonial life-writing has sometimes advanced conceptions of personhood which are highly culturally specific. For example, it has been argued that Equiano's sense of Selfhood is predicated on the Igbo concept of *chi*, familiar to readers of Achebe's *Things Fall Apart* (1958).[57] Equally, the model of personhood in Gandhi's *An Autobiography* is profoundly influenced by Hindu beliefs in *karma*, transcendence of ego and the cyclical reincarnation of souls. The 'regulative psychobiography' which underpins Kamala Das's *My Story* (1976) is equally indebted to (while in some respects also resistant to) Hindu tradition, as Shirley Lim argues.[58] The idea of *chi* makes a powerful return in Buchi Emecheta's *Head Above Water*, surviving the writer's translation from Lagos to London unscathed. However, such explicit articulations of (mono-)culturally specific conceptions of Selfhood are in fact relatively rare within postcolonial life-writing, in European languages at least (Gandhi wrote in Gujarati). Even authors whom one might expect to elaborate such paradigms of personhood often do not do so. Indeed, the model elaborated in Soyinka's *Aké* (1981) in many ways, ironically, conforms to the typology offered by Coe's *When the Grass Was Taller*, despite its invocation of the mythopoesis of Ogun (see Chapter 4).

This pattern does not, however, necessarily support Gusdorf's argument about the essentially derivative nature of non-western life-writing, even in its plotting of autobiographical subjectivity. Rather, the postcolonial sub-genre marks its difference from canonical western norms, in the first instance, by endorsing all three thematics of subjectivity identified by feminist critics in women's life-writing (the important qualifications to this pattern will be discussed in due course). However, the first twist in the argument is that these thematics are equally characteristic of male postcolonial life-writers. Chapter 1 will demonstrate that decentred models of personhood can be traced back to the precursor forms of male postcolonial life-writing, including Equiano's *Interesting Narrative*, beginning with its apparently radically contradictory Self-description on the title page. Equally, if postcolonial women life-writers share the conviction of many western counterparts about the relationality of auto/biographical subjectivity – as their equally recurrent focus on mother/daughter relationships, for example, suggests – Chapter 2 will argue that male colleagues, too, often stress comparably important and explicit links between themselves, their immediate circles and society more broadly. This is particularly obvious in the writing of self-conscious nationalists, where the author may seek to make himself representative of, or spokesman for, the collective to which he belongs – even as he characteristically stresses his 'unique' personal qualifications for doing so. (I don't wish to imply, however, that postcolonial women focus only on the domestic sphere and their male colleagues only on the public, thus repeating the kind of gender distinctions used in traditional Auto/biography

Studies to discriminate against women's life-writing.) As Chapter 3 will argue, much the same argument can be made about the crucial role of embodiment in male postcolonial auto/biographical subjectivity, from Equiano to Said, as feminist critics have offered in relation to women's life-writing.

However useful the taxonomies of auto/biographical Selfhood provided by feminist critics may be in the first instance, it is also further necessary to recognise that each thematic of subjectivity is often inflected quite differently in the postcolonial context by writers of *both* genders. For example, if feminist criticism of women's life-writing characteristically ascribes the dispersal of the Subject to the specific patterns of cultural insertion and socialisation of western women, the explanation is sometimes quite different in postcolonial life-writing. There, decentred subjectivity is often represented as one effect of the material histories and relations of colonialism, in which new and occasionally radically conflicting identities are inscribed in palimpsestic fashion on the subaltern, sometimes by force. Equally, in the context of debates about the relationality of auto/biographical Selfhood, it is extremely rare to find contemporary western women's life-writing espousing nationalism as an axis of (self-)identification. In relation to issues of embodiment, finally, it is even more unusual to find any discussion of ethnicity as a dimension of western women's auto/biographical subjectivity, whereas in postcolonial life-writing by both genders, this is a standard issue.

Such postcolonial inflections of these three thematics of auto/biographical subjectivity need, however, to be complemented by attention to other dimensions of personhood which have played little part in feminist reinterpretations of life-writing. For example, almost nothing has been made of the constitutive importance of geo-cultural location to the formation of identity in western women's autobiography, with the limited exception of working-class writing.[59] By contrast, imperialism and its contemporary successors are nothing if not projects for physically restructuring the world and redistributing its populations, as a consequence radically altering the affective and psychic connection of innumerable subjects to their places of origin or affiliation. Indeed, as Ashcroft, Griffiths and Tiffin (1989) argue, postcolonial literature in general is in large measure distinguished by its degree of engagement with issues of (dis)location: 'It is here that the special postcolonial crisis of identity comes into being; the concern with the development or recovery of an effective identifying relationship between self and place.'[60] In keeping with such perspectives, Chapter 4 will therefore explore the thematic of place and displacement as this bears upon the construction of postcolonial auto/biographical subjectivity.

The issue of the distinctiveness of postcolonial life-writing needs, however, to be extended beyond consideration of thematics of subjectivity to questions of style. Again, feminist interventions within Auto/biography Studies offer productive pointers in this regard. As Chapter 5 will demonstrate, it is often argued that western women's life-writing can be differentiated from its male equivalent by the degree of its formal experimentations with the genre of autobiography as traditionally conceived. This may seem counter-intuitive, given the hand-wringing about definitions in Auto/biography Studies mentioned earlier. However, among traditional liberal-humanist male critics, at least, there has been little challenge to Lejeune's influential anatomy of the genre (largely adopted from Misch[61]) as 'a retrospective prose narrative produced by a real person concerning his own existence, focusing on his individual life, in particular on the development of his personality'.[62] Further, Lejeune asserts, the genre is characterised by a 'pact' between author and reader, whereby the latter can assume that the 'author (whose name designates a real person) and narrator are identical'.[63] Rather, the hand-wringing arises in respect of the bewildering variety of writings which nonetheless conform to these basic criteria. By contrast, subversion of these fundamental rules is sometimes seen as characteristic of women's life-writing. As Benstock puts it: 'Writing that works the borders of definitional boundaries bears witness both to repressive inscription under the [patriarchal] law of genre and to the freedom and dispossession of existence outside the law.'[64] Women's life-writing questions Lejeune's 'pact' at several levels (not least its implicit masculinism – in translation at least). For example, the emphasis on relationality of personhood in women's life-writing necessarily erodes the boundaries between autobiography and biography. Equally, women life-writers deploy other genres, notably fiction and historiography, to a degree which threatens to take their work altogether beyond the boundaries of autobiography as traditionally conceived.

However, Chapter 5 will suggest that a similar degree of inter-generic traffic and experimentation characterises postcolonial life-writing, by men and women alike. Here I will also suggest that historiography and fiction, the first two genres I examine, operate in strategically distinctive ways *vis-à-vis* their roles in western women's life-writing. If marshalling the conventions of historiography reinforces the emphasis on the social dimensions of Selfhood in both western women's and postcolonial life-writing, in the latter case it also remedies the deficiencies of western historiography or contests its conception of (parts of) the non-western world as being without, or even outside, history.[65] In the case of fiction, postcolonial life-writing also deploys the genre to challenge the epistemological status of authorial/autobiographical identity as outlined by Lejeune, and thereby to contest the wider truth claims conventionally made by, and on behalf of, canonical autobiography. However, it is further deployed to foreground some writers' conviction of the essentially constructed and provisional nature of postcolonial identity as a result of the erasure or disruption of foundational affiliations by colonialism. To complement such arguments, I will then go on to consider the relationship to postcolonial life-writing of travel writing, a genre which has played little part in feminist critical analysis of generic experimentation within women's life-writing. Postcolonial authors at times use travel-writing to challenge the resolution of conflicts of identity which is traditionally understood to structure western male autobiography, thereby in the end producing a stable subject position through which the Subject accedes to full self-knowledge. However, if they employ the genre to stress instead the processual and unfinished nature of identity-formation, in the manner often claimed for women auto/biographers, postcolonial life-writers also use travel-writing as a counter-discourse, in a way which exceeds the ambitions of their western counterparts. For instance, the genre provides the grounds both for *auto*-ethnographical challenges to western representations of the non-West and for an ethnography of the West itself.

Some of these stylistic attributes might be deemed to provide strong evidence against Gusdorf's strategic position that non-western autobiographical writing can only be imitative of what already exists in the West. Conversely, however, it could be argued that historiography, fiction and travel-writing are themselves all originally western forms which, like autobiography, are now being used to 'defend' the non-West. To further develop my counter-argument to Gusdorf, therefore, I will explore in Chapter 6 the way that certain examples of post-colonial life-writing, at least, can be distinguished from their western analogues (both masculine and feminine) by their incorporation of non-western narrative modes and linguistic resources. To this extent the sub-genre often works in the same way as postcolonial fiction and poetry, drawing on local forms, metaphors, tropes and discursive traditions as well as hybridising the languages of the former coloniser by integrating indigenous tongues into their standard forms. Given the crucial role of narrative and language in the formation of subjectivity, I will suggest that the 'ideological "I"' of some postcolonial life-writing is further constituted differently to its western analogues by virtue of such features. For example, the deployment of indigenous narrative templates which emphasise spatial relations over temporal ones, or which privilege non-linear temporalities, has important implications for conceptions of Selfhood, notably in respect of its positioning in the social world and development in time. By contrast, while French theory has elaborated theories about *écriture féminine*,[66] there has been no serious suggestion in feminist inflections of Auto/biography Studies that women life-writers draw on narrative forms and language(s) which are exclusive to women as a collective, in the way that certain forms of masquerade or Yoruba are the properties of Soyinka's community, for example.

The third main issue which establishes the specificity of women's life-writing in the eyes of feminist critics concerns the cultural politics and social functions of the sub-genre. According to many observers, as Chapter 7 will show, canonical autobiography is a conservative form, not least because of its complicity in the marginalisation and 'Othering' of women. Conversely, life-writing has been claimed to play an important part in the emancipation of women and in the articulation of their continuing needs and demands as unequal citizens in patriarchal society. For Julia Swindells, for example, women's life-writing characteristically 'moves beyond the life-story of the key individual, and focuses the use of autobiography as part of a political strategy to produce change'.[67] Again, postcolonial life-writing offers clear parallels in this regard, as a number of chapters below will demonstrate. Thus, in her attempt in 1984 to define 'the peculiarities' of 'Commonwealth' auto/biography, MacDermott concluded that much of it could be described as 'protest literature'.[68] But once more, there are sometimes important differences of emphasis between the two sub-genres in this regard. Many postcolonial life-writers write from a context of deep political disempowerment in which the political rights enjoyed by most western women simply do not exist. While some write in exile from dictatorship, others are prevented from writing, even incarcerated, by repressive regimes and others still live under extreme and constant existential threats to their personal security in a situation of ongoing colonialism (see Chapter 7). In terms of women's experience more particularly, there is simply no contemporary western analogue to the more extreme forms of material deprivation and patriarchal oppression suffered by large numbers of women in the non-western world – nor for the sanctions often endured there for advocating women's rights (see Chapter 3).

Before proceeding to more detailed and nuanced investigations of aspects of the debate which has been set up here in preliminary fashion, a number of cautions are necessary. In the first place, it is important to recognise that the term 'women's life-writing', the body of work on which my comparative investigation primarily relies, is as homogenising and totalising as 'Woman', and does not do justice to the multiplicity of sub-forms which exist in the contemporary West. This is a danger which some feminist critics themselves recognise, as in Regenia Gagnier's warning that much feminist Auto/biography Studies is premised on the study of class-specific modes of women's life-writing.[69] Equally, I do not wish to suggest that postcolonial identity always over-rides issues of gender (or class), thereby creating a binary opposition between postcolonial and western women. Indeed, as suggested earlier, the primary target of many postcolonial women life-writers is often (indigenous) patriarchy rather than (neo-)colonialism. Nonetheless, readers will have to forgive a certain level of generality if I am to accomplish my aims within the space of a single monograph.

Second, I do not wish this monograph to be understood as a hostile account of the ethnocentricity of Auto/biography Studies, whether in its mainstream versions or feminist revisions. While criticism will be offered where necessary of the neglect of postcolonial texts and perspectives in that critical field, it is crucial to recognise that Postcolonial Studies also has much to learn from this adjacent sub-discipline. As a token of this recognition, I will reconsider the generic identity of Frantz Fanon's *Black Skin, White Masks* (1952), the only serious competitor to Said's (1978) *Orientalism* as the foundational text of modern Postcolonial Studies. While primarily read as a work of political philosophy and psychoanalytic critique, it also describes some of the existential trajectories and experiences through which Fanon came to understand himself as a human being and colonial subject, thus providing some of the material grounds of the cultural and political theory for which he is best known.[70] As C.L. Innes points out, in *Black Skin* Fanon 'ask[s] the question constantly "Who am I?"'[71] Indeed, insofar as it provides a template for so much subsequent postcolonial life-writing in relation to both theme and form, I will use it as a touchstone in order to set the terms for particular debates in the chapters which follow. To this extent, critical approaches established in Auto/biography Studies potentially enable new readings of this canonical text of postcolonial theory. Thus, while Anjali Prabhu, for example, usefully explores 'some significant ways in which the narrative shifts in this text operate an aesthetic and ethical pressure on salient understandings of hybridity', she misses the opportunity to demonstrate how Fanon's experimentation with auto/biographical genres itself dramatises that pressure.[72]

Above all, perhaps, it is important not to go to the other extreme from Gusdorf and claim that postcolonial life-writing is a completely independent form, which exists in binary opposition even to its western male equivalents. If colonialism imposed new, at least partly westernised, identities on so many of its subjects, no postcolonial author considered in this monograph wholly disavows the influence of western culture on his/her formation. That most of my chosen texts are written as a matter of choice in languages enforced by colonialism, albeit in sometimes hybridised forms, is testimony to this fact and should make one hesitate to propose any Manichean division between postcolonial life-writing and its western analogues. Indeed, some cultural nationalists might argue that this aspect of the sub-genre alone carries Gusdorf's argument. Thus, Ngugi, for example, insists that: 'Language carries culture, and culture carries ... the entire body of values by which we come to perceive ourselves and our place in the world.'[73] Consequently any narration of Self in European languages could be deemed a form of subservience to and reproduction of western cultural authority.[74]

Language aside, there is certainly evidence of the explicit inspiration provided by western models for some postcolonial life-writing. Thus, R.C.P. Sinha begins his study of Indian autobiography in English by asserting that while the genre pre-dates contact with Europe, its 'full flowering ... take[s] place only after the coming of the English to India'.[75] Such perspectives have been seconded by certain postcolonial life-writers themselves. For example, Mulk Raj Anand's preface to his *Autobiography* (1985) argues that:

> In the *Bri Hadaranyaka Upanishad* the sage enjoins the disciple to ask 'Who am I? Where have I come from? And where am I going?' But the inquiries into the self soon become the search for *Atman*, the higher Self. And it was ordained that the ego is not a free agent. Introspective analysis was discounted. Anonymity prevailed.
>
> Only after the impact of the West did we begin to marvel at finding ourselves on the earth earthy [*sic*]. Gandhi, Tagore and Nehru wrote autobiographies, with much honesty, courageously facing the fact [*sic*] about their lives, including facts about their sensual desires.[76]

Similar inferences might be drawn from V.S. Naipaul's comments on Nirad Chaudhuri's *The Autobiography of an Unknown Indian* (1951, discussed in Chapter 5): 'No better account of the penetration of the Indian mind by the West – and by extension, of the penetration of one culture by another – will be or now can be written.'[77] Indeed, it could be argued that even Said's *Out of Place* (1999; see Chapter 7) is in many ways a fairly conventional autobiography, both formally and, in certain respects, in its thematics of subjectivity (although I will argue that the significance of such examples is more complex than one might assume from a Gusdorfian perspective). Moreover, the material conditions of the production and circulation of postcolonial life-writing bind it to the West in ways which inevitably influence its modes of Self-representation. Indeed, most of the texts I examine were first published in the West, many postcolonial life-writers have been located there for substantial lengths of time and the majority of their readers are, in all probability, westerners. Any attempt to challenge Gusdorf's argument must take these factors on-board.

Finally, it is necessary to signal that in a book of this length, with so much basic ground to map, I can make no claims to definitiveness or comprehensiveness. My argument relies on relatively few examples. These have been chosen to reflect the wide variety of periods and locations within which postcolonial life-writing has been practised, rather than to establish a canon. The relatively small number of texts further reflects a conviction that it is better to accord a few works the kind of space and attention that close, theoretically informed, reading demands than to attempt something more wide-ranging but inevitably more superficial. Further, the overwhelming majority of chosen works are either by writers or academics who are thereby not necessarily representative of postcolonial life-writing – or experience – as a whole (who is?). My justification in this respect is that in attempting to establish for the first time a reasonably detailed poetics of the sub-genre, I am more likely to succeed by using writing that is self-conscious about its relationship to the genres within which it chooses to situate itself than is the case with the memoirs of professional politicians, for example. Whatever other interest this latter work might hold, literary skill and self-consciousness are, with some notable exceptions, rarely among their attributes.

I therefore offer this monograph not as a conclusive set of answers to the questions I pose, but rather as a series of intellectual provocations to colleagues in the sub-fields of both Postcolonial and Auto/biography Studies. My hope is that they will find signposts here for further and perhaps more detailed investigations of particular aspects of the debate or raise issues that I have been unable to consider because of constraints of space – or have simply overlooked! Whether subsequent critics will even ask the same questions, let alone arrive at the same answers, remains to be seen. Nonetheless this book will serve its purpose if it generates greater critical engagement with a sub-genre which has so far been insufficiently recognised for its distinctive contribution both to postcolonial literature and to auto/biography, as well as for the degree to which its poetics requires rethinking of some of the conceptual frameworks which characterise the two critical formations surrounding those fields.

1   Centred and decentred Selves

Turning to the first thematic of subjectivity identified in the Introduction, feminist critics within Auto/biography Studies have persistently complained that male colleagues have traditionally promoted a normative view of autobiographical Selfhood as centred and unified (as well as 'sovereign'). Sidonie Smith, for example, claims of canonical autobiography that it is presumed historically that 'the teleological drift of selfhood concedes nothing to indeterminacy, to ambiguity, or to heterogeneity'.[1] There is ample evidence to support such arguments across the history of the critical field. Thus, more than a century ago, Misch argued that: 'In this single whole all [elements of the personality] have their definite place, thanks to their significance in relation to the whole.'[2] At mid-century, Gusdorf insisted that the task of the autobiographer was 'to reconstitute himself in the focus of his special unity and identity across time' in order to express the 'mysterious essence of his being'.[3] Such perspectives persist into the most recent phase of the critical field, despite the advent of post-structuralism.[4] For example, Spengemann asserts that the genre provides the 'ground upon which conflicting aspects of the writer's own nature might be reconciled in complete being'.[5]

For many women critics, such a model of Selfhood is clearly gendered. Mary Evans, for instance, argues that the 'project of masculinity emphasizes ... the completed self'.[6] Indeed, its privileged status is often invoked to explain why women's life-writing has traditionally been marginalised within the male-dominated formation of Auto/biography Studies. In turn, feminist critics have claimed that women life-writers tend to construct more dispersed and decentred models of auto/biographical subjectivity 'as the means to counter the centrifugal power of the old unitary self of western rationalism'.[7] Further, Brodzki and Schenck claim that the postmodernist decentring of the subject in Roland Barthes's autobiography 'can be said to have something in common with the strategies of some women autobiographers dating as far back as the fifteenth century'.[8] Comparable arguments have been extended to minoritarian women's writing in the West. For instance, Lee Quinby suggests that such work tends to construct 'a subjectivity that is multiple and discontinuous' in order to resist the 'modern's era's dominant construction of individualized selfhood'.[9] Equally, Françoise Lionnet argues that postcolonial women's life-writing generally promotes 'the creation of a plural self, one that thrives on ambiguity and multiplicity, on affirmation of differences, not on polarized and polarizing notions of identity'.[10]

While such positions represent the prevailing pattern of claims about this aspect of Selfhood in women's auto/biographical writing, some feminists have nonetheless cautioned against premature celebration of the 'death of the Subject' in relation to female experience. Thus, Linda Hutcheon warns that 'those radical postmodern challenges are in many ways the luxury of the dominant order which can afford to challenge that which it securely possesses'.[11] Such doubts have fed into feminist revisions of Auto/biography Studies. For example, Gilmore argues that '[M]any women autobiographers tend to attribute to speech, presence, political enfranchisement, and cultural authority the same tonic effects contemporary critics associate with the (more or less) free play of signifiers.'[12] This suggests that to appropriate the speaking positions, narrative modes and paradigms of Selfhood associated with the hegemonic regime of social power advances claims to equality for those traditionally denied full subjectivity (and therefore humanity) by the established institutions of cultural authority – which include both autobiography as a genre and the critical field associated with it. This stance is echoed by bell hooks with respect to minoritarian constituencies in the West. While by no means wholly unsympathetic to postmodernism, she asks: 'Should we not be suspicious of postmodern critiques of the "subject" when they surface at a historical moment when many subjugated people feel themselves coming to voice for the first time?' [sic].[13] A similar suspicion of the over-valorisation of fragmented subjectivity in relation to some postcolonial women's life-writing is expressed by Kateryna Longley who sees it as a wholly negative consequence of colonialism in relation to Aboriginal women.[14]

Postcolonial life-writing more broadly demonstrates the same mixed attitude about the centred Subject. This is illustrated, for example, in the contradictory accounts of Caribbean subjectivity provided by John Thieme and Sandra Paquet. In Thieme's view, '[T]he fragmentary, heterogeneous nature of the society precludes the possibility of ... a unitary Cartesian self.'[15] For Paquet, by contrast, it is precisely such factors which under-write the 'diaspora quest for wholeness' in so many Caribbean life-writers.[16] This ambivalence in fact extends back to the earliest theorisation of postcolonial subjectivity in *Black Skin, White Masks*. On the one hand, Fanon suggests that the appropriate response to the psychic disintegration inflicted on so many colonial subjects is to resist it through a strategy of Self-reconstitution as a whole being. Assaulted by racial discourses which fracture him into a 'triple person', Fanon claims: 'I [must] put all the parts back together.'[17] On the other hand, he denies that wholeness can be recovered by an appeal to essences, especially racial ones: 'Negro experience is not a whole, for there is not merely *one* Negro, there are Negroes.'[18] Consequently, Fanon refuses to disavow the western influences in his formation; instead he celebrates 'the zebra striping of my mind'.[19]

In the remainder of this chapter, I will explore some ways in which more recent postcolonial life-writing by both women and men engages with such debates. In doing so, I hope to determine whether the sub-genre can be differentiated from both its canonical and women's equivalents in the West on the basis of this aspect of auto/biographical subjectivity.

The centred Self: Sally Morgan, *My Place* (1987)

There can be little doubt that the narrator of *My Place* aspires to the kind of unified, centred and 'sovereign' Self which many feminist critics have identified as characteristic of canonical male western autobiography. This aspiration begins in early life, during which Sally already feels 'that a very vital part of me was missing'.[20] The text focuses primarily on her quest for that 'missing part', so that after journeying back to grandmother Daisy's ancestral homelands, she at last understands the place of her Aboriginal ethnicity within the 'jigsaw' of her identity (*MP*: 232): 'How deprived we would have been if we had been willing to let things stay as they were. We would have survived, but not as *whole* people' (*MP*: 233; my emphasis). This aspect of the text has elicited strong criticism. Eric Michaels has questioned whether such an apparently Eurocentric model of subjectivity is appropriate for the representation of Aboriginal personhood.[21] Other commentary has claimed that it embodies the class ideology of bourgeois individualism in mainstream Australian mythography, which celebrates the continent as a land of opportunities available to anyone willing to conform to its supposedly ethnically neutral values of hard work and self-improvement. Morgan's fellow-Aboriginal author Mudrooroo Narogin, for example, summarises the 'plotline' as follows: 'Poor underprivileged person through the force of his or her own character makes it to the top through own efforts … the concerns of the Aboriginal community are of secondary importance.'[22]

However, such interpretations of this model of auto/biographical Selfhood seem reductive in the light of Longley's reading of the fractured experience of Aboriginality within which Morgan's formation as a subject must be contextualised. As Carolyn Bliss argues,[23] *My Place* represents the predicament of those of mixed-race descent, more specifically, as one of psychic and cultural amputation. This is explained largely in terms of the policies of forced assimilation inaugurated with the grotesquely misnamed Aborigines Protection Act of 1905, extended and strengthened in 1936. Such legislation promoted the separation of mixed-race children from their mothers (whether 'full-blood' like Sally's great-grandmother Annie, or, themselves of mixed descent like Daisy) in order to 'redeem' them through adoption by white families or incarceration in missions and children's homes. (According to Russell West, between 10 and 30 per cent of all mixed-race children were removed from their mothers in the period 1905–65.[24]) Daisy and Sally's mother Gladys thus both belong to 'the stolen generations', the belated subject of a major government inquiry in the 1990s. Only after the findings were published in 1997 did mainstream Australian society begin to face up to issues which *My Place* had addressed ten years earlier, on the eve of the bicentennial celebrations of Britain's invasion of the continent (and two decades after Aboriginals had so belatedly acquired citizenship rights in their own land). To this extent, as Anne Brewster argues, Morgan's text, like much Aboriginal life-writing, constitutes 'a counter-discourse to … white Australian nationalism'.[25]

In polemically pursuing claims for restitution, both psychic and material, the genre has sometimes been criticised for its stylistic naivety,[26] a charge also laid against Morgan. Carolyn Bliss, for example, complains about her 'artless primer prose'.[27] *My Place* is, however, a good deal more artful than such comments suggest, a fact recognised by Elvira Pulitano, who notes that Morgan's narrative 'operates on multiple levels'.[28] This is especially the case in its treatment of Sally's aspiration to wholeness/unity of Selfhood. Thus, the issue of psychic amputation is broached with great delicacy in the opening chapter, in a manner which demonstrates the integration of a seemingly unself-conscious diaristic realism with allegory and symbolism which characterises Morgan's whole narrative. Visiting her father in hospital, the 5-year-old is repelled by the disabled veterans of the Second World War. Nonetheless, Sally's intuitive sense of her own lack of 'wholeness' is figured in both an unconscious identification with them (she wonders how she would cope without one of her own limbs) and her bodily 'dis-ease' during the visit. As she arrives, she catches glimpses of her 'distorted shape' (*MP*: 11) in the chrome fittings of the hospital. The protagonist is self-conscious about her height, dislikes her 'monkey' limbs and feels 'wrinkled inside' (*MP*:16). Three particular aspects of such 'dis-ease' are flagged in this scene as obstacles which she must overcome if her quest for unified Selfhood is to succeed. First, again providing a link with the veterans, Sally feels physically immobilised during much of her visit. Second, her 'colour' is emphasised by the sterile whiteness of the ward: 'I was a grubby five-year-old in an alien environment' (*MP*: 11). Finally, Sally must overcome her fear of falling 'in pieces on the floor' if she dares to speak (*MP*: 12).

The crucial link between silence/concealment and trauma is further developed in this opening scene. It is initially adumbrated in relation to Morgan's father, Bill Milroy, who is exceptional among the patients in being physically 'in one piece' (*MP*: 284). Yet Sally already senses that 'the heart had gone out of him', leaving only an empty 'frame' (*MP*: 12). Indeed, Morgan's investment in traditional ideas of the whole/centred Self can be explained partly in terms of Sally's developing awareness of the consequences of her father's psychic fragmentation. His mind 'broken' by his experiences as a prisoner-of-war, Bill Milroy is prone to alcoholism, depression and violence against his family. While the explanation for these facts emerges later, his trauma is signalled at the outset by his inability to communicate during his daughter's visit.

The silence of father and daughter suggests a comparable psychic abjection (later, Sally describes herself as 'a crazy member of the family who didn't know who she was' [*MP*: 141]). However, whereas Bill's trauma derives from an inability to escape his memories, Sally's arises from being cut off from her past, so that her narrative becomes a process of 're-membering' an amputated identity. The aetiology of her trauma is again revealed with discreet symbolism. Despite the temperate climate of Perth, she must sleep under a 'mound of coats' to supplement her bed-clothes (*MP*: 13). When her grandmother wakes her to listen to the 'special bird' which represents Daisy's Aboriginal affiliations, it is a struggle to peel these 'layers' off. The clothing under which Sally is buried has traditionally signified the culture of the coloniser, in Australia as elsewhere. (One of the earliest examples of Aboriginal writing is Bennelong's 1796 letter to Lord Sydney's steward, requesting clothes from London.[29]) Even in Arthur and Daisy's youth, shirts remained prized objects of Aboriginal aspiration (*MP*: 182). Indeed, when the adult siblings argue, Daisy disparages her 'blackfella' brother by commenting that he does not 'dress decent' (*MP*: 147). This early incident in Sally's life therefore foreshadows the process of 'dis-*covering*' which she must go through to reconnect with her Aboriginal heritage. The young girl has been assimilated to the dominant culture to such an extent that on this first encounter with the totemic bird, she seeks ocular verification of its existence. Conversely, the distance she travels towards integrating her different ethnic identities into a single new whole is measured by the fact that when the 'special bird' returns at the end of the text, Morgan no longer needs such material corroboration: '"Oh, Nan," I cried with sudden certainty, "I heard it, too. In my heart, I heard it"' (*MP*: 358).

Sally's potentially tragic predicament of disinheritance ironically derives from the fact that the 'cover-up' of her cultural heritage is effected in the first instance by her mother and grandmother, owing to fear of being open about their mixed origins (*MP*: 163). Mother and grandmother, too, have suffered the psychic amputation which such self-repression entails. Thus, after their trip to the Pilbara, Gladys comments: 'All my life, I've only been half a person. I don't think I really realised how much of me was missing until I came North' (*MP*: 233). Silence and disguise, crucial weapons in the battle for survival, can also, as Sally eventually persuades her mother, lead to extinction of cultural identity. In a sense Gladys's silence hitherto is the very theme of the narrative she finally agrees to tell, which turns on her anxiety that the kind of separation which she and Daisy both endured was still possible in Sally's childhood. Despite his own exposure to Jewish suffering during the war, which initially leads him to overlook Gladys's 'colour', Bill Milroy soon reverts to the prejudices of mainstream Australian society. He tries to expel Daisy from the family and prevents Gladys from leaving by reminding her that if she does, he – as a 'proper' (white) Australian – will get custody of the children. As Joyce Zonana argues, Morgan's family life thus 'offers a parable of the relations between white men and black women in Australia'.[30]

Morgan's investment in a traditional model of unified Selfhood can, then, be understood primarily as a means to mitigate the psychic fracturing experienced by Aboriginals which Longley invokes. This is enforced by the strategies of stratification and division which structure both the discursive regimes and material structures of colonialism. For example, Arthur recalls that when he arrives at the Swan mission, the children so recently torn from their mothers are further segregated by gender and shade of skin colour (*MP*: 184). Equally, Morgan advocates traditional auto/biographical sovereignty of Self to counter the historical status of Aboriginals as objects to be possessed. Daisy asserts that in her youth, 'we was owned, like a cow or a horse' (*MP*: 336). Gladys laments that even in 'care', 'when I was sick, I belonged to the Native Welfare Department' (*MP*: 250). But Morgan inflects a potentially conservative emphasis on Self-possession by reconfiguring the idea of 'ownership' to include connotations of 'owning up' in two distinct senses. First, it expresses the need for mainstream society not only to acknowledge its responsibility for the current predicament of Aboriginals, but also to recognise the role of the latter in the building of modern Australia. As Arthur argues, 'no-one can say the blackfella didn't do his share' (*MP*: 211). On the other hand, it also requires mixed-race, assimilated urban-dwellers like Sally to acknowledge their Aboriginal communities of origin.

This embrace of 'sovereign' Selfhood is emphasised by Morgan's deployment of the conventions of crime fiction. At one point, Gladys comments to Sally that 'you're like a bloody detective' (*MP*: 238). As Sheila Collingwood-Whittick argues: 'Proleptic hints of the otherness which Morgan will later have to integrate into her perception of her self are regularly posted in the early part of *My Place*.'[31] Entering adulthood, Sally awakens to the fact that her identity has been constructed on the basis of 'a little white lie' (*MP*: 135), a term which in this context has bitterly ironic connotations. After Sally realises that Daisy is part-Aboriginal, the protagonist proceeds like a private investigator, sifting truth from falsehood, following chance leads, interviewing material witnesses, researching in archives and visiting crime-scenes. This structure provides much of the narrative tension of the text as well as metaphorising the dynamic of Sally's identity-formation. This, after Arthur's first visit of her adult life, Sally acknowledges that: 'We were very confused, we knew that the small pieces of information we now possessed weren't the complete truth' (*MP*: 158). Through her own agency, she cumulatively adds missing pieces to the 'jigsaw', generating an increasingly synoptic overview of events, so that by the end of the text, the overall contours of her identity, at least, are clear. For example, speaking to Billy in Pilbara provides 'one more precious thing that added to our sense of belonging … It was like all the little pieces of a huge jigsaw were finally fitting together' (*MP*: 232).

However, as West argues,[32] in deploying the conventions of the detective genre, Morgan reworks them from a postcolonial (and gendered) perspective. In doing so, she further inflects the traditional idea of 'sovereign' autobiographical subjectivity, not least in questioning her status as the subject of a social system ultimately governed by an alien Sovereign. Most obviously, Sally does not represent the officially sanctioned (white) system of law and order. Indeed, she positions herself explicitly in opposition to it when she attempts to research her family history in the Battye archives. Here, she finds access blocked by police authority, which is keen to preserve the public (mis)perception of its role as 'Protectors of the Aborigines', rather than acknowledge its instrumentality in the destruction of Aboriginal society and culture. As this suggests, Morgan is also therefore a victim of the crimes she is investigating. Further, and equally uncharacteristic of the genre, what is being investigated is less the actions of individual suspects (Howden Drake-Brockman is, in any case, long dead), than a *collective* crime perpetrated by a social and ideological system, colonialism itself. Finally, of course, the crime in question is real, not fictional.

Despite Morgan's aspiration to a traditional model of unified and 'sovereign' autobiographical Selfhood, this is not definitively achieved. This is partly because, further contradicting the conventions of the detective genre, certain 'secrets' are never resolved, including the fate of Gladys's sister and the identity of their father. Arthur confidently hints that this is Howden Drake-Brockman and there is corroboration in the resemblance between the photograph of the land-owner and Gladys. This challenges the surviving Drake-Brockmans' ascription of paternity to 'Maltese Sam', who has, conveniently, long disappeared. Daisy, however, takes the truth to her grave. Consequently it also remains unclear whether Gladys is the incestuous product of a liaison between Drake-Brockman and his daughter Daisy. To this extent, Morgan is in the end unable to reclaim the whole history, even of her immediate family, and is thereby frustrated in her quest for full belonging. Yet Morgan not only comes to disavow the importance of legitimation through the paternal line but, more radically, to disown essentialist conceptions of belonging founded on blood genealogy. Early in her quest, Sally asks: 'What did it really mean to be Aboriginal? ... What did it mean for someone like me?' (*MP*: 141). Despite the success of the trip north, the answer appears to be contingent and provisional. Morgan asserts her Aboriginality through discursive processes of 'owning up', in which performative autobiographical *acts* of narrative confession play the constitutive part. After Arthur's recollections, for example, she asserts: 'I'll put it all together, because we've got bits and pieces all over the place' (*MP*: 165).

As this *collective* focus suggests (see also Chapter 2), insofar as Morgan seeks to establish a unified and 'sovereign' Self in *My Place*, this is not in order to reaffirm all the values traditionally associated with this thematic of subjectivity, especially as conceived of by Gusdorf. Instead, the trope is primarily put in the service of a sustained critique of colonial discourse and contemporary Australian racism which, Arthur argues, continues unabated (*MP*: 212). The terms in which this critique is framed could hardly be more emotive and powerful. Thus, despite Sally's initial disavowal of the link (*MP*: 105), the Australian Aboriginal experience becomes implicitly associated with the Holocaust. Further, it is compared with the worst excesses of American slavery. Such parallels are the more effectively drawn by being only hinted at in small symbolic details. For example, the Holocaust is invoked when Gladys describes how stolen children were roughly loaded on a cattle-truck before being taken away (*MP*: 264), slavery in the 'slave cap' of the black doll offered to Gladys (*MP*: 261) and names given to Aboriginal workers, like 'Old Pompee' (*MP*: 326).

As has been seen, at the outset of the text, Morgan fears that speaking in her own voice would reduce her to 'pieces on the floor'. By the end, the effectiveness with which she has *un*covered and learned to articulate that voice constitutes a vindication of the politically progressive potential of a *strategic* embrace of canonical models of autobiographical Selfhood in the postcolonial context. In keeping with her ethics of integration (stylistic, psychological, and political), Morgan seeks to make not only herself – and her family and the people to which they belong – 'whole' by dealing with past traumas. Perhaps more remarkably, in seeking to expand the text of 'Australianness' to include Aboriginality, she offers the chance of healing to her people's oppressors. As Daisy argues, mainstream Australia's failure to properly integrate Aboriginals and their particular civilisational values means that 'the white man' suffers from a comparable degree of psychic and cultural amputation to his victims, such that he is 'only livin' half a life' (*MP*: 344). If this suggests a further revision of the norms of the detective genre, in that Morgan seeks reconciliation rather than retribution for the collective crimes committed against Aboriginals, *My Place* nonetheless distinguishes crucially between integration and assimilation as the path towards this.

The wider political allegory implicit in Morgan's discourse of integration per-haps remains the best defence against what Graham Huggan warns is one possi-ble danger faced by those who write of 'the stolen generations'. This is that they 'run the risk of being stolen all over again'[33] by being pressed into the service of a project of reconciliation which simply reinscribes the old colonial doctrine of assimilation. Morgan demonstrates the crucial difference between that and her conception of true integration in the lessons Gladys Corunna draws from her daughter's search: 'I suppose, in hundreds of years' time, there won't be any black Aboriginals left … as we mix with other races, we'll lose some of the physical characteristics that distinguish us now' (*MP*: 306). This suggests that the broader cultural and ethnic differences represented by 'physical characteristics' will be sublated through a process of dialectical progression, resulting in the material as well as psychic synthesis of a new and more inclusive Australian identity. Thus, if the physical markers of Aboriginality are to disappear (a prospect that many readers may feel uneasy with), the implication is that mainstream Australian eth-nicity will thereby also be changed in crucial ways: 'I like to think that, no matter what we become, our spiritual tie with the land and the other unique qualities we possess will somehow *weave their way through* to future generations of Australians' (*MP*: 306, my emphasis).

The decentred Self: Equiano, *The Interesting Narrative* (1789)

Reading *My Place* alongside Olaudah Equiano's *The Interesting Narrative* makes even more shocking Morgan's account of the predicament of Australian Aboriginals in the early/middle twentieth century, in that so many events and situations she describes are directly comparable to Equiano's experiences one hundred and fifty years earlier. The convergence between the two writers is further evident in their use of life-writing as an instrument to both protest against such abuses and to advance the reclamation of personhood deformed by colonialism. However, the two texts differ in important respects, notably in terms of their protagonists' life-experience. Equiano is not only male but, to use the term of *My Place*, 'full-blood'. He also claims[34] to have been involuntarily transported across the globe from his native land to an entirely new culture, where he is legally a chattel.

Nonetheless, Equiano faces a similar range of options to Morgan in terms of his identity-construction as an auto/biographical Subject, ranging from an affirmation of 'native roots', to complete assimilation to the dominant formation. So enthusiastically does Equiano pursue the latter option, according to some critics, that he ends by embracing a singular British identity. Tanya Caldwell, for example, argues that he 'takes every opportunity to repudiate any fundamental difference between himself and the culture in which he developed as a self-conscious being'.[35] Certainly, as one might expect of a vulnerable abducted boy, Equiano sets himself urgently to the task of learning the values and customs of his captors. One haunting example of Equiano's ensuing identification with the dominant occurs in Guernsey, where he becomes dazzled by the 'rosy' complexion of his hosts' daughter Mary. In a passage which anticipates the description in *My Place* of Daisy's friend Nellie, who takes peroxide baths in the hope of 'whitening' herself (*MP*: 337), Equiano records: 'I therefore tried oftentimes myself if I could not by washing make my face of the same colour as my little play-mate ... but it was all in vain; and I now began to be mortified by the difference in our complexions.'[36] It is a measure of how far he has internalised such values that by the time he encounters his first fellow-black in England, Equiano 'turned a little out of his way at first' in what seems to be a gesture of embarrassed disavowal (*IN*: 85).

This pattern continues into adulthood, when the narrator regularly conceives of England in highly idealised terms as home. Thus, Jesús Benito and Ana Manzanas insist that Equiano 'never thinks of Africa as his final destination'.[37] Indeed, the adult protagonist at times resembles a quintessentially imperial Englishman. On the voyage to establish plantations on the Musquito Coast (to be worked by slave labour which he has himself helped procure), for example, the author proselytizes like a missionary to the Indian prince. Later, he aligns himself with one hero of colonial exploration in employing 'a stratagem ... [he] had read in the life of Columbus' (*IN*: 208) to quell a riot. Elsewhere, Equiano proclaims the virtues of trade with Africa not simply as a means of providing an alternative to the slave trade, but of assimilating Africans to the superior civilisation represented by 'British fashions, manners, customs, &c.' (*IN*: 233) which he appears to have so readily absorbed.[38] It is therefore little surprise that he is regarded as belonging to the dominant ethnicity by other subalterns. For example, when questioned about his religious backsliding, the Indian prince retorts to Equiano: 'How comes it that all the *white men* on board ... swear, lie and get drunk, *only excepting yourself?*' (*IN*: 204; my emphasis).

Some commentary sees Equiano's turn to autobiography as further evidence of his assimilation to the cultural dominant. For example, Caldwell argues that by its very nature as a (supposedly) exclusively western form, autobiography 'denies the black author any access to an authentic African self'.[39] Certainly, the designation of Equiano as 'the black Christian' (*IN*: 92) perhaps inevitably invokes the protagonist of Bunyan's *Pilgrim's Progress* (1678), locating Equiano squarely within a metropolitan Protestant tradition of spiritual self-inquiry.[40] While Adam Potkay acknowledges that Equiano provides one or two 'twists' to the rules of spiritual autobiography, he detects no real contestation in his primary conception of the genre as 'a theological quest', which determines the author's vision of belonging: 'His final home, in *The Interesting Narrative*, is thus Christianity and its exegetical methods.'[41] One might, then, legitimately infer that the author's apparent endorsement of the ideology of the genre and obedience to its 'rules' illuminate a broader pattern of acceptance of the norms of the dominant culture which is symbolised by the highly conventional bourgeois persona who gazes out from the engraving at the front of his text.[42]

However, to over-emphasise such evidence of Equiano's assimilation to Britishness is to simplify the protagonist's negotiation of his autobiographical identity. As Geraldine Murphy suggests, *The Interesting Narrative* is both 'written within and against the terms of the dominant culture'.[43] The complexity of Equiano's formation as an ethnic subject, in particular, is apparent even in the incidents already described. Once over his surprise at the black youth's over-enthusiastic approach on the Isle of Wight, Equiano and his 'fellow-countryman' become 'very happy in frequently seeing each other' (*IN*: 85). Moreover, even as the Indian prince reads Equiano as 'white', he sharply distinguishes his interlocutor from the latter's fellow-adventurers. Between them, these incidents suggest on the one hand Equiano's continuing identification with his culture of origin and, on the other, a widespread perception of his outsider status *vis-à-vis* mainstream white society, patterns which persist throughout the text.

Equiano's assimilation to Britishness is partly frustrated by the discrimination he experiences from other Britons. Some of those he encounters are aggrieved precisely by the degree of his apparent assimilation. For example, Captain Doran threatens violence because Equiano 'talked too much English', a complaint repeated in Savannah (*IN*: 94, 159). Long after manumission, Equiano is reminded that his 'blackness' leaves him vulnerable to rejection, for example, when he applies to serve as a missionary in Africa. Despite an excellent reference from the former Governor of Cape Coast, and his knowledge of 'the manners and customs' of his homeland, 'some certain scruples of delicacy', as Equiano puts it – with scrupulous delicacy (*IN*: 223) – lead the Bishop of London to decline him. However, even more benevolently disposed whites often insist on Equiano's difference. For instance, after encountering Daniel Queen, from whom he receives Biblical instruction, Equiano is not recognised simply as a co-religionist but distinguished as 'the *black* Christian' (*IN*: 92; my emphasis). Similarly, when approached to help return poor blacks to Africa, it is Equiano's 'difference' that clearly helps earn him consideration. Thus, while the author considers himself 'almost an Englishman' (*IN*: 77) within a short period of being abducted, he is never allowed fully to become one, whether by those sympathetic or antipathetic towards him.

Benito and Manzanas argue that as a consequence of such experiences, Equiano 'maintains a detached and ambivalent position towards whites'.[44] The author's sometimes hostile attitude to the dominant ethnicity is marked from the outset. In Africa, he asserts, 'whiteness' is synonymous with deformity. Describing his first encounters with Europeans, Equiano deploys the kind of counter-stereotyping which characterises later postcolonial writing. In particular, he constructs his captors as potential cannibals.[45] Deep anger understandably informs his descriptions of the slave economy in the West Indies (and the version of Christianity to which it pays lip-service). Despite the risk of alienating contemporary British 'moderates', Equiano comes close to legitimising insurrection against plantation slavery (*IN*: 111–12; compare 139–40). Further, while clearly represented as a better place for a black man than the West Indies, Equiano's sometimes disobliging experiences in London encourage him to consider seriously settling in Turkey (*IN*: 179, 181). Indeed, the necessity of the proposed Sierra Leone expedition demonstrates, *pace* Caldwell, that freedom for blacks cannot be achieved 'within English traditions and institutions'.[46]

On the other hand, Equiano's consistent awareness of his culture of origin also prevents complete assimilation to the dominant ethnicity. At the end of the text, significantly, he insists that he can still speak his mother tongue (*IN*: 222). The affective power of his putative memories of an African childhood supports the author's claim that all the adversity he experienced thereafter served only to 'rivet' them in his mind (*IN*: 46; the image has nicely ironic connotations in this context). Throughout the text, chance incidents reinforce these links to his past. For example, Queen's readings in the Old Testament 'tended to impress our manners and customs more deeply on my memory' (*IN*: 92). Indeed, at the climax of his conversion crisis, Equiano suddenly remembers his mother (*IN*: 191). Contradicting Caldwell, the writer's unwillingness to disavow his non-European identity is explicitly marked from the first lines of the text, which insist that he is a 'stranger', a self-positioning immediately reinforced by Equiano's heavily ironic comment that 'did I consider myself a European, I might say my sufferings were great' (*IN*: 31). When he assumes responsibility during the shipwreck on the Bahama banks, he describes himself as 'a kind of chieftain' (Equiano's family was aristocratic), not a 'kind of captain' (*IN*: 151). Even late in his narrative, Equiano continues to define himself not as an Englishman or Briton, but as 'an obscure African', 'a black man' and an 'oppressed Ethiopian' (*IN*: 229, 232). In the course of negotiating over the Sierra Leone expedition, Equiano also explains why he has not, hitherto, considered Africa as his desired final destination. He is understandably fearful of getting entangled once more with slavers if he was to go 'home'. It is an index of his continuing identification with Africa that in the end Equiano is nonetheless prepared to face this and other dangers to return.

To some critics, therefore, Equiano's embrace of 'Britishness' is to be understood as primarily strategic, reflecting his self-confessed propensity to 'stratagem' (for example, *IN*: 125, 180, 208). Clearly, it ensures his greater utility – and therefore better treatment – at the hands of his masters. Later, it is a crucial element in his attempt to enlist sympathy for the cause of abolition. In this respect, the more Equiano can close the gap between 'Africanness' and the self-identifications of his audience (for example, by stressing the parallels between his culture of origin and those of Jews, Greeks and Highlanders – which align him progressively more closely with his readers), the more not only the slave trade, but the system of slavery itself, seem not just inhumane but 'un-British'. Equiano's appropriation of the form of spiritual autobiography can be seen as consonant with this larger strategy. Against Caldwell and Potkay, it could be argued that Equiano disrupts generic rules, 'converting' the form to radical new uses. His opening address 'to the Lords Spiritual and Temporal' indicates the *dual* focus of the text which follows. This is maintained to the last chapter, which is as much concerned with material matters of economy and politics as it is with spiritual ones. Indeed, in questioning Equiano's adherence to the norms of eighteenth-century spiritual autobiography, Susan Marren makes the point that commerce succeeds where Christianity signally fails to secure Equiano's freedom.[47] Moreover, despite the seeming importance of the conversion scene in Chapter X, the question must be asked, from what is Equiano being converted here – and to what? Whether or not he fully understands the meaning of his early baptism, he is clearly a 'proper' Christian at least from the time of his friendship with the Miss Guerins. In any case, it is difficult to appreciate what is damnable about Equiano's life between his baptism and Chapter X (let alone before; as Douglas Anderson notes, someone who has been abducted and enslaved is clearly more sinned against than sinning[48]). The redundancy of the conversion episode, structurally crucial to conventional spiritual autobiography, is further suggested by the fact that Equiano is again given what appears to be the same 'Guide to the Indians' which he received on baptism. That the conversion may be no more than a token gesture of generic conformity might also help explain the uncharacteristic stylistic flatness of this part of his narrative, about which critics have complained since Mary Wollstonecraft's early review of the text.[49]

That Equiano is using the sub-genre of spiritual autobiography subversively is supported by other evidence in the text. For example, while expressly forbidden to do so, he continues to write his journal during the voyage to the Arctic (*IN*: 173). Consequently, Self-narrativisation becomes implicitly associated with rebellion against (white) authority. Equiano's revisionary impulses are further signalled in his adaptation of the text of *Paradise Lost*, which adapts Beelzebub's rebelliousness to speak to the issue of contemporary slavery (*IN*: 112). William Mottolese argues that in another such example of inter-textual appropriation, Equiano's narrative 'mimics and subverts' the 'Guide to the Indians' itself, redirecting it towards a domestic British audience. The first part of its full title (which Equiano never divulges) is *The Knowledge and Practice of Christianity Made Easy to the Meanest Capacities*, a phrase which might as easily describe his own text.[50] Appreciation of Equiano's subversive energies, rather than innate racism, might just explain why he was not accepted as a missionary to Africa. Indeed, such qualities lead some critics to the opposite extreme from Caldwell's assertion of the author's full assimilation to white culture. Robin Sabino and Jennifer Hall, for example, argue that Equiano's 'world view remained Igbo throughout his life span',[51] notably in relation to his reliance on the traditional idea of *chi* to understand his life-trajectory.[52]

William Samuels asserts that such evidence supports the argument that the author adopts 'the mask of a docile slave' in order to consolidate a '"single self" … an idealized African identity that Equiano wishes to reclaim'.[53] Others also contend that *The Interesting Narrative* is organised by a model of unified Selfhood, even when they disagree with both Caldwell and Samuels as to the orientation of Equiano's self-identification. For example, Carretta argues that the text constructs 'an integrated essential self abstracted from the disparate and sometimes conflicting particular details' of his life.[54] Helen Thomas, by contrast, suggests that Equiano 'achieved a creolised (re)construction of "himself"' based on the principles of 'synthesis' and 'fusion'.[55] Against such readings, I would argue that the model of Selfhood which he elaborates differs quite radically from the emphasis of *My Place* on integration of personhood. At the very end of the text, Equiano states that his 'life and fortune have been extremely chequered' (*IN*: 236). The image of the chequer-board figures a model of hybrid identity in which his ethnicities remain consciously juxtaposed but distinct, rather than – as is the case with Morgan – becoming 'miscegenated' into a new, unified whole figured in the image of the (largely) resolved 'jigsaw'.[56]

This is consonant with the narrator's painful predicament throughout *The Interesting Narrative* (as well as helping explain its sometimes disjunctive form[57]). On the one hand, Equiano must assert his similarity to the dominant in order to advance the argument that the enslavement of Africans is barbaric. On the other, he must assert his difference from that dominant in order to support his authority as a witness to the horrors he has experienced. Equiano's emphasis on this duality of being is in fact registered on the very title page of his text,[58] which reads: *The Interesting Narrative of the Life of Olaudah Equiano, or Gustavus Vassa, the African. Written By Himself*. There is much to note here. First, Equiano's use of his African name is a deliberate act of (af)filiation in which he first proclaims his identity as a 'stranger' to his metropolitan audience. Its significance in this context is suggested by Carretta's observation that: 'Outside of his autobiography, the author of *The Interesting Narrative* almost never called himself Equiano.'[59] Elsewhere, the author explains how he resisted the Latin slave name first given him by Lieutenant Pascal, before physical coercion obliged him to adopt it, becoming the name 'by which I have been known ever since' (*IN*: 64). However, Equiano does not take the opportunity offered by writing his life-story to disavow it definitively. This may be partly for commercial reasons (Equiano would have been a name unknown to the public) but also, perhaps, because of its connotations (Gustavus Vassa being the Swedish monarch who led his subjugated people to independence). Nonetheless, the *conjunction* 'or' equally signifies *disjunction* between the identities implied by Equiano's African and European names, posing them as distinct, if not as alternatives. Finally, the ascription 'Written By Himself' (contrast the implications of the consistent first-person voice in *My Place*), while not unprecedented in eighteenth-century autobiographical texts (Vico, for example, uses an identical sub-title), foreshadows the disjunctive narrative perspective of the text which shortly ensues. Its opening pages, with their symptomatic slippage between first and third person in the account of Africa, in turn set the terms for what follows, allowing the author to embrace both his 'original' and acquired ethnicities without subordinating either. Like Fanon, then, Equiano clings to the 'zebra striping' of his identity and in doing so, contravenes one of the primary strategies of traditional spiritual autobiography, the attainment of unity of personhood. There could scarcely be a stronger disavowal than Equiano's of the anti-Manichean thrust of Augustine's conception of personhood in *Confessions*, widely recognised as the founding text of spiritual autobiography: 'You gathered me together from the state of disintegration in which I had been fruitlessly divided. I turned from unity in you to be lost in multiplicity.'[60]

Conclusion

The texts considered in this chapter indicate the complex relationship of this first thematic of subjectivity in the postcolonial life-writing *vis-à-vis* its inscriptions in western autobiography. On the one hand, there is a distinct pattern, across the geo-cultural and historical range of the sub-genre, of the decentred model of identity found in Equiano. For example, towards the end of *Out of Place* (1999, see Chapter 7), Edward Said proclaims: 'I occasionally experience myself as a cluster of flowing currents. I prefer this to the idea of a solid self, the identity to which so many attach so much significance.'[61] Conversely, the centred and unified conception of auto/biographical subjectivity elaborated by Morgan is also widely apparent. Thus, Sindiwe Magona's *To My Children's Children* (1991) reflects the epistemology of personhood in traditional Xhosa culture, where individual as well as social Being is figured in terms of 'connectedness and oneness'.[62] As the comparison between Morgan and Equiano further suggests, one should also be cautious of assuming that there is 'progress' from 'naïve' models of centred personhood towards more 'modern' conceptions of decentredness, in the way Majeed asserts is the case with the evolution of Indian nationalist autobiography.[63] My own analysis suggests that this trajecory does not apply to postcolonial life-writing more generally. Rather it corroborates Whitlock's argument that '[T]he hybrid and the syncretic always coincide with identifications that pursue authentic, continuous, and homogenous self-identities.'[64]

The cultural/political meanings of these contrastive models of Selfhood are equally complex. Some might see the reproduction of models of the centred Self found in canonical western autobiography as evidence in support of Gusdorf's conviction of the 'belated' nature of non-western auto/biography. Equally, the decentred Self of much contemporary postcolonial life-writing might be considered to be imitative of postmodernist elaborations of 'the death of the Subject'. Both accounts are too simple. As the example of Magona suggests, the inscription of the centred Self at times reflects an emphasis characteristic of a variety of non-western cultures. Thus, Léopold Senghor, the theoretician of African *négritude*, claimed that the African philosophy of Being is grounded in the principle of 'synthesis'. For the African writer, accordingly, 'Man is therefore a composition of mobile life forces which interlock: a world of solidarities that seek to knit themselves together.'[65] Conversely, Equiano's *Interesting Narrative* obviously long predates postmodernism. Neither this, nor later postcolonial texts featuring a comparable model of Selfhood, celebrate decentredness in the abstract philosophical terms which characterise postmodernist discussions of personhood. Rather, as already suggested, they reflect the material effects of the histories of colonialism, which often enforced fragmentation and multiplicity of identity on subjectivities that – as Senghor suggests – had hitherto been centred, if not foundationally rooted, by indigenous cultural tradition.

Further, one could argue that both models of Selfhood, far from being evidence of a complicitous assimilation to the cultural dominant, are at least potentially politically oppositional. Paul Smith observes of postmodern debates about the Subject that, with the exception of feminist contributions, 'all the discourses I have focused on presume and construct their appropriate "subject" in a way which ultimately leaves little room for consideration of resistance.'[66] By contrast, the attributes of decentredness enable the (post)colonial life-writer to evade the fixed identities through which (neo-)colonial stereotype, in particular, seeks to fix the (post)colonial subject in an inferior relation to the 'centre'. As Whitlock argues, 'thinking in terms of origins and authenticity, centre and periphery, and the separation into consistent and homogenous identities are fundamental to colonizing discourses.'[67] (The same might be argued about certain 'indigenous' discourses which seek to fix its subjects in particular identities, as is often the case with nationalism in respect of women, for example.)

However, Whitlock's argument needs refinement insofar as deployment of a centred and unified conception of auto/biographical Selfhood could be interpreted as having equal oppositional potential to its decentred analogues.[68] In the first place, such a model of subjectivity could just as well be understood as a riposte to colonial discourse, which historically sought to deny (post)colonial subjects membership of humanity on the basis of their supposed lack of the unified, centred and sovereign subjectivity characteristic of canonical autobiography. In this context, the appropriation of the constructs which underpin the West's dominant economy of self-representation is a significant gesture of resistance. Here one might adapt Jeanne Perreault's argument about recourse in western women's autobiography to the centred Self: 'Feminist [and, by implication, postcolonial] gestures towards cohesion may be grounded in the desire for a "point of departure" and indeed, a point of arrival, that embrace a process of transformation as a revolutionary concept.'[69]

Consonant with this argument, both texts provide clear evidence that the fracturing experience of colonialism on (post)colonial subjectivity can be turned to advantage. Whether through synthesis of aspects of 'native' and colonial cultural identities in order to construct a new, integrated, personhood (Morgan), or by emphasising a disjunctive conception of Selfhood which refuses sublation of its different elements into a single new whole (Equiano), postcolonial life-writing expresses its subjects' agency and capacity for self-renewal. Further, and as is typical of the sub-genre as a whole, both Morgan and Equiano eschew the temptation of constructing a singularised conception of identity based on what Edouard Glissant calls 'a single, unique root'.[70] Whether figured as 'weaving' (Morgan), 'chequering' (Equiano) or 'striping' (Fanon), postcolonial auto/biographical identity rarely seeks to utterly disavow the effects of colonialism on its constitution.

Nonetheless, there is a powerful strain of melancholia in both Morgan and Equiano. As has been seen, her failure to get Daisy to reveal all means that Sally is condemned to some measure of continuing 'amputation'. Equally, *The Interesting Narrative* supports Rushdie's reminder that hybrid identity is not only a means to 'straddle two cultures', a posture which Morgan arguably achieves, but also involves the danger of 'fall[ing] between two stools'.[71] Texts considered later in this monograph suggest that one should beware of too hastily concluding that either model of identity is innately empowering. For example, Nawal El Saadawi (see Chapter 3) and Shirley Lim (Chapter 4) seek to escape the highly restricted and static models of female identity enforced in their respective natal cultures. By contrast, V.S. Naipaul (Chapter 5) consistently despairs at the seeming impossibility of grounding Caribbean identity in terms solid and stable enough to provide security and self-esteem. Like Naipaul's *A Way in the World*, Said's *Out of Place* (Chapter 7) offers a more radical version of the decentredness found in Equiano, who always seems in control of the relationship between the twin aspects of his identity. For Said, Lim and Assia Djebar (Chapter 6), no less than Naipaul, decentredness is productive, both psychically and creatively. However, it also has the potential to cause the severest existential discomfort, as is suggested by Said's depressions, Djebar's self-doubts, Naipaul's oscillations between self-aggrandisement and self-loathing, or Lim's mental breakdown soon after arriving in the United States from Malaysia.

In its divided and ambivalent relationship to the conception of Selfhood characteristic of canonical western autobiography, postcolonial life-writing offers many parallels with its western women's analogues. As has been seen, feminist criticism is split over whether women's life-writing does, or should, embrace both models of Selfhood. Nonetheless my analysis suggests that the dilemma between embracing models of centred or decentred subjectivity is not confined to women life-writers in the postcolonial context. The fact that male colleagues also employ both models of Selfhood (as will be seen in Chapter 2, C.L.R. James is directly comparable to Morgan in his conception of personhood, as Brendan Behan is to Equiano) complicates western feminist claims about the gendered particularity of this thematic of subjectivity. The strategic question of the derivativeness or otherwise of postcolonial life-writing cannot be settled, therefore, without investigation of other aspects of auto/biographical subjectivity. This will be the task of the next three chapters.

2 Relational Selves

In both texts analysed in the previous chapter, the achievement of individual Selfhood, whether understood as centred or decentred, is not their protagonists' sole, or perhaps even prime, objective. Thus, Equiano constructs himself even on his title-page in a *representative* role as 'the African'. Equally, Morgan increasingly de-centres herself to make room for other first-person family voices, which comprise nearly a third of *My Place*, thereby shifting it away from individual towards collective auto/biography. Indeed, the privileging of the latter focus is implied in the epigraph: 'How deprived we would have been if we had been willing to let things stay as they were. We would have survived, but not as a whole people. We would never have known our place' (*MP*: n.p.). The addition of the indefinite article 'a' suggests a crucial change of emphasis from the source of the epigram in the text itself, which reads: 'We would have survived, but not as whole people' (*MP*: 233).

Such preoccupations point to a second thematic of auto/biographical subjectivity, which will be the focus of this chapter. Auto/biography Studies has traditionally advanced a view of autobiographical personhood as monadic and autonomous. For example, Gilmore argues that historically the canonical Subject is deemed to be 'contained within a set of boundaries that distinguish it from everything else around it'.[1] There is considerable support for such interpretations within the history of Auto/biography Studies. At the beginning of the twentieth century, Misch proposed that the objective of the autobiographer is to 'stand as an I, or, more exactly, as an "I"-saying person, *over against* other persons and living beings'.[2] During the second phase of Auto/biography Studies, Gusdorf corroborated this argument. The 'conscious awareness of the singularity of each individual life', which he saw as the primary impulse animating the genre, could not exist if 'the individual does not oppose himself to all others ... does not feel himself to exist outside of others, and still less against others'.[3] Such attitudes are repeated among male critics in the most recent phase of the critical field, despite the advent of postmodernism.[4] Thus, Olney, in recognising in women's life-writing 'a quite different orientation towards the self and others from the typical orientation to be found in autobiographies by men', reinforces the perspectives of his predecessors about this aspect of canonical autobiographical subjectivity.[5]

For many feminist critics, this conception of the autonomy of autobiographical identity is as clearly gendered as the emphasis on unified and centred Selfhood which traditionally accompanies it in Auto/biography Studies. By contrast, they have almost unanimously argued that subjectivity in women's life-writing is primarily relational rather than monadic. For example, Brodzki and Schenck assert that 'Self-definition in relation to significant others, is the most pervasive characteristic of the female autobiography.'[6] Indeed, Mary Mason proposes that what she calls the 'grounding of identity through relation to the chosen other'[7] characterises women's life-writing from its origins at the turn of the fifteenth century with *The Book of Margery Kempe*. Complementing the initial focus of attention on the auto/biographer's communion with God and/or family relationships, recent feminist criticism has explored the concept of relationality in terms of gender as a collective identity. For instance, Perreault suggests that much contemporary western women's life-writing demands recognition of 'who and what is meant by that written "I" as an element in the "we" of feminist communities'.[8]

Comparable arguments are often made about minoritarian women's life-writing in the West. Thus, Lourdes Torres claims of US Latina work that: 'The subject created is at once individual and collective.'[9] Postcolonial women's life-writing is often held to demonstrate similar, or even enhanced, attributes of relationality. Equally, Doris Sommer asserts that in Latin American women's *testimonio*, the autobiographer never considers herself as 'one isolated being' but as representative of a community.[10] Indeed, according to Longley, 'it is impossible to think of autobiography as an individual activity in traditional Aboriginal society' (an argument confirmed in the case of Morgan).[11] Furthermore, the emphasis on relationality in these different branches of women's life-writing is recognised as having important formal implications for traditional understandings of the genre. In the first place, the emphasis on relational or collective identities erodes the traditional boundary between autobiography and biography, which Olney claims is one that 'every writer on autobiography would feel it necessary to maintain'.[12] Issues of multi-authorship in women's 'life story', more specifically, create what Carole Boyce Davies describes as a 'scandal' for traditional theories of autobiography as an individual performance, such as Lejeune's.[13]

In emphasising the relational dimensions of women's life-writing, however, some observers caution against the same dangers of reification which attend discussions of the issue of (de)centred subjectivity. Thus, Regenia Gagnier complains that Woolf's conception of autobiography is limited by middle-class values of individualism and detachment which over-ride her identification with women of different classes.[14] In the postcolonial context, moreover, women's life-writing does not embrace relationality as a matter of course, or sometimes limits its operations. For example, Mary Seacole (see Chapter 5) barely mentions her parents, husband or daughter. In *Head Above Water*, Buchi Emecheta's identification with fellow-Nigerians in London is severely circumscribed by issues of ethnicity inflamed by the Biafran war, which pitted Emecheta's Igbo East against the Hausa North and Yoruba West. Equally, her work reflects deep tensions within London's black community between those of Caribbean and African origin. Among some (post)colonial societies, furthermore, women may be marginalised and anonymised by an indigenous patriarchy to an extent that a fiercely individualistic conception of autonomous Selfhood becomes – strategically and temporarily, at least – legitimate, even necessary. For example, Merle Hodge argues that: 'From the very beginning of West Indian history the black woman has had a de facto "equality" thrust upon her – the equality of cattle in a herd.'[15] Equally, Shirley Lim (see Chapter 4) suggests that to be able to write auto/biographically, a postcolonial woman 'may have to develop the "consciousness" of a gap between [her]self and others'; only thus can she escape 'the rule of her community' and the 'doubly colonial world' to which her gender may be confined.[16] This is the case not only with Lim, but with writers as diverse as Emecheta, Sindiwe Magona and Nawal El Saadawi (see Chapter 3).

In the rest of this chapter, I apply feminist debates about this second thematic of subjectivity to postcolonial life-writing by men, in order to explore whether it conforms to the patterns of (non-)relationality detected in both canonical autobiography and its female analogues. Having considered the sometimes contradictory evidence which C.L.R. James and Brendan Behan provide, I will then explore its implications for the primary strategic issue of my text, the question of the specificity of postcolonial life-writing. In this respect, I am again prompted by Fanon, whose *Black Skin* adumbrates what Edouard Glissant calls a characteristically postcolonial 'poetics of relation'[17] on a number of levels. Perhaps the most striking axis Fanon conjures is the assertion that the black man 'must be black in relation to the white man'.[18] This might seem both an unfortunate illustration of Fanon's tendency to masculinism (although in this particular instance it may be primarily a problem of translation[19]), as well as unwittingly supportive of Gusdorf's argument about the secondary and dependent nature of non-western life-writing. (This argument will be contested in due course.) Nonetheless, it usefully raises the theoretical issue of whether (post)colonial subjectivity is necessarily constructed along this relational axis, as a consequence of the material histories of colonial acculturation, thereby inflecting established conceptions of auto/biographical representations of personhood. However, as one might expect of a thinker steeped in psychoanalytic thinking and immersed in issues of language and ideology, Fanon's conception of relationality goes much deeper, deriving in the last instance from what he considers to be the inalienably *social* character of Selfhood: 'Hence we are driven from the individual back to the social structure.'[20] Thus, while deeply preoccupied by his individual experience and formation, Fanon is also concerned with the predicament of the Antillean, even of the colonised subject as a whole.

Self and nation: C.L.R. James, *Beyond a Boundary* (1963)

In certain respects, the centred and sovereign Self ostensibly constructed in James's text, like Morgan's, corresponds to what is widely considered to be the normative model of the Subject in the western canon of autobiography. Unity of Being characterises those figures whom James most admires. Of William Hazlitt, for example, he comments that 'he is not a divided man ... He takes his whole self wherever he goes'[21]. By contrast, despite inspiring James as a cricket and music critic, Neville Cardus is represented as 'a victim of … that division of the human personality, which is the greatest curse of our time' (*BaB*: 196). Like Augustine's *Confessions*, *Beyond a Boundary* represents James's trajectory towards self-knowledge and psychological maturity in terms of a progression from division to integration of Self. James acknowledges that, as a boy: 'Two people lived in me: one, the rebel against all family and school discipline and order; the other, a Puritan who would have cut off a finger sooner than do anything contrary to the ethics of the game' (*BaB*: 28). Nonetheless, the author suggests, he had already intuited the principles of synthesis and holism which were to become the hallmark of his later conception of personhood: 'Somehow from around me I … selected and fastened on to the things that made a whole' (*BaB*: 18). Anna Grimshaw argues that *Beyond a Boundary* 'completed the search for integration which James had begun … some sixty years before'.[22] So important did the principle of unity of Being become for its author that she explains her subject's defection from the revolutionary Marxism, in which he was active for over two decades, in terms of James's increasing conviction that it 'separated essential aspects of his being'.[23]

Consonant with the argument of feminist critics discussed above, James's autobiographical Self apparently displays a characteristically masculine tendency not just towards acquisition of 'sovereignty' but to monadism and isolation (compare N.C. Chaudhuri, see Chapter 5). This appears to be corroborated by the neglect in *Beyond a Boundary* of the author's immediate 'Others'. Confined largely to the first three chapters, James's birth family makes a brief reappearance at the end, where his unnamed second wife (Constance Webb) and son are introduced, only to be summarily dismissed. 'I do not feel inclined to go into all that here,' James comments laconically (*BaB*: 254; neither his first nor third wives are mentioned at all in the narrative). Aside from Learie Constantine, furthermore, few personal friends are given much attention. Such factors invite one to (mis)read *Beyond a Boundary* in the same way as Morgan's *My Place* (or even Equiano's *Interesting Narrative*), as a record of the process by which a talented individual(ist) from the margins secures a position of social distinction by conforming to dominant norms and values.

James's apparent investment in a conventional model of sovereign, monadic Selfhood might be read as one symptom of his well-nigh total assimilation to western culture. Farrukh Dhondy proposes that he was 'the only intellectual of the black diaspora unequivocally to espouse and embrace the intellectual, artistic and socio-political culture of Europe'.[24] Ultimately simplistic though Dhondy's interpretation is, a selective reading of *Beyond a Boundary* certainly provides evidence to support it. Recounting his immersion in the public-school ethos of his schooling and devotion to British writing, from school-boy yarns to classical figures – notably Thackeray – James describes himself as: 'A British intellectual long before I was ten, already an alien in my own environment among my own people, even my own family' (*BaB*: 18). If he later became a 'declared enemy of British imperialism' (*BaB*: 45), the terms in which his enmity were framed were nonetheless heavily indebted to the western Marxist thought he first encountered in England and developed in the US. Marxism also enabled James to theorise his early intuitive grasp of the all-important principles of holism and integration. In one letter, he quotes Marx's dictum that: 'The truth is in the whole.'[25] However, as the same letter's reference to 'the incomparable Hegel'[26] suggests, it is to Marx's predecessor that James ultimately looks for the synthesising, dialectical method which was to underpin his political and intellectual projects, including his life-writing. James's recourse late in life to the autobiographical mode in *Beyond a Boundary* might be considered in turn as evidence of a retreat to his early pattern of positive identification with the culture of the coloniser, after he became disillusioned with revolutionary Marxism. Gestures towards the same Puritan tradition of spiritual autobiography drawn on by Equiano (and, later, Emecheta) can be detected in James's acknowledgement of how he 'worshipped at the shrine of John Bunyan' (*BaB*: 20). Early in life, James not only considered it his 'moral and religious duty' to improve himself (*BaB*: 21), but embarked on a consistent process of self-examination which, arguably, culminates in *Beyond a Boundary*.

However, James's apparent investment in such a model of autobiographical Selfhood cannot be seen unproblematically either as a function of his gender or as a sign of his assimilation to the dominant in the terms Dhondy proposes.[27] As with Morgan, his conception of personhood operates in the first place as a *critical* response to the psychologically fragmenting forces of colonialism. Paul Buhle argues that because of its particular histories, during which it fell successively under Spanish, French and British rule, together with the importation of large numbers of African slaves and Indian indentured labourers, 'perhaps more than any other Caribbean society [James's home island of Trinidad was] the victim … of multiple identities'.[28] (See also the discussion of the implications of this argument for Naipaul in Chapter 5.) But while deprecating the fracturing effects of racial theory on identity, of which Morgan and Equiano also complain, James's conception of Selfhood is further mobilised against the threat posed to individual psychological integrity by both the capitalist and totalitarian systems dominant in the mid-twentieth century. According to Grimshaw, James believed that 'never before had the individual personality been so fragmented and restricted'.[29] Conversely, Brett St Louis rightly suggests that James's high valuation of classical Greece derived in large measure from his conviction of its commitment to the psychic wholeness of its citizens. Thus, James 'grieves the loss of the integrated personality that was not an accident of Greek antiquity, but a result of its direct democracy that cultivated individuals who understood and exercised their rights, liberties, freedoms, and possibilities in relation to their community'.[30]

More importantly for the focus of this chapter, the Self constructed in *Beyond a Boundary* is not set 'over against' its 'Others' in the terms described by Misch, Gusdorf and Olney, any more than Morgan's. For James, integration *of* Self is the desired effect and goal of the individual's integration *into* society. This underpins his distinctive conception of 'personality *in* society' (*BaB*: 3, my emphasis), a theme announced on the first page of the text, where it is also dramatised. Like some of the nineteenth-century 'condition of England' novels which he so much admired, *Beyond a Boundary* begins with a panoramic long-shot of the community in which the boy James is situated, before narrowing its focus to the protagonist. He is first glimpsed perched on a chair, which enables him with equal facility to reach for the bookshelf and look out of the window onto the cricket ground opposite. Inner and outer, ideational and material, private and public worlds are thereby related, if not seamlessly conjoined, as are the principles of self-reflection and social (inter-action). Instead personality is the effect of the system of relations embodied in all forms of social organisation in which the individual is involved. This includes sport, James's organising metaphor in *Beyond a Boundary* for conceptualising Car-ibbean society. He was therefore to dismiss the argument that Garfield Sobers, possibly the most talented cricketer of the post-war era, was anything other than

> the most typical West Indies cricketer that it is possible to imagine. All gen-iuses are merely people who carry to an extreme definitive [*sic*] the char-acteristics of the unit of civilization to which they belong and the special act or function which they express or practise.[31]

This fundamentally relational conception of personhood has crucial implica-tions for James's conception of autobiographical form, involving the necessity of going 'beyond the boundaries' of the genre as conventionally understood. James's Preface asserts that what follows is 'neither cricket reminiscences nor auto-biography' (*BaB*: n.p.) and justifies his hybrid, 'in-between' mode of writing on the basis that: 'To establish his own identity, Caliban ... must himself pioneer into regions Caesar never knew' (*BaB*: n.p.). This foregrounds not only the text's unconventional style but offers an explanation for it in terms of both the relation between James as an individual and his *representative* identity as (rebellious) Car-ibbean archetype, and between the author and the coloniser (in the manner Fanon describes). Autobiography may have provided James with a preliminary 'grammar' in which to articulate his Self, much as Caliban was taught by Pros-pero to express himself; however, in keeping with his dissident forerunner, James subverts its rules to the extent that what the Preface describes as 'the auto-biographical framework' (*BaB*: n.p.) becomes severely attenuated in the service of exploring those social *relations* which structure James's own formation.

Most obviously, the revisionary nature of *Beyond a Boundary* is represented in its concern to provide a gallery of portraits (or group-portrait) of cultural figures and cricketers, many of whom James did not know personally, who contributed to his intellectual and political development. Pre-eminent among them, although in this case someone he did know, is Learie Constantine, who is given such emphasis that James at one point admits: 'Biography is my subject' (*BaB*: 134). Further contrary to what one might expect, the 'Epilogue and Apotheosis', moreover, provide no summative account of James's reflections on his life and experience, but focuses instead on the Melbourne Test match between Australia and the West Indies in 1961. In turn, despite the apparent influence of Bunyan, the text lacks the kind of intimately self-reflective 'conversion' scenes found in Equiano which might explain, for example, James's decisive turns to and from Marxism/Trotskyism. A further deviation from generic norms is the inclusion of an index, which pushes his text towards historiography rather than personal narrative. His apparent desire to diminish the subjective aspects of his writing is reinforced in remarks about another genre on which he draws. 'Any extended cricket analysis which is not based on historical facts or the techniques of the game,' James states dismissively, in asserting the difference between his own text and run-of-the-mill cricket reminiscences, 'tells us more about the writer than what he is writing about' (*BaB*: 171).

Thus, as Ato Quayson argues, even insofar as *Beyond a Boundary* can be understood as an autobiography, it offers an 'explicit collocation of the individual personality with an entire historical process'.[32] This gives James's text its epic scope, sweeping from ancient Athens, through Victorian Britain to the contemporary Caribbean, as the author seeks to establish his conception of the relationship of the general to the particular, including his individual Self. The economy with which this objective is accomplished derives primarily from the author's focus on the game of cricket. For James, as Aldon Nielson argues, cricket is 'a dramatic spectacle in which the dialectical relations between the one and the many are continually re-enacted'.[33] It therefore provides rich matter for reflection on the wider problems of 'relationality' which interest James as an historian, cultural theorist and political philosopher as well as autobiographer. In the first place, cricket embodies the same system of morality and laws which both constrain and enable the individual in relation to social structures of more obvious kinds. Further, it demands the co-operation between the members of the team towards a collective goal, which for the writer is the very essence of meaningful social organisation (*BaB*: 197).

Within the conditions of Caribbean life more specifically, these aspects of the game also enable it to become a medium for anti-colonial politics. James describes how, through the influence of Constantine, he became increasingly aware of the gap between the theoretically meritocratic ideals of cricket and the actuality of its manipulation as a social institution to preserve white privilege and power. This disjunction provides the site for nationalist sentiment to develop, a gathering mobilisation in which James eagerly participated once he reached England. Despite being a product of colonial acculturation, cricket offered itself as the basis of an independent national culture partly because of its mass audience and partly because of its integrative dynamic. Even during colonial times, James shows, the otherwise stratified classes and racial groups in Trinidad came together to play, although the different clubs still reproduced these inherited social divisions in respect of their membership. Inter-island and international competition nonetheless steadily broke down these stratifications, providing the basis for the emergence of a common sense of 'West Indianness', which reached its apotheosis with the appointment of Frank Worrell as the first black captain of the West Indies. In this development, *Beyond a Boundary* suggests that James, as editor of *The Nation* newspaper, plays a direct, significant and representative role, thereby also enhancing his personal feelings of belonging after many years in exile.

However, cricket further illustrates James's conception of nationalism as merely a stage in the larger dialectic of human development towards a culture of 'universal' relations which would make such particularist forms of identification redundant. As Grimshaw argues, James 'understood the movement of the modern world to be one of increasing integration'.[34] One symptom of this was the writer's enthusiastic support for a West Indian Federation, which partly explains James's focus on cricket as the prime pan-Caribbean cultural practice (at least in its Anglophone parts) rather than on calypso or Carnival, as one might have expected from a specifically Trinidadian nationalist. Influenced by both Marxism and Pan-Africanism, James further proposes a model of international relations which seeks to sublate the old binaries of coloniser and colonised into a new synthesis. Cricket is particularly useful to James's argument insofar as it symbolises the culture shared (increasingly, at least theoretically, on equal terms) between former masters and bondsmen.

This multiplicitous emphasis on integration (compare Morgan) in turn suggests that *Beyond a Boundary* may in fact be more structurally coherent as an auto/biographical text than might seem on first reading James's Preface. In the course of exploring his social concerns, the sources of the ideas and structures of feeling which define James's particular ways of seeing and being also emerge very clearly. For example, his personal investment in cricket is related to its promise to bring to an end what he describes as the 'war between English Puritanism ... and the realism of West Indian life' (*BaB*: 21), which raged within him during early life. In this light, the generic disjunctions become less glaring. Thus, the 'Epilogue and Apotheosis', which initially appears to have little bearing on the author's own development, can in fact be read allegorically as heralding the emergence of the social conditions necessary for the very possibility of an auto/biography like *Beyond a Boundary*. It is only once the West Indies has 'made a public entry into the comity of nations' (*BaB*: 261) that James can complete a text which is at once linked to the historical traditions and conventions of western autobiography while simultaneously radically questioning them. (Indeed, it is only at this moment of decolonisation that James can assert a Self which is 'sovereign' in political as well as epistemological terms.) Equally, only at this particular conjuncture can James's formation in *Beyond a Boundary* be read in representative terms as an allegory of the growth of Trinidad, the West Indies and, indeed, the whole colonial world, towards independence and thence to the genuine integration implied in the concept of the 'comity of nations'. These are clear manifestations of the 'connected pattern' (*BaB*: 7) which James's text seeks to construct at the formal as well as thematic level. Like Grimshaw, St Louis judges the quest for synthesis a success, arguing that, it 'seamlessly combines [personal] memoir and West Indian social history'.[35]

This does not mean that James's project is without contradictions. In the first place, integration of Self is achieved partly by significant omissions, not just in James's personal, but public life. Grant Farred suggests that James's barely acknowledged American sojourn (1938–53) was nonetheless 'crucial to his conception of *Beyond a Boundary*'.[36] Indeed, he goes on to argue that the unified Selfhood that James so assiduously constructs is compensation for a life of often severe dislocation and upheaval. The society into which James wishes to insert his

integrated Self is also curiously incomplete. He makes strenuous efforts to promote cultural practices (auto/biographical writing as well as cricket) capable of
relating to and integrating the variety of communities of which the Caribbean is
comprised. He is not perhaps entirely successful in terms of racial groups (the
overwhelming majority of cricketers he discusses are black Caribbeans), even if his
awareness of the racially-mixed character of the region, and Trinidad more specifically (where 40 per cent of the population is of East Indian origin), means that
he explicitly eschews the foundational identity offered by *negritude*. More problematic still is James's treatment of gender. At the time *Beyond a Boundary* was written,
cricket was a game played almost exclusively by men. Roughly half the population of the Caribbean, therefore, are positioned as passive onlookers (at best),
rather than active participants in James's model of national culture, just as some
of the women he was intimately involved with play no real role within his account
of his formation. Nonetheless, it is clear that James consistently aspires to forms of
relation with a variety of 'Others', which leads him to go 'beyond the boundaries'
which canonical autobiography and traditional Auto/biography Studies alike characteristically police. As James argued of Walt Whitman, his 'passion to identify
himself with his fellow countrymen did enable him to create a new social medium'.[37]

Self and class (and sexuality): Brendan Behan, *Borstal Boy* (1958)

While nation is the collective axis with which James is primarily concerned in
terms of his development as an auto/biographical Subject, *Beyond a Boundary* also
engages with ideas of class affiliation. Cricket is thus represented as a social form
which potentially transcends class as well as racial polarisations in the name of a
new national community-in-the-making. In Brendan Behan's *Borstal Boy* (1958),
these axes of self-identification are reversed in terms of their importance. The text
elaborates a process whereby what initially seem to be the impregnable claims of
nation on the individual are increasingly complicated by Behan's awareness of
solidarity with some social fractions within the home of the empire which has for
so long oppressed his country. Indeed, barely a third of the way into his narrative,
this leads him to an apparent outright disavowal of the commitments which gal-
vanised him to participate in a terrorist campaign on the British mainland: 'I'd
sooner be with Charlie and Ginger and Browny in Borstal than with my own
comrades and country-men any place else.'[38]

Behan's self-construction at the outset of the text, which opens in November
1939 with his arrest in Liverpool as a 16-year-old Volunteer on a sabotage mission,[39] situates him squarely within a family tradition of involvement in Irish liberation politics (his father was imprisoned for IRA activities, his maternal uncle
wrote Eire's national anthem and a grandmother and two aunts were jailed in
Britain on terrorist charges soon after his arrest). While on remand, Behan for-
tifies himself by remembering the sacrifices of previous 'martyrs' to the cause and
singing nationalist songs. Equally, when charged, he frames his defiance explicitly
in the discourse of 'speeches from the dock' (*BB*: 4) made by earlier generations

of activists captured by the British, being particularly inspired by the example of the 'Invincibles'. Moreover, in representing British atrocities in Ireland after the First World War as being of a piece with the Amritsar massacre (*BB*: 2), Behan aligns himself with a world-wide nationalist struggle against imperialism. Indeed, his preliminary counter-discursive invocations of British colonial writers like Rider Haggard and Kipling (*BB*: 82–3)[40] align Behan with much of the new post-colonial writing emerging at the same time as *Borstal Boy*, as decolonisation accelerated in Africa and Asia.

Even at this early stage, however, there are signs of conflict within Behan's nationalist identifications. He thus expresses strong hostility towards those who see Irish nationalism as inseparable from Catholicism. While taking comfort from religious services (when allowed to attend them), Behan is unable to forgive the Church for its hostility to the IRA (he follows his father, along with many others opposed to the Irish Free State's 'appeasement' of Britain over Ulster, in being excommunicated for belonging to the organisation). These fissures in Behan's sense of 'Irishness' are exacerbated in other ways. He comes to recognise both the intractable difference of Northern Irish Catholics like Lavery (*BB*: 184–7) and the antipathy towards 'Dublin jackeens' like himself of rural 'Culchies' such as Parry (*BB*: 258). He is further unsettled by growing awareness of his difference from Irish emigrants settled in England, especially those within the hierarchy of the penal establishment. Father Lane and Warder Mooney exemplify a disorienting dis-identification with Ireland among some emigrants which is echoed by certain prisoners of Irish extraction, notably Dale. Insofar as these prisons are metonyms of the British state, Behan is eventually forced to acknowledge the complicity of some of his fellow-countrymen in the system of imperialism from which his nation supposedly continues to suffer: 'And some of the worse [*sic*] bastards running it are the Irish' (*BB*: 301).

Nationalism is compromised primarily, however, because of Behan's increasing identification with his fellow-prisoners along the axis of class. He brings with him from Ireland an already well-developed sense of class identity, inherited from his painter father. In a letter, Behan recalls a school-teacher debating a book entitled *Could Ireland Become Communist?* and comments: 'For giving a very definite answer in the affirmative, I got a kick in the neck.'[41] At CID headquarters, Behan claims that he has come to fight for the Irish Workers' and Small Farmers' Republic, making a clear distinction between 'the left-wing element in the movement', and the 'craw-thumpers' who 'would be hopping mad at me giving the impression that the IRA was Communistic' (*BB*: 4–5). That his political philosophy is as much socialist as nationalist in character is further indicated by recurrent praise for the Spanish Republican cause, for which Behan had once hoped to fight.[42] However, the fact that he comes from the hard streets of Dublin's North Side appears to be the determining factor in an increasing sense of solidarity with his fellow-prisoners:

I had the same rearing as most of them; Dublin, Liverpool, Manchester, Glasgow, London. All our mothers had all done the pawn – pledging on

Monday, releasing on Saturday. We all knew the chip shop and the picture house and the fourpenny rush of a Saturday afternoon, and the summer swimming in the canal and being chased along the railway by the cops.

(*BB*: 232)[43]

Such sentiments pose two particular problems for nationalist ideology. In the first place, it challenges the discrimination traditionally insisted upon between 'political' prisoners and common criminals, a distinction which his fellow-IRA detainee Lavery is keen to enforce (*BB*: 187). Much more damagingly, however, Behan's solidarity with his fellow-inmates might be understood as fraternisation with the enemy, if not 'a sort of 'igh treason' (*BB*: 11).

In fact, Behan never abandons belief in the nationalist cause. Rather, he comes to question the IRA's strategy of armed struggle at a time when Nazism was the more pressing enemy. However, Behan's shift from nation to class as his primary axis of self-identification is confirmed as he works through successive stages of the prison system. In Walton jail, the carceral regime is mapped primarily in terms of empire, reinforcing his sense of 'Irishness'. For example, the Governor's office 'was a sort of viceregal apartment' (*BB*: 48) and Behan ridicules the man himself as 'this tired old consul, weary from his labours among the lesser breeds, administering the King's justice equal and fairly to wild Irish and turbulent Pathan' (*BB*: 82). Borstal, by contrast, is conceived essentially in class terms, where national identity is less of an issue. The timbered building reminds Behan of 'a Tudor great house' (*BB*: 203); the Governor is known to all as 'the Squire' and runs his institution on the lines of a public school, with 'Houses' (ironically, Behan is assigned to St George's), a Matron and dormitory captains. Here, he learns more sophisticated forms of class-analysis, primarily through Tom Meadows, who lauds the class-consciousness and organisation exemplified by Robert Tressell's *Ragged-Trousered Philanthropists*. Nonetheless, Behan increasingly demurs from Meadows's cold objectivity towards their fellow-inmates, whom the latter dismisses as 'lumpen proletariat' (*BB*: 336). Against such perspectives, the protagonist protests that 'the blokes are only working-class kids the same as ourselves' (*BB*: 294), an identification reciprocated by many of the English Behan encounters. While there are moments when he is taken to task for his IRA membership, Charlie sets the prevailing tone of solidarity among his fellow-prisoners, even in Walton: 'I don't care, Paddy, if you were in the IRA or what you were bleedin' in. You're my china, Paddy' (*BB*: 63).

Class identification, however, is only one reason for Behan's attraction to Charlie, which soon develops into a clearly homoerotic relationship. The homosocial world of prison in turn becomes a powerful vector for Behan's progressive disenchantment with an Irish nationalism which polices sexuality in coercive ways. Behan's can be seen as 'problematic' from the outset of the text. Contradicting the self-disciplining discourses of nationalist mythography, he is unable to subdue his erotic urges while on remand. After first being interrogated, Behan masturbates in his cell, wondering guiltily what previous 'martyrs' would have thought of him doing so. One could argue that Behan's sexuality is only channelled towards other males because of the prison environment. His immediate appreciation of Charlie's 'long dark eyelashes' (*BB*: 10), however, seems too spontaneous to be explained in this way. Such evidence of Behan's 'unruly' sexuality is perhaps supported by the letter 'from a boy in Dublin' (*BB*: 2) found on him at the time of his arrest. Despite Behan's disclaimers, it seems especially significant in the absence of any equivalent from his alleged girl-friend, Shiela [*sic*]. The letter's contents are not spelled out, but one might infer that Behan's homosexual orientations precede his incarceration in English institutions. If heterosexuality is strictly policed within nationalist discourse (Shiela reminds Behan tartly that he is a Volunteer when he makes unwelcome advances [*BB*: 66]), homosexuality is an affront to the discourses of 'Mother Ireland' and the maiden Erin. Indeed Colbert Kearney describes it as 'an obscene insult to the good name of republicanism'.[44] The Belfast IRA man Lavery reminds Behan unambiguously that: 'The prisoners ... talk about things, aye, and do things ... that the lowest ruffian in Ireland, Catholic or Protestant, wouldn't put his tongue to the mention of' (*BB*: 186).[45] From the orthodox nationalist point of view, the scandal of Behan's same-sex relationships is, of course, compounded by the fact that his objects of desire are English. Charlie is not only like 'a typical English boy in an advertisement' (*BB*: 164), however, but a member of the colonisers' armed forces, an identity which is reinforced each time he dons his uniform for official occasions.

The increasing complexity and hybridity of Behan's (self-)identifications, reminiscent of Equiano's decentred model of subjectivity, is partly suggested in the rich range of inter-texts which *Borstal Boy* draws on. These suggest a multiplicity of national, ethnic and class affiliations which progressively undermine singularising notions of unified personhood and national belonging alike. These include not just the Irish tradition of prison narratives represented by 'martyrs' like Tom Clarke (*BB*: 42, 64),[46] but British works as diverse as Bunyan's *Pilgrim's Progress* (written in Bedford jail and another link with Equiano, as well as James) and Woolf's fictional biography of the bi-gendered *Orlando* (which furnishes Behan's densely teasing epigraph). Perhaps the most significant inter-text, however, is Behan's fellow-Dubliner and co-exile, James Joyce, first mentioned after Behan is beaten up for taking Father Lane to task (*BB*: 68) and later the subject of Behan's prize essay at the 'Eisteddfod'. There are certainly enough specific echoes of *A Portrait of the Artist* to justify seeing Behan's text as 'A Portrait of the Artist as a Young (ex-)Nationalist'. Specific echoes include the Christmas sermon in Walton (compare Chapter 3 of *A Portrait*) and Behan's revelatory experiences on the seashore at Hollesley Bay (compare Chapter 4 of *A Portrait*). *Borstal Boy*, too, describes the formation of an artist's mind, in the process of which Behan repeats the lesson that Stephen draws: in order to succeed, he must escape the nets of nationality and religion. In exile, moreover, Behan often survives through the silence (*BB*: 13, 221) and cunning (*BB*: 348–9) which Stephen advocates. Nonetheless, while this might seem to be evidence of Behan's turning away from the kinds of relationality described earlier, he represents such strategies as ultimately political in nature and collectively-oriented: 'I thought it better to survive my sentence and come out and strike a blow in vengeance … than be kicked to death or insanity here' (*BB*: 131).

Above all, Behan's affinities with Joyce's cosmopolitan conception of a decentred, postnational, but still relational conception of identity can be traced in the linguistic hybridity which does so much to reflect the protagonist's shifting negotiations with various collectives. At one point, he refers to Poynings' law of 1495, which 'forbade the native Irish to keep up their own language and customs' (*BB*: 283). This perhaps explains Behan's pride in his Gaelic, expressed not only in songs but also diction like 'airt', 'shoneen', and 'garsun' (*BB*: 3, 199, 122). But he also brings with him distinctive versions of Irish English, whether 'corruptions' like 'eejit' (*BB*: 171), proverbs and sayings such as 'he'd mind mice at a cross-roads' (*BB*: 180) or 'short and sweet as an ass's gallop' (*BB*: 135). Onto this is grafted the more particular class dialect of Dublin's North Side, which he distinguishes from what he dismisses as 'Abbey Theatre bogman [country] talk' (*BB*: 97).[47] This is especially apparent when Behan slips into interior monologue, as if to suggest that this is his authentic 'voice':

> Yous have enough songs out of yous about the boys that faced the Saxon foe, but bejasus, when there's one of them there among you, the real Ally Dally, the real goat's genollickers, yous are silent as the tomb.
>
> (*BB*: 85)

It might be considered symptomatic of Behan's 'hunker-sliding' (*BB*: 118) towards sympathetic identification with England, therefore, that towards the end of the text he uses not the first-person, but third-person, plural formulations like 'As they say in Irish' (*BB*: 327) to preface certain instances of 'native' language use.[48] Certainly, his language becomes inflected by a new range of class-specific 'Englishes' acquired from fellow-prisoners. Shortly after his arrest, Behan boasts that: 'I speak it like a native, English, in two days and a bit' (*BB*: 15). Soon afterwards, he describes them smoking 'as Charlie said, "like lords' bastards"' (*BB*: 29). From Charlie, Behan also picks up 'Cockney' rhyming slang, often abbreviated, as in 'china' ('china plate'/mate) or 'flowery' ('flowery dell'/cell). Onto this in turn Behan grafts aspects of dialect from other parts of Britain, often rendered phonetically in order to bring out their distinctive accents.

However, at least to some extent, Behan's linguistic shifts must be understood as a defensive form of mimicry, making him less vulnerable among English prisoners whom he fears initially will prove 'very nationalistic' (*BB*: 70). In this sense it can be understood as a stratagem of self-concealment of the kind which some critics argue was favoured by Equiano. Conversely, in contrast to Equiano, one might claim that Behan 'displaces' standard English as deliberate strategy of cultural/political self-assertion which is consonant with his continuing nationalist affiliations. His unorthodox English usage, notably a flagrant disregard for the 'rules' of grammar and syntax, is clearly subversive of the cultural authority represented by the official English of the prison system (itself a metaphor of colonial rule), in a manner which foreshadows the experimentations of postcolonial writers. Like contemporaries such as Achebe, moreover (*Things Fall Apart* was published in the same year as *Borstal Boy*), Behan asserts resistance through appropriation of the master-texts of the colonising culture. A particularly striking example of this comes in his performance of Hardy's *Under the Greenwood Tree*, during which Behan sings the Christmas carol to 'the air of the "Famine Song"' (*BB*: 88). He 'translates' other passages from the novel into Irish English (*BB*: 80–1), to the extent that, Kearney argues, 'even Hardy's prose is colonised'.[49] Behan's affiliations with postcolonial discourse are also reinforced through associations with Caliban, another colonial subject who has had his island usurped. Behan is linked to Caliban in being an object of 'reform' within a comparably 'benevolent' carceral regime. They also share both a proclivity for 'sweet airs that give delight' (Behan is forever singing traditional Gaelic songs) and cursing. Behan's curses are as inventive and pointed as his predecessor's: 'If you're half right it's too good for you, you jackamanape's scourings of a lock hospital piss pot' (*BB*: 260; compare 82, 96, 297).[50] Once again, such language constitutes a form of cultural 'disobedience' which expresses resistance just as obviously as Behan's sexual 'deviance' and political ideology.

The complexity of the author's (self-)identifications thus powerfully challenges narrowly conceived models of the relation between individual and collective in some anti-colonial discourse. As John Brannigan argues: '[Irish] Nationalist narratives of imprisonment tend to suggest the unequivocal identification of the individual with the nation.'[51] However, Behan's deviation from this model does not amount to his full assimilation to English culture. If his early release signals that the British state no longer considers him a threat, Behan is nonetheless deported and forbidden to return to the United Kingdom. The final scene, which finds him all alone on Irish soil once more, just as he was when he arrived in England on his sabotage mission, might seem to affirm Behan's final embrace of a masculinist and monadic conception of self-sufficiency, signifying his achievement of autobiographical maturity. In this respect, the changing conception of Selfhood which accompanies Behan's trajectory through the prison system appears to have come full circle. In Walton, as an apparently freelance and independent Volunteer, he is placed in solitary confinement, which largely suits his initially solipsistic sense of autonomy and difference. In Feltham, he shares a cell with others, before moving into a crowded dormitory in Borstal. These increasingly populated scenes of confinement allegorise his gradual opening up to the principle of relationality as a precondition of personal growth and development as he moves towards something resembling a normal society in Suffolk.

In this light, however, the ending is more complex and melancholy than an initial reading might suggest. When the Irish immigration officer comments that it must be wonderful to be free, Behan retorts ambiguously: 'It must' (*BB*: 372). If his physical liberty is restored, it is by no means clear that Ireland will offer him the intellectual and emotional (and sexual) freedoms paradoxically available in a carceral bastion of the empire which continues to prevent the reunification of his homeland. Just as his homeland appears in a 'haze' (*BB*: 371), so Behan's corresponding inner uncertainties arise primarily from an intuition that he is now cut off from precisely those solidarities and axes of identification which were so instrumental in his formation.

Conclusion

The texts analysed here suggest that postcolonial life-writing stands in a complex relationship to western women's auto/biography in respect of this second thematic of subjectivity, too. While both sub-genres contrast with the canon in terms of their construction of an auto/biographical Self which is fundamentally relational, this is sometimes conceived in rather different terms in the two sub-genres. Thus, James and Behan to some degree corroborate the argument of feminist critics that intimate varieties of inter-personal relationships are less important in the construction of male auto/biographical Selfhood than is the case with women writers. For example, Behan greets the news of Charlie's death in the war with brief and stoic under-statement. James offers even less insight into his affective life, a paradigm equally evident in texts from Claude McKay's *A Long Way from Home* (1937) to Chaudhuri's *Autobiography of an Unknown Indian* (1951; see Chapter 5). However, there are important exceptions to this pattern. Thus, whereas feminist critics have pointed to the importance of the mother–daughter relationship as a prime instance of the characteristic relationality of women's life-writing, a corresponding father–son axis can be found in some of its male equivalent, for example, Said's *Out of Place* (see Chapter 7) and Hanif Kureishi's *My Ear at his Heart: Reading My Father* (2004).[52] V.S. Naipaul, too, devotes considerable, if ambivalent, attention to his father in *Finding the Centre* (1984; see Chapter 5), a relationship which the author has since excavated in greater detail.[53]

The general absence or marginalisation of immediate 'significant Others' in male postcolonial life-writing is, however, often compensated for by identification and solidarity with a variety of groups in relation to which the writer constructs his sense of Selfhood. As the example of James suggests, this is perhaps most strikingly evident in political claims to representativity and relationality at a national level (an issue which will be returned to in Chapter 7). Spectacular examples of such claims include Nkrumah's *Ghana: The Autobiography of Kwame Nkrumah* (1957) and Lee Kuan Yew's *The Singapore Story: Memoirs of Lee Kuan Yew* (1998), in which auto/biographer and nation are breathtakingly conflated. As has been seen, class is a further important axis of individual/collective (self-)identification in male postcolonial life-writing and racial/ethnic collectives another. Thus, the final chapter of McKay's *A Long Way from Home* is entitled 'On Belonging to a Minority Group', as if to suggest that, despite his scepticism about 'Negro politics' as constituted at the time of writing, he remains willy-nilly bound within this axis of (self-)identification (not least by the gaze of others).

While engaging with collective identities based in gender and – to a lesser extent – class,[54] western women's life-writing rarely espouses those associated with nation to the same degree as its postcolonial analogues. Although not an autobiography, Woolf's *Three Guineas* (1938) sets the pattern in this respect, with the narrator's famous declaration that: 'As a woman I want no country. As a woman, my country is the whole world.'[55] Woolf is equally little interested in ethnicity or race as grounds for solidarity, whether among women or between the genders. In this respect, minoritarian and postcolonial women's life-writing often converges far more closely with its male analogues than with western women's life-writing. For example, Hertha Wong claims that while Native American women's life-writing has powerful elements of relationality, 'instead of identifying as a (universal) woman, a Native woman is far more likely to identify herself by tribal, national, or cultural affiliation'.[56] Such collective (self-)identifications are also widely found in postcolonial women's writing considered in this volume, as the examples of Morgan and Amiry (Chapter 7) suggest, although often, as with Behan, in qualified form (see, for example, the work of Lim and El Saadawi, discussed in Chapters 3 and 4). There is therefore some justice in Lionnet's observation that in postcolonial life-writing as a whole, 'the individual necessarily defines him – or herself with regard to a community',[57] whether of ethnic, racial or national kinds. Indeed, the Indian critic G.N. Devy has asserted that:

> if a [postcolonial Indian] writer cannot relate himself meaningfully to his culture, his society, the whole purpose of writing an autobiography is lost. Such a book ... cannot succeed in creating organic links with the society which should be the aim of an autobiography.[58]

However, as suggested in the introduction to this chapter, one should not characterise all postcolonial life-writing, even by women, as inevitably relational or seeking representativity at this level. While Olney was, laudably, one of the first westerners to recognise non-western life-writing, like Lionnet, he has an unfortunate tendency to essentialise it in this respect. Thus, he argues that, like western minoritarian life-writing, it 'renders in a peculiarly direct and faithful way the experience and vision of a people, which is the same experience and the same vision lying behind and informing all the literature of that people'.[59] This is unconvincingly homogenising. Many postcolonial politicians do not narrate themselves in the grandiose fashion of Nkrumah and Lee. For example, in the epilogue to the autobiography he published at a moment of powerful nationalist upsurge in India, Nehru insists that: 'I often wonder if I represent anyone at all.'[60] Equally, while writing of his father – and also partly corroborating Fanon's argument, cited at the outset of this chapter, insofar as he constructs himself in axial relation to the metropolitan centre – Naipaul's autobiographical texts (see Chapter 5) offer no sympathetic negotiation whatsoever with the collective identities represented by nation and ethnicity (or, indeed, class). Instead, emphasising both the 'cruelty of extended-family life', and what it sees as the vacuity of decolonisation politics, *A Way in the World* (1994), in particular, charts the process whereby Naipaul learns to 'belong to [him]self'.[61]

Such examples of non-relationality should not necessarily be dismissed as reactionary deviations from the norms of male postcolonial life-writing, any more than Lim and El Saadawi can be castigated for their strategic and occasional embrace of individualism. Parallel with some western women colleagues' evasions of the essentialising terms of patriarchal discourse, the postcolonial writer's embrace of autonomy and singularity could be interpreted in the first place as a riposte to the tendency in colonial discourse to stereotype subject peoples as homogenised and indistinguishable collectives (for example, 'the wily Oriental' or 'the noble savage'). Conversely, however, it could be understood as an attempt to escape the sometimes coercive emphasis on collective identity within 'indigenous' social groups to which the writer is affiliated, whether clan, class, ethnic group or the nation itself, of the kind Lim and El Saadawi describe. Such pressures underlie the impatience of some minoritarian and postcolonial writers with what has been described as 'the burden of representation'.[62] To this extent, however, paradoxical though it may seem, even the apparently detached and monadic subject constructed in the life-writing of a figure like Naipaul supports Robert Fraser's contention that, in the postcolonial context, 'to separate questions of personal and political identity is essentially impossible'.[63]

As with Chapter 1, the texts considered here provide mixed evidence in relation to the strategic issue of the distinctive identity of postcolonial life-writing in terms of this thematic of subjectivity. However, analysis of James and Behan suggests reason for scepticism towards reifying claims that relationality is a special characteristic of western women's life-writing. Conversely, the parallels between the two sub-fields in this respect also make distinguishing sharply between them problematic. The major difference appears to consist not in terms of the discourse of relationality itself but in the different degrees and kinds of relation espoused by western women authors, on the one hand, and their postcolonial colleagues – male and female – on the other. Investigation of further thematics of subjectivity is therefore required to advance the project of establishing a poetics of postcolonial life-writing.

3 Embodied Selves

For James, West Indian nationalism is expressed in significant measure through the medium of the Body. Insofar as cricket is a physical contest, it allows a distinctively Caribbean identity to be asserted through the particular styles in which West Indians play the game, notably in batting and bowling. Equally, Behan's rebellion against nationalism, in the name of other kinds of community, is often expressed through (the erotic energies of) his body. To this extent, embodiment is clearly an important thematic of some auto/biographical subjectivity, even if it is one which, feminist critics have complained, has been largely ignored within mainstream Auto/biography Studies. Sidonie Smith, for example, suggests that in their concern to promote a putatively universal Subject, male critics have historically conceived of auto/biographical Selfhood 'irrespective of or despite the bodily surround'.[1] Gilmore claims that this emphasis derives from canonical autobiography itself, where the Body is 'so frequently absent' as a subject of investigation; insofar as it is present, she argues, corporality 'has functioned as a metaphor for soul, consciousness, intellect, and imagination', rather than a material and cultural reality.[2] Feminist critics often explain this in terms of the genre's roots in the confessional tradition of Christianity, which privileges the life of the Spirit over that of the Body, a dualism inherited by secular philosophy from the time of the Renaissance. Thus, for Descartes, according to Shirley Neuman, the Self is represented as something 'whose whole essence or nature is only to think, and which, to exist, has no need of space nor of any material thing or body'.[3]

Lack of attention to embodiment as a dimension of identity is certainly evident in Auto/biography Studies throughout its history. Misch does not mention it, emphasising instead qualities like the subject's 'clarity of consciousness' and arguing that a text becomes canonical only when it represents 'the contemporary *intellectual* outlook'.[4] Gusdorf follows suit. While stressing that the genre 'recomposes and interprets a life *in its totality*', he focuses exclusively on autobiographical truth conceived 'as an expression of inmost being', and of the 'spiritual capacities of the writer'.[5] The third phase of Auto/biographical Studies is similarly unforthcoming in this respect, whether in its humanist or post-structuralist inflections. One searches in vain through the work of critics as diverse as Olney, Spengemann and Sprinker for any detailed engagement with issues surrounding the Body.

Feminist auto/biography critics suggest that the historical occlusion of this thematic of subjectivity, too, is clearly gendered in its causes and implications, providing a further explanation for the historical marginalisation of women's life-writing. Thus, for Mary Mason, the emphasis on spiritual and intellectual transcendence of the Body in canonical autobiography 'does not accord with the deepest realities of women's experience'.[6] Conversely, Gilmore asserts, female auto/biographers 'have found the body to provide rich grounds for thinking through the relationship between identity and representation'.[7] This is primarily because, as Fedwa Malti-Douglas puts it, for feminists, the Body is 'a physical reality that in itself possesses no necessary moral or social meaning but is then invested with a moral value. This investment, in turn, dictates social conclusions.'[8] Such perspectives have been applied across the historical range of western women's life-writing, leading Sidonie Smith to claim that '[S]ome kind of history of the body is always inscribed in women's autobiographical texts.'[9] These arguments have been extended to minoritarian women's life-writing in the West. Thus, of Asian American women's work, Shirley Lim (see Chapter 4) observes that 'to recognize a material self is to begin to write politically'.[10] In turn, they have been applied to its postcolonial analogues. For example, John Beverley argues that by virtue of its oral qualities, 'something of the experience of body itself inheres in [Latin American] *testimonio*'.[11] Similar patterns have been detected even in the precursor forms of postcolonial women's life-writing. For example discussing *The History of Mary Prince* (1831), Paquet reminds one that at the centre 'of Prince's public account of self is the body of a female slave'.[12]

As Lim's comment suggests, important political, as well as psycho-affective, capital has been claimed for this emphasis in women's life-writing. In particular, it allows women writers to revalue the female Body so often demeaned in patriarchal culture and, more specifically, in canonical autobiography (for example, in Rousseau's construction of Zulietta). The agency this focus implies is, significantly, recurrently expressed in a preoccupation with the bodily attribute of 'voice', the claiming of which – as was seen in Morgan's case – has become a signature of feminist mobilisations across the globe. Nonetheless, Neuman cautions that the attempted recuperation of the female Body in women's life-writing risks reinscribing the patriarchal synecdoches of femininity, namely 'birth, belly and body'.[13] The same caution holds true for postcolonial counterparts, especially in view of the characteristically demeaning sexualisation of the female 'Other' in colonial discourse.[14] Such dilemmas are also, however, widely apparent in male postcolonial life-writing, perhaps unsurprisingly given that colonial (and contemporary) raciology recurrently constructs the non-western Man in ways parallel to patriarchy's conception of the female Body. Whether as a source of labour, in terms of sexual performance, or even as the figure of the non-human, such discourse traditionally (mis)represents the colonised male, in particular, in terms of his deviation from those qualities which underwrite the West's characteristic self-image – notably Mind, Reason and Spirit. Like their women counterparts, male postcolonial life-writers have chosen to negotiate the risk in different ways, as I will demonstrate.

Fanon once again formulates the theoretical parameters for postcolonial life-writing (by both genders) in this respect. Noting that 'the corporeal schema' is discursively constituted by a 'historico-racial' one,[15] Fanon anticipates the feminist argument that the Body is a construct as much as a material object and therefore subject to change and reappropriation. Consequently, while he repeatedly shows how the 'Negro' is oppressed in and because of his Body, he also hails that Body as a potential site of resistance, pleasure and Self-revaluation. In doing so, *Black Skin* also anticipates feminist auto/biography criticism in its rebuttal of the traditional Christian and Cartesian dualism of western culture (and, by implication, of canonical autobiography). Instead, he asserts that: '[F]or us the body is not something opposed to what you call the mind. We are in the world. And long live the couple, Man and Earth.'[16]

In this chapter I analyse two examples of postcolonial life-writing by authors of different genders in the light of these debates. I will consider whether they treat the Body to a different degree or in different ways to what is claimed in relation to canonical autobiography and assess the extent to which such variations can be mapped in the gendered terms elaborated by feminist revisions of Auto/biography Studies. I will further consider whether postcolonial women's life-writing represents the Body in the same way as western women colleagues or if it instead reflects aspects of experience which are specific to the different material and social contexts of the postcolonial world. Such analysis will then be used to shed light on the larger strategic question which animates this book, the differences of postcolonial life-writing from its western analogues.

Gandhi, *An Autobiography or the Story of My Experiments with Truth* (1927–29)

More than any other text analysed in this book, perhaps, Gandhi's *An Autobiography* engages with bio-mechanical aspects of the author's existence, ranging over themes as diverse as sexual (in)activity, personal hygiene, physical exercise, labour and diet. Many chapters focus on issues of ingestion, digestion or, indeed, defecation (at one point, Gandhi describes the pain caused during evacuation by anal fissures, at another an attack of dysentery during which he suffered 'thirty to forty motions in twenty-four hours'[17]). Despite the abundance of such material, his text has tended to be read as a classic example of spiritual autobiography which turns from engagement with its author's identity-formation in a specific historical world, towards elaboration of abstract truths applicable to humanity as a whole. Thus, the Indian critic K. Chellappan argues that *An Autobiography* dramatises Gandhi's experience of 'the essential anguish of the eternal Self',[18] an emphasis also commonly offered by western commentators. Jeffrey Meyers, for instance, suggests that: 'Constantly seeking the path of salvation, Gandhi meditates on his sense of moral weakness and the stages of his spiritual development, his conversion experience and awareness of grace.'[19]

Such approaches view Gandhi's conception of the Body as simply a particularly obdurate aspect of individual identity which must be overcome if the author is to achieve 'true' Selfhood (or transcendence of it). Through learning to school the physical appetites which link him to the animal world, it is implied, his proper identity as a *mahatma* ('great soul') emerges like a butterfly from its ugly pupa. However, the relationship of issues of embodiment to autobiographical Selfhood in Gandhi's text is more complex than these readings suggest. From his Introduction, which flags the text's subsequent engagement with 'non-violence, celibacy and other principles of [bodily] conduct *believed to be distinct from truth*' (*AA*: 15, my emphasis), Gandhi is evidently seeking to rethink the oppositional relationship between the realms of Spirit and Body which so often shape readings of *An Autobiography*. For example, the suspicion of conventional western medicine, which becomes increasingly marked as his text proceeds, is driven by Gandhi's perception that it damagingly separates these two aspects of identity in its diagnostic procedures. Moreover, insofar as his body is the laboratory within which the vast majority of Gandhi's 'experiments with truth' are conducted, there is a strong suggestion that some kinds of 'truth' can only be reached *through* the Body. For example, as Joseph Alter observes, Gandhi argues that '*brahmacharya* and *ahimsa* would have no meaning in the absence of the body'.[20]

There is certainly a strong personal and psychological dimension to Gandhi's thematic investment in the Body in *An Autobiography*. Perhaps the clearest analogue of the 'crisis' scenes of western spiritual autobiography is the early account of the night of his father's death, of which the author comments: 'It is a blot I have never been able to efface or forget' (*AA*: 44). The moment is made traumatic not simply because of Gandhi's loss of his parent, but by the fact that the writer is making love to his wife in an adjoining room when death occurs: 'I saw that, if animal passion had not blinded me, I should have been spared the torture of separation from my father during his last moments' (*AA*: 44). The fact that Kasturbai is pregnant compounds Gandhi's sense of guilt, which is further intensified when the child dies a few days after birth. As Erik Erikson's magisterial psychobiographies of Gandhi make clear, this event is central to the development of the author's personality and helps to account for the obsession with Bodily self-discipline which often takes centre stage in *An Autobiography*.[21]

However, the importance of the Body in *An Autobiography* extends to the fact that it is not simply Gandhi's private property, an aspect of personal identity or the avenue to a particular individual's enlightenment. It is also a *socialised* interface between those domains and the broader cultural forces shaping the writer's world, in relation to which he takes on progressively more public and representative roles (compare Chapter 2). The intimate link between individual body and the wider 'Body Politic' is indicated in Gandhi's acknowledgement that it is primarily his experiments with the former 'from which I have derived such power as I possess for working in the political field' (*AA*: 14). These experiments respond in considerable measure to Gandhi's growing awareness through corporeal experience of his status as colonised subject. His sense of the humiliating injustice of foreign rule is initially expressed in shame at his feebleness compared with the 'white body' of colonial authority (*AA*: 34). Time and again in his early life, Gandhi is physically reminded of that feebleness. His first meeting with a British administrator after returning to India from London ends with him being man-handled out of the office (*AA*:103). In South Africa, Gandhi suffers colonial vio-lence more persistently and directly, whether in being barged off the pavement by a white security guard, hauled out of coaches and trains to make way for racial 'superiors', or pelted with stones, brickbats and rotten eggs by a settler mob on his return to Natal in 1897. The writer experiences other modes of physical con-straint and surveillance, for example, when he is variously prevented from tra-velling to the Transvaal (and later to the Punjab) by the imperial system of permits familiar from Morgan and Equiano. The physical regulation of subject bodies is more graphically evident in Gandhi's multiple experiences of imprison-ment. And as his engagement in the Zulu 'rebellion' (and later the Amritsar protests) makes plain, colonialism's ultimate sanction when faced with resistance is the destruction of the bodies of its subjects.[22]

Conversely, Gandhi's elaboration of distinctive forms of mass anti-colonial politics also derives in significant measure through mobilisation of the Body. Oppressed by his cowardliness, the adolescent Gandhi allows himself to be tem-porarily persuaded that 'meat-eating was good, that it would make me strong and daring, and that, if the whole country took to meat-eating, the English could be overcome' (*AA*: 35). From the outset, then, *An Autobiography* conjoins 'reform' of Gandhi's individual body with the struggle against foreign domination. Indeed, his desire for mastery of bodily appetites provides a template for developing the self-control and self-discipline necessary not just to attain self-rule in the political sphere, but to remain worthy of it. As Parama Roy argues, diet is the 'terrain on which his politics would be inaugurated'.[23] Experiments in this sphere prepare the ground for the vow of *brahmacharya* taken in South Africa, which is in turn 'a preliminary as it were to Satyagraha' (*AA*: 291), both there and in India. Thus, the adoption of fasting as a technique of individual bodily purification evolves into one of Gandhi's most effective weapons of anti-colonial resistance, although within the time-frame covered by *An Autobiography* it is still being used primarily to resolve disputes of a more local nature. The doctrine of non-violence is a further illustration of how Gandhi's concern with the Body inflected his political praxis. In stark contrast to the physical excesses of colonial power, illustrated in its repri-sals against the Zulu 'rebellion' and the Amritsar protests, for Gandhi, one 'truth' of politics is that care for the bodies of opponents is no less an obligation than for those of his supporters (compare Morgan's forgiving attitude to 'white' Australia).

However, the Body is also mobilised in Gandhi's critique of traditional Indian society. If he soon abandons his early flirtation with meat-eating, he never loses the desire for 'reform' of his native culture. This episode is symptomatic in that the perceived need for change arises from the apparent deficiency of 'the Indian Body' and the discursive regimes which surround it. Indeed, the author's first public act of rebellion against tradition is provoked by his caste community's prohibition on travel overseas, an injunction with ironic parallels to colonial restrictions on the circulation of subject bodies.[24] Gandhi's critique of 'the Indian Body' often brings him into conflict with institutionalised religion. Indeed, the worst derelictions of basic hygiene are often associated with high-caste Hindus.

During the plague in Rajkot, for example, Gandhi draws a disobliging contrast between the latrine arrangements of 'the upper ten' (*AA*: 165) and those of the poor. He is particularly disgusted by the disregard for sanitation in the holy places of Benares, seeing this is a clear example of a degenerate deviation from 'true' Hindu law. Out of his first experience of a Congress meeting, which demonstrates that even among the more progressive elements of Indian society there was 'no limit to insanitation' (*AA*: 212), emerges Gandhi's decision to make the cleaning of communal latrines a key symbol of his political programme.

The Body also provides the grounds on which Gandhi articulates his most radical critique of indigenous 'biopolitics' and perhaps his most fundamental conflict with institutionalised religion. In Bihar, for example, Gandhi is strictly forbidden to draw water at a well for fear that he may compromise customary law. He fulminates against religious sanction for such practices: 'If untouchability could be a part of Hinduism, it could but be a rotten part or an excrescence' (*AA*: 136). Outraged by such prohibitions, he welcomes a family of 'untouchables' to the ashram at Sabarmati, despite the risk that he will lose the support of upper-caste patrons. Increasingly, however, Gandhi poses the problem not only in spiritual or ethical, but in macro-political terms, seeing analogies between the caste system and colonialism, with 'the upper ten' exercising equivalent controls over the lowest orders of Indian society through the medium of the Body. Equally, the caste system exemplifies for Gandhi the divisions in Indian society which allow colonialism to more easily maintain control. As with hygiene, however, the issue also becomes central to the 'reform' of Gandhi's private life as well. At one point he employs an 'untouchable' cook to prepare his meals and even 'inter-dines' with this servant. Later, he humbles himself by 'scavenging' the latrines alongside those who traditionally perform this function.

A further aspect of Gandhi's life which vividly illustrates the intersection of public and private concerns on the site of the Body is the issue of gender politics. Gandhi represents himself at the outset of the text as a willing beneficiary of the traditional system of patriarchy in which he has been brought up, primarily because it allows him to indulge 'the [male] passions that flesh is heir to' (*AA*: 25). In order to do so, Gandhi confesses, 'I had to make good my authority as a husband!' (*AA*: 27). The writer unflinchingly describes a whole range of behaviour designed to enforce his mastery over Kasturbai and his enjoyment of her body. It is 'lustful love', he remorsefully explains, which leads to his failure to educate his wife. Conversely, it is also largely through the medium of his own body that Gandhi seeks to dissolve his patriarchal authority and to provide an example to others in this regard.[25] Through the experiment of *brahmacharya*, for example, he 'realized that the wife is not the husband's bondslave, but ... an equal partner' (*AA*: 39). As a result, he comes to condemn a variety of social practices which seek to repress women specifically through control of their bodies, from the general Hindu system of child-marriage to his native Kathiawad's 'peculiar, useless and barbarous *Purdah*' (*AA*: 28).

As part of this process, Gandhi increasingly seeks to incorporate the 'feminine' within his changing conception of Selfhood. This, too, is substantially achieved through bodily practices. One example is the theme of nursing which runs throughout the text, from the boy Gandhi's administration of massages and changes of dressing to his dying father, to the performance of ambulance duties in both South Africa and England, and his care for his sick wife and children in later life. Another is the assumption of a variety of domestic duties, from cooking to laundry to dressmaking, which are also conventionally coded as 'feminine' activities. The principle of non-violence could be interpreted as another aspect of the incorporation of the 'feminine' as part of both Gandhi's personal philosophy and political programme, in contrast to the emphasis on violent 'manliness' among many fellow-nationalists. Indeed, Gandhi once claimed that 'woman is the incarnation of *ahimsa'.*[26] Yet this project is not without contradictions. For example, celibacy is imposed on Kasturbai without any consultation (*AA*: 197). Arguably this desexualises his wife in a way entirely consonant with the prescriptions of patriarchal Hindu tradition. Equally, Gandhi's usurpation of certain 'feminine' roles – he at one point displaces his sister from care of her dying husband, at another he sends away a qualified female nurse during a plague outbreak – is not compensated for by the promotion of women to roles of any significance in his political movement, despite the influence on him of the British Suffragettes.[27] Indeed, they play the subordinate role typical in anti-colonial nationalism more broadly.

As such evidence suggests, the Body is a crucial site on which Gandhi, repeatedly drawing on his own personal experience, mobilises criticism of aspects of both colonial and indigenous Indian culture. Conversely, however, anticipating C.L.R. James, the Body is also represented as a site on which the author proposes that a 'reformed' East and West can work out a more productive relationship than has been the case under colonialism. This is consonant with the broader syncretic and internationalist vision represented by the writer's attempts 'to unify the teachings of the *Gita*, *The Light of Asia* and the Sermon on the Mount' (*AA*: 78). Further, many aspects of Gandhi's programme of 'reform' of 'the Indian Body' (including his own) are strongly influenced by his experiences in the West. As the author points out, despite his parents' strict vegetarianism (which he wilfully flouted during his early experiments as a carnivore), Hindu tradition as he understood it as a young man did not proscribe meat-eating. Indeed 'the *Manusmriti* [Hindu Law as codified by Manu] seemed to support it' (*AA*: 47). Thus, Gandhi's abstinence from meat on arriving in England should perhaps be seen primarily as a personal mark of filial respect for his mother's wishes rather than an affirmation of Hindu/Indian identity. It is only on visiting a restaurant in Farringdon, where he purchases a copy of Salt's *Plea for Vegetarianism*, that Gandhi claims 'to have become a vegetarian by choice' and decides to make the spread of the movement his 'mission' (*AA*: 59). His preliminary convictions confirmed by texts from a variety of other western authorities, Gandhi commences his life-long experiments with diet. South Africa reinforces the lessons of his 'English experiments in vegetarian cookery' (*AA*: 96), sometimes in unexpected ways. For example, denied curry powder and tea and forced to eat his evening meal early while in prison, Gandhi decides thereafter to take no food after dark and to substitute cocoa or water for the signature drink of his community.[28]

This signals complex issues around Gandhi's identity. Paradoxically, it is largely through insertion in the alien cultures of England and South Africa that he gathers the resources to 'become Indian'. These resources extend well beyond the realm of the corporeal. For example, on arrival in Britain, he confesses to having only 'a nodding acquaintance with Hinduism' (*AA*: 79); hitherto he has identified himself primarily by caste position and family status, together with some identification with the region of Kathiawad. It is in London that Gandhi first encounters 'the book *par excellence* for the knowledge of Truth', in the form of Edwin Arnold's translation of the *Bhagavad Gita* (*AA*: 76). Introductions to Madame Blavatsky and Annie Besant further stimulate Gandhi's 'desire to read books on Hinduism' (*AA*: 77). Discovering that Gandhi has not read the history of India, Frederick Pincutt persuades him to begin the task, ironically with Kaye and Malleson's classic account of 'the great rebellion' against British rule in 1857. In London, furthermore, Gandhi meets fellow-exiles from all parts of the sub-continent at the National Indian Association, an institution which, as the name suggests, fostered a political and supra-regional sense of identity. It is through his time in South Africa, above all, that Gandhi forges a conception of India as a collective identity and develops the sense of 'national self-respect' (*AA*: 139) which thereafter leads him towards the Indian National Congress.

Gandhi's definition early in his text of religion as a process of 'self-realization' (*AA*: 45) deploys a term which corresponds with some definitions of the purpose of western autobiography. But while this might seem conclusive evidence to support Gusdorf's argument about the 'belated' nature of *An Autobiography* and, by extrapolation, of postcolonial life-writing more generally, the truth is more complicated. As was seen in the Introduction, Gandhi denied writing an autobiography as traditionally conceived in the West. As was also seen there, one way this deviation is achieved is through his use of 'regulative psychobiographies' drawn from Indian traditions of religious narrative. Such inter-texts have radical implications for western ideas of (autobiographical) self-realisation. Indeed, Gandhi ends his text with a quite contrary emphasis: 'I must reduce myself to zero' (*AA*: 454). In a text which is sub-titled 'Experiments with Truth', one of the most striking is the attempt – like Equiano – to fuse a religious narrative with one which so consistently engages the temporal, material world. A crucial aspect of this hybrid project is Gandhi's refusal to erase the Body, whether as a medium of spiritual enlightenment or the vessel of political being in the world. Julie Codell rightly claims that, to the end of his text, Gandhi 'remained committed to ... the bodily'.[29] Joseph Alter argues that Gandhi thereby turned Hindu scripture upside down 'and made the fact of his "being here" into a kind of embodied, politicized *moksha*'.[30] However, this concern with the Body makes Gandhi's text equally revisionary in relation to canonical autobiography. If his work has no precedent among the *shastras*, it is in this respect equally unprecedented in the western cultural tradition which colonialism imposed on India.[31]

Nawal El Saadawi, *A Daughter of Isis: The Autobiography of Nawal El Saadawi* (1999)

Thematics of the Body are as crucial for El Saadawi as for Gandhi (who is cited as an inspirational anti-colonial fore-runner in *A Daughter of Isis*[32]). Like her predecessor, the Egyptian feminist writer seeks to break down the binary oppositions between Mind and Body endemic in patriarchal culture around the world. Although she views western medicine more positively than Gandhi, El Saadawi, too, insists that physical and mental health are inter-dependent.[33] For example, her own illnesses are demonstrated to occur at moments of intense emotional suffering, usually related to her position as a female subject. The traditional binaries are further undermined by El Saadawi's treatment of memory, which often operates corporeally in *A Daughter*. Thus, once, in exile in North Carolina, the author declares that: 'My body remembers the smell of dust, the touch of the earth under my feet, the glare of the sun hurting my eyes' (*DI*: 30). Equally, intellection is often mediated somatically. Even when too young to know exactly what 'spinster' and 'divorcee' mean, El Saadawi realises that something is seriously amiss with her aunts according to prevailing social norms: 'I understood everything. It went through my body with a shiver' (*DI*: 39). For each writer, furthermore, the Body is a site on which political relations are mediated. El Saadawi, too, traces the oppressions of colonialism and traditional feudal society on the bodies of the non-western poor. Adopting a class perspective consonant with her family nickname, 'Warwar the slave girl', she observes that the peasants in her home village 'died of diarrhoea, of respiratory or of gastro-intestinal infections' (*DI*: 72). As with Gandhi, therefore, the Body in *A Daughter* represents an interface between the public domain and individual subject-formation. Thus, her increasing realisation that 'sickness and poverty are linked to politics' (*DI*: 291–2) underpins El Saadawi's decision to become a rural doctor.

Yet there are crucial differences between *An Autobiography* and *A Daughter* in their treatment of the Body. In part, these derive from the divergent social and ethical-religious norms of the authors' respective cultures of origin. Primarily, however, they ensue from the different gender of each writer. While Gandhi provides some insight into such issues in India, El Saadawi provides a much fuller account of how non-western women are sometimes socially positioned and exploited by indigenous discourses and practices surrounding the Body, particularly in traditional rural areas at the time she was growing up. Thus, the midwife 'would let out a screaming "yoo-yoo" if her eyes fell on a penis' or 'become as silent as the dead if all she could find was a cleft' (*DI*: 20). If such 'lack' portends the inferior status to which infant girls will be assigned in traditional society, their bodies are also, in one crucial respect, 'excessive'. This engenders perhaps the decisive psychosocial event in El Saadawi's life, her circumcision:[34] 'When I was six, the *daya* (midwife) came along holding a razor in her hands, pulled out my clitoris from between my thighs, and cut it off' (*DI*: 11). The event is so traumatic that the author is unable to acknowledge it openly for thirty-five years. Indeed this trauma's persistence can be read in the very brevity and simplicity of El Saadawai's description of her own experience compared with the space afforded to Sittil Hajja's visceral account of the assault she endures:

> Um Mahmoud ... together with four other women, took hold of me, tied me up as though she were trussing a chicken, covered my head with a shawl and pulled my thighs wide apart so she could tear off my surface below ... her finger going through it like a nail cutting into my flesh with a burning pain.
>
> (*DI*: 27; compare 32–3)

Still bleeding on the jolting donkey-ride to her wedding feast, within a matter of hours the 10-year-old Sittil Hajja must endure the additional pain of defloration.

Circumcision is represented as the most spectacular form of patriarchal violence against the bodies of some rural Egyptian women of a certain generation, at least.[35] But it is only one such example. El Saadawi also describes the tradition of husbands beating wives on the wedding night to enforce their authority. The mere advent of suitors requires the depilation of every part of the female Body, including the pubic region, by means of a low-tech equivalent of waxing, so exquisitely painful that El Saadawi contemplates suicide. Failure to produce a male heir, or the reproduction of too many female children, even infertility, are further pretexts for male violence. Thus, Aunt Rokaya is beaten daily because she cannot bear a child (her husband never entertains the possibility that he is the 'problem'). Rape is also a constant threat and its victims are rarely considered innocent, even by other women. Thus, when Shelabaya is impregnated against her will, the girl is sent back to probable death at the hands of her father by Nawal's aunt while the perpetrator, her uncle, remains unpunished.

Aside from the clitoris, according to *A Daughter*, indigenous patriarchy organises in particular relation to two further facets of the Body. The first is the voice, perhaps – as suggested earlier – the most potent vessel and symbol of agency and subjectivity in postcolonial literature. Symbolic of the vocal restraint expected of women[36] is Aunt Rokaya; even among her own sex, she would 'lift the hem of her black *tarha* and dab her eyes, her mouth concealed behind it as she mumbled' (*DI*: 45). Like the 'dumb, lifeless dolls' (*DI*: 44) which the child El Saadawi is given as part of her socialisation, the females of her family are often condemned to dumbness. Grandmother Amna, for example, presides over 'the dead silence' of the Shoukry household in Cairo and her daughters die 'surrounded by silence, without a sound, without anyone hearing of their death' (*DI*: 37, 106). The repression of Egyptian women is further mediated through the economy of the gaze. With the qualified exception of peasant society, which demands their labour out of doors, women in *A Daughter* are often required to be invisible, unless within designated domestic spaces: 'Everything in a woman's life was seen as shameful, even her face. She often hid it behind a piece of material, or the edge of her shawl, or behind the shutters of her window' (*DI*: 10). Conversely, the woman's gaze is required to be averted, a 'properly modest' girl aspiring to the condition of a 'blind kitten' (*DI*: 104). Thus, on her wedding night, Nawal's mother lies with 'her eyes closed, being impregnated with her first child, without taking off her clothes or opening her eyes' (*DI*: 22). By contrast, the male gaze is often represented as an offensive weapon in *A Daughter*. Even as a school-girl, El Saadawi records, men 'never stopped gazing at me, with a stare that was like an arrow going through my chest' (*DI*: 100). It is no surprise, therefore, that she recurrently invokes the inspirational figure of the blind writer Taha Hussayn (1889–1973), whose desirably liberal attitudes are implicitly linked to his necessary exclusion from the prevailing gendered scopic regime.

Yet if the Body is the locus for patriarchal domination in *A Daughter*, as it is for colonial domination in Gandhi, it is also the site on which both female (and anti-colonial) resistance can be mobilised. The text suggests that El Saadawi's experience of circumcision is decisive in shaping many of the writer's personality contours and life-choices, especially in kindling the anger which shapes her future politics. That anger, significantly, 'accumulates in the body' (*DI*: 206), engendering a rebelliousness which is marked early in the author's life. When her relatives pray for her transformation into a boy, for example, El Saadawi bridles: 'I hoped that God did not have the power to change me into a male like my brother' (*DI*: 44). Instead, she seeks to add the social power enjoyed by males to her femininity. Thus, resenting the dolls her father buys, she prefers to play with her brother's pistols. When suitors call during puberty, El Saadawi resists through the Body, blackening her teeth with egg-plant, feigning clumsiness, even spilling boiling coffee over one visitor. She also pretends to be sick in order to skip school classes in domestic economy. Later in life, by contrast, she exploits her 'unfeminine' physique (the adolescent El Saadawi is tall and well-built for her age) to physically strike back at a variety of male harassers.

Further, *A Daughter* explicitly challenges the prevailing discursive regimes surrounding the embodiment of Egyptian women on the very grounds on which these discourses are constituted. In the first place, as a *testimonio*, it seeks to break the silence enjoined on her gender, using one individual voice in a relational and representative manner (see Chapter 2) to speak up about the true condition of many members of her sex. Like Morgan's *My Place* and Assia Djebar's *Fantasia* (see Chapter 5), *A Daughter* restores voice to those whom history has silenced, by weaving first-person accounts of others, notably relatives like grandmother Sittil Hajja, cousin Zaynab and aunt Fatima, into her own (*DI*: 26–7, 32–4, 129, 239). Equally, El Saadawi's text interrupts the prevailing scopic economy in two principal ways. The first is by making visible that which patriarchy attempts to conceal. Thus, the author describes her work as an attempt 'to discover what is buried deep down inside me, to reveal what is hidden through fear of God, the father, the husband, the teacher … through fear of the nation to which we belong' (*DI*: 15). This includes her physical desires, 'unfeminine' anger and professional ambitions. To this end, she aspires to having 'eyes like the eyes of Zarq'a Al-Yamama [a noted female military scout of pre-Islamic times] able to see what remained concealed from others' (*DI*: 209).

As one might also infer from this comment, however, El Saadawi is equally concerned to appropriate the patriarchal gaze in order to reverse it. Like Gandhi, she is sometimes deeply critical of the complicity of traditional religion in the deformation of many Egyptian women, physical and emotional. As soon as she has learned to write her mother's name, the author's father replaces it with his own, describing the new conjunction as 'God's will'. The author comments: 'That was the first time I heard the word God ... I could not love anyone who removed my mother's name from next to mine, who abolished her as though she did not exist' (*DI*: 1). This foreshadows the constant struggle against institutionalised religion which, despite a brief period of spiritual fervour, characterises El Saadawi's subject-formation. Her critique has several strands. Perhaps most radically, she challenges the authority of the Koran itself, in a manner reminiscent of Gandhi's critique of certain Hindu *shastras*. For example, she deprecates the verse which values males twice as much as females and the text's failure to address her sex, or even mention individual historical women. She also satirises the teaching that in paradise a man will enjoy seventy-two virgins, while 'a woman is promised no-one except her husband, that is if he ... is not too busy with the virgins who surround him' (*DI*: 4). Equally, El Saadawi turns her critical gaze on clerical figures such as her paternal uncle, Sheikh Muhammad, who self-servingly cite such scriptural authority to enforce their gender privileges. In El Saadawi's account, the combination of sacred text and cleric engender the kind of fatalism represented by Aunt Rokaya, who concludes the account of her violent marriage with the following homily: 'Everything comes from God, we praise and thank ye, God, for the sweet and the bitter' (*DI*: 45).

El Saadawi's piercing gaze clearly challenges the economy of traditional patriarchy, as does her articulation of a critical voice. Her disregard for custom in these respects has led to accusations that she is therefore not 'properly' Egyptian, even an agent of the West. Like Behan, she is certainly ambivalent about nationalism. At its best, it is represented as a deeply unifying discourse, both socially and psychically (not least because it can break down the barriers 'between body and mind' [*DI*: 229]). She also embraces nationalism insofar, as has been seen, El Saadawi posits a direct link between (neo-)colonialism[37] and the degradation of the Egyptian Body which concerns her as a doctor: 'People become sick because they are poor ... People become poor because we are colonized, and ... our resources are taken away from us.'[38] At Helwan school, she is a ring-leader in the protest against colonialism and at university supports the underground in the occupied Canal zone. During the Suez Crisis, she volunteers as a doctor when Egypt is attacked by the combined Anglo-French-Israeli forces. Her later opposition to the Camp David Accords, in which Sadat reached what she sees as a demeaning accommodation with Israel which rewarded Zionist aggression, might be seen as a further example of El Saadawi's principled nationalism, which led to her imprisonment in 1981.

However, while asserting pride in her country early in *A Daughter*, El Saadawi claims that even as a child, she 'would not believe in a country which robbed me of my pride and freedom' (*DI*: 6–7). In marked contrast to Gandhi, El Saadawi does not view nationalism as necessarily beneficial to women. At many nationalist demonstrations, she notes, she is the only woman present. In the era of Egypt's technical independence, moreover, there are few signs of an improvement in the condition of her sex. Her own efforts to better its lot are met with consistent official resistance, even persecution: 'Every time we started something, a magazine, an association, a cultural society, a publishing project ... they would close it down' (*DI*: 12). More specifically, echoing Behan's rejection of the conflation of Eire with Catholicism, El Saadawi disavows narrowly Islamic models of Egyptian national identity. While Muslim Brotherhood activities are viewed sympathetically when directed against British occupation and the puppet King Farouk, her sense of the multiplicity of Egypt's religious heritage is too strong for an unqualified endorsement. Just as Gandhi seeks to bring Islam, Christianity and Hinduism into dialogue, so *A Daughter* stresses the common ground between Islam, Judaism and Christianity. Thus, the references to 'our Prophet Moses' (*DI*: 26), for example, speak to a multi-cultural inheritance which contradicts the idea of Egypt as exclusively Islamic. It is this vision of her nation, perhaps, as much as El Saadawi's critique of Islamic teaching itself, which led to her being placed 'on a fundamentalist death list' (*DI*: 12) in 1992.

El Saadawi has been further criticised because of her allegedly unreflective endorsement of feminist ideas originating in western culture. As Fedwa Malti-Douglas argues: 'Her anti-patriarchal discourses ... are perceived as fanning the flames of Western anti-Arab attitudes.'[39] One can certainly detect the influence of western literary feminism in *A Daughter of Isis*. There are obvious parallels with *Jane Eyre*, which El Saadawi studies at secondary school. These include the figure of the rebellious female protagonist; the sometimes dismal boarding institution which the author attends, similarly leavened by the affection of selected school-friends; and her quasi-orphan status in the homes of a variety of uncaring relatives in Cairo, where she identifies most with servants like Sa'adeya. Above all, perhaps, the iconic figure of the blind reformer Taha Hussayn has affinities with Rochester as a symbol of a desirably reformed masculinity. Further, the ambivalent relationship between El Saadawi and her favoured, but less talented, brother Tala'at recalls George Eliot's feminist treatment of the rivalry between the Tulliver siblings in *The Mill on the Floss* (El Saadawi studies Eliot alongside Jane Austen and the Brontës).

However, allegations of El Saadawi's Eurocentrism and attendant hostility towards Egyptian Islamic tradition require qualification (not least because of the homogenised and stereotypical version of western feminism which is usually used to beat the author with). In the first place, she emphasises that Muslim women are not the only ones oppressed by patriarchal religion. For example, her Christian school-friend is not spared the devastating experience of circumcision. Equally, El Saadawi suggests that the culture of the large Jewish community in Egypt is deeply masculinist because of its religious traditions. Thus, she argues that the treatment of the 'contamination' of menstruation in the Koran is 'innocent ... in comparison with what was said about it in the Torah' (*DI*: 65–6). Nor is she uncritical of the position of women in western culture. In one interview El Saadawi has claimed that '*all* women are circumcised. Internationally, nationally, everywhere'[40] – whether physically or psychologically, whether by patriarchy, religion or, indeed, capitalism. Although this argument is not fleshed out in *A*

Daughter, it is hinted at in the representation of the principal western character who makes an appearance. Miss Hamer, El Saadawi's primary school head-mistress, is no less repressed – or repressive (she is a great enthusiast for corporal punishment) – than her Egyptian counterparts.

Further, as Amal Amireh demonstrates, El Saadawi has been highly critical of some strands of western feminism for their 'focus on issues of sexuality and patriarchy in isolation from issues of class and colonialism'.[41] In *A Daughter*, the author's circumspection is suggested in her decision to align herself primarily with an autochthonous genealogy of empowered early Egyptian and Arab women rather than western figureheads like Jane Eyre. One example already alluded to is Zarq'a Al-Yamama, invoked on several occasions in *A Daughter of Isis*. Elsewhere El Saadawi dreams of 'reciting line after line of poetry as though I was al-Khansa'a [a pre-Islamic woman poet of the Hejaz]' (*DI*: 209). As her title suggests, the author also summons the ancient Egyptian goddess (of healing, among other qualities) as a symbol of the empowerment to which she aspires. Indeed, from the outset, El Saadawi positions herself as 'a descendant of Isis or her mother Noot', who enjoins her daughter to work for the well-being of the people as a whole (*DI*: 4). But El Saadawi is also inspired more immediately by the women of her family, for example, her widowed grandmother, Sittil Hajja, the daughter of the equally formidable 'Woman from Gaza'. Neither conforms to the model of the obedient, serf-like female widely prized in traditional culture at the time of writing, although Sittil Hajja, in particular, is represented as complicit in many of the customs and attitudes which demean her sex. Nonetheless, she stands up to the village headman when required and strikes the village guard who beats El Saa-dawi's father for no reason. ('The woman from Gaza', in fact, pays with her life for daring to humiliate the village headman.)

Moreover, both Taha Hussayn and each of El Saadawi's parents clearly illus-trate the author's conviction that a critique of the deforming social consequences of custom and institutional religion for many women – and for their bodies more particularly – can arise from *within* Egyptian culture itself rather than being necessarily dependent on ideas, feminist or otherwise, imported from abroad. (More specifically, Hussayn's use of autobiography in *An Egyptian Childhood* [1926–27] to advance such ideas is probably El Saadawi's primary inspiration in *A Daughter*.) Thus, while her father is a devout Muslim, 'the Prophet was not a model for him in everything' (*DI*: 5). Not only does he take only one wife, he treats El Saadawi's mother with sufficient consideration that the author claims only to remember one serious quarrel between them. If the Egyptian woman is to be redeemed from her degraded condition, *A Daughter* suggests, this can be achieved only through disciplining of the male Body, which her father's life represents in a qualified way. Conversely, El Saadawi's feminist programme pro-mises redemption for Egyptian men from a patriarchy which enslaves them, too. (Compare Morgan's attitude to 'white' Australia, and Gandhi's to the colonisers.) As Malti-Douglas argues, El Saadawi's writing demonstrates how 'the rituals of blood and shame imprison men'[42] as well as women. As an 11-year-old, the author plays the part of Isis in a school play, bringing the stricken body of Osiris back to life. The image symbolises the author's ambition for the resurrection of the whole Egyptian Body politic, irrespective of gender, through elaboration of a new regime of the corporeal.

Conclusion

As the texts discussed make plain, some postcolonial life-writing by both genders makes the Body a central element in the construction of auto/biographical identity. Consonant with feminist perspectives, moreover, such work characteristically represents the Body as much as a discursive as a material aspect of subjectivity. A particularly striking example of this conjunction occurs in Soyinka's *Aké* (see Chapter 4), where the youth's initiation ceremonies involve the inscription of his identity as a member of the Yoruba community through the scarification of his body. Some interpretations of Gandhi lend support to the feminist argument that the Body in male autobiography primarily represents an obstacle to the more important processes of spiritual growth and intellectual development. However, in keeping with the positions of critics like Lim outlined at the beginning of this chapter, one could more credibly argue that Gandhi in fact represents the (reformed) Body not only as a crucial aspect of individual personhood, but as a key site of political mobilisation. In this respect, *An Autobiography* anticipates Fanon's *Black Skin*, which famously ends: 'O my body, make of me a man who always questions.'[43] However, this conception of the Body as a locus of resistance, as well as abjection, extends back to the precursor forms of male postcolonial life-writing. Thus, Equiano's engraved portrait in the frontispiece of his text *embodies* his equality with the reader, notably by virtue of its direct (even challenging) gaze. This is aimed at precisely those white readers who are traditionally privileged in scopic terms and anticipates the demand throughout the subsequent narrative that such recognition be extended to Equiano's 'sable brethren'.[44]

The treatment of the Body in postcolonial women's life-writing, by contrast, suggests a complex relationship to its western women's equivalent in this respect. At times, their approach appears to be complementary. Thus, unlike male postcolonial life-writers, whose treatment of Bodily abjection is almost exclusively conceived in relation to the coloniser, women colleagues as diverse as El Saadawi, Lim and Emecheta identify indigenous patriarchy as the immediate, if not prime, cause of their subjection. At other times, however, the relationship between postcolonial and western women's life-writing may be disjunctive. If both constituencies recognise that the Body may be a site of resistance, the modes and degree of female abjection that they respectively discuss are often quite different. Aspects of the condition of some Egyptian women, as described by El Saadawi, are almost unthinkable for the vast majority of their western counterparts. Indeed, from Prince's *History* to *Daughter of Isis*, (post)colonial women's life-writing demonstrates that the bodily oppressions suffered by women vary markedly according to ethnicity, history and geo-cultural location. Thus, the fact that Mrs Wood is one of Prince's most vicious owners supports the argument of many postcolonial feminists that there is no 'universal Woman's Body', in the name of which western feminism has sometimes been accused of mobilising prematurely, not least by El Saadawi herself.

As indicated earlier, there are certainly dangers in the emphasis often placed by postcolonial life-writers, male and female, on the Body as a dimension of subjectivity. Parallel with the 'impossible position' in which Neuman sees patriarchal discourse positioning the would-be western woman auto/biographer,[45] this emphasis risks re-inscribing the negative vision of the Body of the (post)colonial subject in western discourse – and, more specifically, in canonical autobiography (a notable example being the deviant sexuality and animality which Rousseau foregrounds in his representation of the masturbating 'Moor'). Consequently, whereas some postcolonial writers endorse the feminist strategy of revaluing, or re-inscribing, the Body, others marginalise or efface it altogether, particularly its sexual dimensions. Among postcolonial women life-writers, Nayantara Saghal's *Prison House and Chocolate Cake* (1954), for example, is silent on such matters, though they are repeatedly addressed in the extensive body of fiction for which she is better known. Such discretion has long been a feature of the women's tradition. Thus, *The Wonderful Adventures of Mrs Seacole* (1857; see Chapter 5) maintains a studied silence about the author's body (with the exception of consistent self-mockery about her girth). Instead, she constructs her identity in asexually maternal terms, as the 'Mother' of British troops in the Crimean War (whose trauma sometimes also emphatically de-masculinises them). Such reticence can be understood as a powerful form of cultural resistance to colonial discourse and, by extrapolation, to its successor regimes. For example, Seacole's silence about her own sexuality needs to be placed in the context of her knowing awareness of conventional western stereotypes about her 'hot-blooded' Creole lineage.[46] Conversely, she shows no such compunction in her depiction of white women, notably Lola Montez, whom she meets in Panama. As well as their propensity to drunkenness, dishonesty and violence, Seacole particularly emphasises their sexual licence. In this respect, too, she is also implicitly 'writing back' against colonial discourse, which tends to construct a binary opposition between the angelic propriety of white women in the empire and their 'improper' native counterparts, male and female.[47]

Male postcolonial life-writing also sometimes severely circumscribes or represses discussion of the Body. Equiano's silence about his sexuality, like Seacole's, is framed in terms of a self-conscious rebuttal of stereotypical metropolitan ideas about Black males. At the outset of *The Interesting Narrative*, he is at pains to describe the orderly regulation of sexual relations in traditional African society, insisting that 'incontinence' outside marriage is almost unknown..[48] By contrast, Equiano emphasises the violent and animalistic sexual behaviour of slavers and masters towards their chattels. However, it is perhaps in McKay's *A Long Way from Home* (1937) that the political significance of autobiographical silence about Black male sexuality is most explicitly spelled out. For McKay, the prurient interest of mainstream white society in the 'bugaboo of sex – the African's sex' is something he simply refuses to indulge: 'I think the Anglo-Saxon mind becomes morbid when it turns on the sex life of colored people.'[49] Such discretion is all the more striking in the context of McKay's close relationship with the Irish-American literary entrepreneur Frank Harris, whose autobiography *My Life and Loves* (1922–27) had become notorious for its boasting about matters sexual.[50]

The texts considered here once more provide mixed evidence in relation to the strategic issue of the distinctiveness of postcolonial life-writing from its western equivalents. Analysis of Gandhi and Behan suggests some reason for scepticism towards claims that a preoccupation with embodiment is a distinctive property of western women's life-writing. One might, conversely, argue that the specificity of postcolonial life-writing in this respect is partly registered in a consistent pre-occupation with 'colour' as a metaphor of the ethnic/racial and cultural differ-ences which partly determine the (post)colonial world. As Sidonie Smith remarks, in her discussion of Woolf's autobiographical 'A Sketch of the Past', the text 'never mentions the colour of the skin that needs escaping'.[51] Thus, there is nothing in western life-writing, by men or women, to compare to Fanon's trau-matic chance encounter with the white child in *Black Skin* (anticipated in McKay's experience and repeated in Emecheta's), in the course of which 'the crushing objecthood' of 'inferior' racial identity is experienced through the child's sponta-neous focus on Fanon's 'blackness'.[52] In turn, however, the many parallels in relation to their treatment of aspects of this thematic of autobiographical sub-jectivity also make it difficult to distinguish sharply between postcolonial life-writing and its western women's analogues. Investigation of further dimensions of subjectivity remains necessary, therefore, in order to help settle the question of the distinctiveness of postcolonial life-writing.

4 Located Selves

In both *An Autobiography* and *A Daughter*, the Body is often conceptualised in terms of specific locations and topographies. Thus, Gandhi's bodily 'experiments' vary considerably depending on whether he is in London, South Africa or India. The link between aspects of embodiment and 'place' is equally strong for El Saadawi, whether in the recurrent association of femininity with the kitchen, or the remembered smells of Cairo which plague her in exile. To this extent, these texts corroborate the insights of recent materialist-feminist work in the field of 'critical geography'. Gillian Rose's *Feminism and Geography* (1993), Doreen Massey's *Space, Place and Gender* (1994) and Linda McDowell's *Gender, Identity and Place* (1999) exemplify its focus on the ways that women's subjectivities are partly determined by their insertion within a variety of socio-spatial locations. In descending order of scale, these range from global diasporas, through nation spaces, cities and rural areas to domestic dwellings and, indeed, the Body.[1] As McDowell argues, in such work, 'place' is not conceived simply as 'a set of co-ordinates on a map' but must also be understood as a conjunction of 'practices that … result in overlapping and intersecting places with multiple and changing boundaries, constituted and maintained by social relations of power and exclusion'.[2] Nonetheless, while 'place' is never limited to geo-spatial co-ordinates in feminist 'critical geography', it is rarely entirely divorced from them.

Somewhat surprisingly, such work appears to have had little impact on feminist inflections of Auto/biography Studies. While Sidonie Smith observes that 'bodies locate us *topographically*, temporally, socioculturally as well as linguistically in a series of transcodings along multiple axes of meaning',[3] little work has been done on 'place' as a thematic of subjectivity in feminist analysis of the canon. On the face of it, this is a surprising omission, given that it offers another potential avenue to decentre the canon's putatively 'universal' Subject, which by implication transcends the particularities of socio-geographical location as well as time. As was seen in the last chapter, according to Neuman, the canonical Self is represented as something 'whose whole essence or nature is only to think, and which, to exist, has no need of *space* nor of any material thing or body'.[4] However, the same lacuna is also evident in discussions of western women's life-writing, with the limited exception, as noted in the Introduction, of working-class texts. Thus, one searches in vain in the indices of the feminist overviews of the field provided by Marcus and Anderson for categories such as 'place', 'space', or '(dis)location' in relation to the female writers they discuss.[5]

Instead, such critics tend to conceive of 'location' in primarily figurative terms. For example, Nancy Mairs suggests that: 'The body is itself a dwelling place … Through writing her body, woman may reclaim the deed to her dwelling.'[6] Among colleagues, there has been much comparably metaphorical discussion of the 'siting' of women life-writers in terms of 'a standpoint, a terrain, an intersection, a network, a crossroads of multiply situated knowledges'.[7] Such analysis is, however, overwhelmingly directed towards discussion of *discursive* spaces denied or aspired to by female auto/biographers. For example, Brodzki and Schenck assert 'the imperative situating of the female subject in spite of the postmodernist campaign against the sovereign self'.[8] Yet as Brodzki makes clear, this strategy is not conceived within a materialist epistemology, despite its implicit critique of post-structuralist assertions about 'the death of the subject'. Indeed, she claims – in terms which are both essentialising and idealist – that 'The autobiographer is always a displaced person; to speak and write from the space marked self-referential is to inhabit … no place.'[9] In similar vein, Benstock defines the key issue posed by her edited volume as follows: 'how is the "self" opened to question in the self-positioning act of writing?'[10] This attests to the methodological preponderance of post-structuralism in her collection of essays. As one contributor, Felicity Nussbaum, explains, such theory characteristically 'redefines the individual as a position, a *locus* where discourses intersect'.[11]

The politics of enunciative sites are, of course, a key issue in all forms of cultural production, including auto/biography.[12] However, too narrow a focus on such a conception of 'location' downplays at least equally important material kinds of 'place' in the narrative construction of subjectivity. To this extent, feminist interventions within Auto/biography Studies have largely replicated the silence on such issues of male critics as dispersed (geographically and temporally), as Misch, Gusdorf and Weintraub. As has been seen, both Misch and Gusdorf offer geo-cultural explanations for the growth of the genre 'proper' in the West; and Misch expends considerable energy on non-western life-writing of the classical period. But neither explores in any detail the constitutive role of specific geo-cultural locations in the formation of the canonical writers they discuss.[13] They focus instead on what Gusdorf calls 'interior space',[14] an emphasis repeated by Weintraub, whose insistence on the transcendent ineffability of Selfhood necessarily diminishes not only the importance of the Body, but of 'place' understood in the ways defined above.[15] While Spengemann indeed considers (western) *national* traditions of autobiography, in practice, he is equally little interested in the specific ways that concrete geo-cultural locations inflect individual autobiographical subjectivities.[16]

The main exception to this general pattern is the third feminist overview of the genre identified in the Introduction, Smith and Watson's *Reading Autobiography*. This clearly recognises that in some life-writing, 'geographical location strongly inflects the story being told'.[17] This is illustrated with brief reference to immigrant life-stories, narratives of city dwelling and prison testimonies. Further, Smith and

Watson argue that an emphasis on socio-spatial location characterises some minoritarian and postcolonial women's life-writing. For example, among Aboriginal authors, 'physical displacement and cultural dislocation' are accepted as contexts within which the life-writers from the community characteristically negotiate their identity (a thesis confirmed in earlier discussion of Morgan). Nonetheless, Smith and Watson conclude that this thematic of subjectivity is 'as yet rarely studied by critics who tend to see [socio-spatial location] as a backdrop' to more important dimensions of the subject's formation.[18]

By contrast, from within Postcolonial Studies, Edward Said proclaims that: 'If there is anything that politically distinguishes the imagination of anti-imperialism, it is the primacy of the geographical in it.'[19] Consequently, Warley argues, 'the forgetting of the locatedness of the subject speaks of an imperialist assumption of centrality that has never been possible for the post-colonial [life-]writer.'[20] Such arguments recognise that colonialism was uncompromisingly an enterprise of material expansion and displacement across the globe, which involved the penetration and restructuring of the cultural as well as physical spaces inhabited by pre-conquest populations. The redistribution of indigenous inhabitants to exploit their land and resources, the creation of new administrative units, notably nation states, as much as the imposition of alien languages and value-systems, had profound consequences for subject peoples' understanding of their identities. In the case of Palestine (see Chapter 7), for example, the creation of the State of Israel in 1947–48 created 750,000 refugees, whose diasporic descendants now number some five million, many of whom are keen to return to the homeland from which they were ethnically cleansed.[21] In its contemporary guise of globalisation, colonialism continues to be responsible for the creation of millions of political and economic refugees (throughout 2006, the Iraq War alone produced nearly 100,000 new refugees every *month*, reaching a total of 1.8 million between the outbreak of hostilities in 2003 and the end of 2006[22]). To these can be added huge numbers of migrants who move country for less immediately pressing reasons, such as to improve their education or economic opportunities. This pattern reflects the continuing structural inequality of social and economic provision between 'the West and the Rest' within the the neo-colonial system of globalisation.

In its concern with this thematic of subjectivity, *Black Skin* once more offers a template for later postcolonial life-writers, male and female. As previously stated, Fanon is clearly interested in both Black and colonised experience in general, and in promoting a reconceptualised 'universal' humanism (or, as he puts it symptomatically, 'restoring man to his proper *place*'[23]). Nonetheless, he consistently locates the evolution of his thinking in terms of the specific existential experience of both his ('French') Caribbean origins and subsequent life in Lyons (indeed, *Black Skin* barely alludes to other European colonialisms). Early on, Fanon proclaims that 'my conclusions are valid only for the Antilles' and, towards the end, insists that his whole inquiry is framed partly in immediate relation to 'the lives of the eight-year-old children who labor in the cane fields of Martinique or Gaudeloupe'.[24] In between, he insists repeatedly that the geo-cultural particularities of the non-western world undermine the false universality of western psychoanalysis and Marxism alike. (While deploring western Marxism's sublation of race into the class dialectic, he nonetheless commends its scrupulous attention to class differences, for example between the colonised doctor from Guadeloupe and the dock-worker of Abidjan.[25])

In the light of these debates, I will now compare two examples of postcolonial life-writing which offer divergent conceptualisations of the relation between geo-cultural (dis)location and auto/biographical identity. The comparison aims further to demonstrate how the issues in question are inflected by the gender and ethnicity of their authors, as well as the cultural norms of the societies from which they both derive and travel to. In conclusion, I will explore how this segment of analysis bears on the larger strategic concern of this monograph with the distinctiveness of postcolonial life-writing.

Wole Soyinka, *Aké: The Years of Childhood* (1981)

The importance of 'place' to Soyinka's autobiographical identity is foregrounded in the very title of his text, Aké being an abbreviated, familiar rendering of Abeokuta, the small town in which the author was brought up and educated until the age of 11. The mutually constitutive relationship between location and Self is explored from a variety of angles. For example, on the one hand, places are often 'selved' in the text, especially in the earlier part of the boy's life. Thus, as part of the process by which Aké acquires an 'extended persona'[26] in Wole's consciousness, even the rock where he regularly seeks sanctuary is strongly anthropomorphised. Jonah is 'solitary and private' like himself and later the older child grieves 'the passing of a unique confidant, the loss of a replete subsuming presence' (*A*: 64). Conversely, the unruly Paa Adatan is conceived as part of the local nigerian landscape, in terms of 'a rugged terrain which had to be captured, then secured tree by tree, hill by hill, boulder by boulder' (*A*: 114). More significantly, Soyinka's growth as a Subject is indexed in terms of his increasing consciousness of being 'situated' in a variety of senses. At its simplest, and consonant with Tim Cribb's suggestion that the author's recreation of his past is framed largely 'within the perceptual range' of a growing child,[27] Soyinka's cognitive development is initially plotted partly in terms of learning to navigate his body within its immediate physical surroundings: 'I knew where to go whenever the sounds from an event carried into the house' (*A*: 36). Wole matures partly by progressively more ambitious explorations of physical space, a process through which change and temporality also come to impinge on his consciousness. For instance, after his first solo expedition outside the family compound, which takes him all the way to Ibara, the child feels 'markedly different from whatever I was before the march' (*A*: 50).

A further stage in his developing Self-consciousness is represented by Wole's coming to appreciate that 'places' are locations inscribed with social meanings and circumscribed by discursive as well as material boundaries. One of his first lessons in this regard is that the human world is partitioned from that of 'spirits and ghommids' (*A*: 2), the walls of the parsonage constituting the immediate border between the two orders of existence. While the supernatural entities will tolerate humans entering their domain of bush, such hospitality is clearly bounded. As Eniola recalls, 'we were to stay off any area beyond the rocks and that clump of bamboo by the stream' (*A*: 6). Within the human realm, Wole further begins to understand, 'place' demarcates social difference, establishing complex sets of insiders and outsiders in relation to whom the boy must also locate himself as a Subject. 'Home', for example, is partly defined by its exclusion, except under extreme duress, of government officials, notably Tax Inspectors. The child initially begins to situate himself in class terms by virtue of the fact that visiting traders from Isara are confined to the back-yard of the family home. Perhaps the most forceful and tragic example of Soyinka's growing appreciation that 'place' is discursively as much as physically constituted involves the outcast Sarowanke. Initially tolerated, her makeshift dwelling beneath the communal mango tree is destroyed once the 'madwoman' falls pregnant, demonstrating that domestic and public spaces must be kept rigorously separate.

As one might infer from this example, a further important aspect of Soyinka's identity-formation involves the realisation that 'place' is also gendered. This begins with the child's perception that his parents have separate bedrooms, to which the male and female children have varying degrees of access at different stages of their lives. Outside the home, similar distinctions obtain, although in ways which complicate the traditional (western) binary coding of the domestic sphere as feminine and the public as masculine. For example, a significant proportion of economic activity, represented by the shops and market stalls in Abeokuta, is conducted by women, even if the political sphere of the Akala's palace remains male-dominated, at least until invaded by the irate women traders towards the end of the text. (Insofar as their revolt is also implicitly directed against the British, by virtue of their guaranteeing the Akala's position, women in fact penetrate deep into the wider public sphere of nationalist struggle.) If the streets of Abeokuta are gender-neutral in everyday life, on certain occasions they become explicitly masculinised, notably during the *egungun* rituals when women must remain indoors for fear of nuisance. Another resolutely masculine formative sphere are the locally-staffed single-sex secondary schools Wole attends, where regular corporal punishment and the intimidation of older 'papas' enforce a system of patriarchal discipline reminiscent of colonialism itself, with its male District Officers and policemen. Similarly, Isara, his father Ayo's birth-place, is experienced primarily as a male sphere by the growing child. Here traditional norms of masculinity are enforced through activities like hunting – from which women are excluded. The initiation ritual which the child undergoes here specifically performs Wole's insertion into Ijebu manhood; taken from his mother to an exclusively male hut the night before the ceremony, during the scarification itself Soyinka is enjoined not to betray his gender by crying like a girl.

As this suggests, 'place' also grounds the various geo-cultural systems among which Wole must locate himself. Isara represents one pole of identification. In this 'second home', where he is initially gently mocked for being too 'English' (*A*: 135; compare Equiano), Soyinka takes 'several steps into the past' (*A*: 66–7), discovering that his identity is deeply shaped by the values of traditional life. Indeed, by naming the grandfather who performs his initiation a supplementary 'Father', the boy proclaims a filiation which is returned in the promise that 'Ogun protects his own' (*A*: 140). At the opposite extreme are the specifically colonial locations which the child enters only once during the narrative, when he stumbles into the police post during his solo expedition through Abeokuta. On the same journey, Wole passes the 'Residency', a forbidding building guarded by constables, which houses the District Officer (whom the boy encounters for the first time in the flesh towards the end of the text). Set 'well back up a hill, part hidden by trees' (*A*: 13), its position reflects the initial remoteness of colonial rule from the child's immediate everyday concerns.

Mediating between these geo-cultural poles is Abeokuta and, more specifically, the cluster of buildings in the compound round the church, which Soyinka has described elsewhere as 'a sort of semi-hermetic … Christian conclave'.[28] Corresponding to Mpalive-Hangson Msiska's description of Soyinka's family as being 'part of the modernizing class of the mission-educated élite',[29] his parents' negotiations with the modernity represented by colonialism are conducted in both material and ideological terms. Thus, while water is still stored in calabashes half-buried in the garden, the arrival of the radio and telephone figure the increasing connectivity between the minute particularity of 'local' life and the global economy and polity. For example, the radio brings news of the Second World War, the transformative and (dis)integrative effects of which are also felt in the presence of Congolese troops in Abeokuta and the departure of Uncle Dipo to fight in Burma.

In *Aké*, colonialism clearly transforms traditional identities associated with 'place' to a significant degree. This process can be seen in its hybridisation of nature itself. Thus, bougainvillea, originally from the Pacific, grows in Essay's garden and his orchard also boasts the pomegranate, introduced to the region by a previous bishop. Substituting for the Edenic apple in local eyes (*A*: 3), it symbolises the temptations of foreign knowledge which will eventually lead to Wole's departure from Abeokuta. A more explicit example of the impact of colonialism on the social meanings of place comes when Paa Adatan draws his cutlass and scrapes a boundary across the earth in front of Wild Christian's shop to keep away German soldiers whom he fears may mount a surprise attack: 'If they try cross this line, guns go turn to broom for dem hand' (*A*: 110–11). Once again, Wole is reminded not only of the crucial importance of borders, but that they are contingent and, because primarily discursive, subject to change.

However, this process works both ways. Despite its obviously sympathetic orientations to British rule, the parsonage compound is as much the site of hybridisation of the alien culture as the converse. As Derek Wright argues, Soyinka thereby represents 'the colonial impingement as an assimilation or translation into another order of experience instead of an obliteration of one culture by another'.[30] An obvious example is the 'wild' Christianity of Wole's mother. Only on the anniversary of the missionaries' arrival does she actually proselytise on the streets. The rest of the year, her faith accommodates a good deal of traditional metaphysics. For example, on the family visit to Isara, her dread of poisoning is an implicit acknowledgement of the power of traditional 'magic'. (Essay, too, relies on all manner of 'medicine' from Isara in the parsonage.) Similarly, the presence in the Reverend Kuti's household of uncle Sanya, despite his strong links to local cults, represents the characteristic tolerance of the Christian community. Consequently Wole is not forced to ground himself within any singular cultural identity. Indeed, selecting as he pleases from each tradition, he also proves himself capable of rebellion against both (whether by refusing to prostrate himself before the *Odemo* or by stealing the collection money). This pattern is reflected more widely in his family. While 'Wild Christian' occasionally denounces 'superstition', she also plays a prominent part in the revolt against the tax regime which is imposed, the women believe, by the government in Lagos (*A*: 182). Indeed, her sister-in-law Beere provides perhaps the most damning criticism of colonial racism when she furiously demands of the District Officer why Japan and not Germany was made to suffer the Atom Bomb: 'I know you, the white mentality: Japanese, Chinese, Africans, we are all subhuman' (*A*: 224).

The largely benevolent nature of these varied lessons about the discursive meanings of 'place' and their relationship to Self are responsible for the affirmative tone of Soyinka's reconstruction of his younger life. Neither tradition nor colonialism, the familiar or the foreign, weigh upon the child in oppressive ways, the kindliness of 'Father', for example, being anticipated in the kindness of the white policeman who rescues the lost child at the beginning of the text. Biodun Jeyifo argues that Soyinka's text cannot be read as a *Bildungsroman* because it expresses none of the disillusion which characterises that genre; and Ato Quayson insists on 'the essential humour and lightheartedness of the narrative'.[31] While *Aké* certainly contains abundant affirmative and comic qualities, these are partly offset, however, in its framing of the narrative of childhood, where the mature writer meditates on the changes that time has wrought on his former home and, by implication, insofar as 'place' has been so closely linked to personhood, himself. If modern Abeokuta seems shrunken so, too, the older Soyinka seems diminished, the expansively open and physically active boy transformed into a comparatively immobile adult observer.

The melancholy derives primarily from the fact that the text's representation of 'location' is inflected by its antithesis. The reasons for Soyinka's displacement are never specified, any more than the motivation for his return. However, *Aké* plots a trajectory of increasing separation, physical and affective, from Soyinka's initial grounding in a specific quarter of Abeokuta in pursuit of successively more ambitious educational opportunities. This suggests complex issues around the naming of Soyinka's text. By choosing *Aké* for his title, Soyinka appears to wish to construct a relational Self of the kind discussed in Chapter 2, which recognises the determining influence on his formation not just of 'place', but also of the community he grows up in. However, this idea is complicated by the process of individuation which the child Wole enthusiastically embraces. As has been seen, even at primary school, Wole seeks out private places of sanctuary, notably Jonah, causing his mother anxiety that he spends too much time alone. Wole is particularly disturbed by his experience of 'the communal mat' (*A*: 83) on which the children of the house and their symptomatically unnamed troupe of 'cousins' sleep: 'I would wake up in the night after a violent struggle with pythons that had tied up all my limbs, suffocating under slimy monsters from a mythical past, unable to utter the scream for help which rose in my throat' (*A*: 84). Such early experiences of feeling stifled by the collective partly impel Wole's restlessness to leave home. Travelling has been associated with agency, freedom and individuation ever since the narrator's first solo expedition beyond the walls of the family house. Government College in Ibadan is therefore welcomed as 'another liberating step' (*A*: 153) in his quest for autonomy.

Nonetheless, a relational Self is clearly implied in the sense of loss inscribed in the adult Soyinka's perspective on the Abeokuta of his childhood. This is not simply a response to the physical decay of the place over time: 'An evil thing has happened to Aké parsonage. The land is eroded, the lawns are bared ... on a depleted landscape, full of creaks, exposed and nerveless' (*A*: 3–4). It is also the consequence of his perception of the town's increasing insertion into the 'space/time compression' which characterises globalisation.[32] The Abeokuta to which Soyinka returns is now the site 'of a global waste industry' which has severely compromised its former identity; instead of the 'hundred varieties' of cultural forms of his childhood, Soyinka now finds that homogenisation and 'identicality' reign (*A*: 157–8). Swamped by the ersatz products of an unequal world trading system, the original character of the town is almost effaced: 'Along the same midnight walk of Dayisi the guitarist now darts the young hawker, releasing into the faces of passers-by through his finger on the caller's button, the dulcet chimes of Made-In-Hong-Kong doorbells' (*A*: 150). Even the most basic signifiers of cultural difference, such as food, have been distorted. For example, the traditional milk-curds have given way to fake ice cream, exciting Soyinka's withering disgust: 'The quick-profit importer of instant machines is content to foist a bed-pan slop of diabetic kittens on his youthful customers and watch them lick it noisily, biting deeper into the cone' (*A*: 156). In place of the former emphasis on the mutual hybridisation of local and foreign cultures has come a grovelling mimicry of an 'instant-culture' (*A*: 157) with no affiliations to 'place'. Thus, Dayisi's distinctive 'juju-band' rhythms have ceded to 'yet another local imitation of foreign pop' (*A*: 157). Given Soyinka's emphasis on the corporeal inscription of cultural difference during his initiation process, the more recent surrender of the Nigerian Body to the influences of globalisation is particularly telling. Representative of this process are the girls bleached by skin-tone creams who gather in the 'neighbourhood' McDonald's or, with hair sizzled straight congregating over their Kentucky fried chicken.

Such perspectives raise the issue of whether the displaced adult Soyinka has himself escaped the deleterious influences of globalisation. After all, the very conceptual tools which enable him to identify Abeokuta's diminished place within the world system are gained through his own experience of separation from his natal town. Indeed, James Gibbs suggests that *Aké* is 'the work of a man under attack for being "too European" in the eyes of some of his countrymen'.[33] If this is the case, a defence could be mounted for Soyinka partly on the 'site' of language. This may seem an unpromising claim, given his choice to write in the language of the former coloniser, as well as that of the prevailing forces of globalisation. Nonetheless, it is obvious that the author is not conforming to the 'rules' of these hegemonic versions of English any more than Behan. From his youth, Soyinka paradoxically experiences Standard English as an *alienated* form of the 'proper' version spoken at home. Thus, on meeting the white policeman at the end of his first solo journey from the parsonage, Wole comments that it was 'difficult to understand him all the time but by straining hard, I could make sense of his questions' (*A*: 46). From later in his childhood, Soyinka nostalgically remembers the 'strange language' of the choir he temporarily joins, 'a mixture of English, Yoruba and some celestial language that could only be what was spoken by those cherubs in the stained-glass windows' (*A*: 152; compare the school song, *A*: 22). Soyinka's continuing loyalty to the hybridising dynamic of his childhood culture is reflected in the adult author's replication of such linguistic experimentation. Thus, the writer peppers his discourse with translated Yoruba metaphors: 'You are going to eat the cane tonight' (*A*: 65). Conversely, Yoruba diction is also often left untranslated: 'New Year was palm wine, *ebiripo, ikokore*' (*A*: 67). This register is leavened with the reported 'pidgin' speech of characters like Paa Adatan, leading Robert Fraser to argue that 'despite the fluency of the English medium in this book, the norm is not perceived to be English, but Yoruba'.[34] Yet it is more complicated than this. Like Behan, who draws on a comparably wide linguistic range, Soyinka leavens his writing with neologisms such as 'resorb' and 'motorped' (*A*: 79, 168) and recondite diction such as 'ghommids' (*A*: 2). Also like Behan, Soyinka's discourse is often encased in a poetically flighty syntax which corresponds to 'the language of the cherubs' – or the artist.

Thus, if it is possible to read *Aké* as in part reflecting an alienation from birth-community which exceptional educational achievement and colonial acculturation so often entails in the postcolonial context, it could be argued by contrast that Soyinka remains loyal to the traditions of his youth. For example, his trajectory corresponds closely to the 'regulative psychobiography' enacted in Yoruba mythopoesis. Claimed for Ogun by his grandfather, as has been seen, Soyinka reaffirmed this identification the year after winning the Nobel Prize (and three years after the publication of *Aké*).[35] Thus, in an important sense, the much-travelled adult Soyinka continues to claim perceptual and affective roots in the value-system associated with the Yoruba deity. Paradoxically, the significance of this lies in the fact that Ogun represents *both* the integrity of autochthonous tradition *and* the principle of change and adaptation. Thus, Derek Wright sees Ogun as 'the god of transition, the archetypal crosser of boundaries'.[36] In similar vein, Msiska comments that: 'For Soyinka, Ogun is the god of all spaces of transition, the in-between spaces that need to be inhabited, transgressed and overcome as one moves between one mode of existence and another.'[37] As this suggests, for Soyinka displacement is not necessarily the antithesis of spaces of filiation. Rather, it can provide a new location from where inherited identities and values can also be preserved and reaffirmed. If, as Louis James argues, 'the place [Aké] ...

underlies the boy's opening consciousness' [*sic*], it continues to ground the mature writer in crucial ways.[38]

Shirley Geok-Lin Lim, *Among the White Moon Faces: Memoirs of an Asian American Woman* (1996)

There are considerable areas of overlap between the life-writing of Soyinka and Lim in terms of the role ascribed to issues of place and displacement in the formation of postcolonial subjectivity. Both texts provide a detailed account of childhood in a colonial location which is conceived, especially early in life, as an integral aspect of their authors' identity. Comparable to the 'selving' of place in *Aké*, the child Lim experiences Malacca 'not as a town but as a familiar spirit, a space extending from the family, and familiarity encompassing territory'.[39] In both works, moreover, the birth-place is being increasingly transformed by the politics of decolonisation and intimations of globalisation. This entails similar dilemmas for both autobiographical Subjects in terms of the contrasting attractions of traditional culture and a modernity imposed from abroad. Further *Aké* and *Among the White Moon Faces* alike stage their protagonists' increasing dislocation from their cultures of origin in pursuit of educational opportunity, in the context of which dynamic the early growth of a future writer's mind is carefully elaborated.

Yet there are also significant differences between Lim and Soyinka's treatments of both the cultural politics and psycho-social effects of (dis)location. In the first place, she is a good deal more conflicted about her native culture and place of birth, an ambivalence in which gender issues play a crucial role. In her Chinese-Malayan community, girls are valued little more than in El Saadawi's village on the Nile:

> Girls were interchangeable. They fetched, obeyed, served, poured tea, balanced their baby brothers and sisters on their hips while they stood in the outer circles of older women. Unnecessary as individuals, girls need concern nobody, unlike sons, especially first sons, on whose goodwill mothers measured their future.
>
> (*AWMF*: 14)

If there is also an echo here of the rivalry with an older brother in *A Daughter of Isis*, Lim's early development is structured by comparable negotiations with – and subsequent rejection of – 'the only one shape' (*sic*; *AWMF*: 99) available for females in her culture. This process is signalled in the (Self-cancelling) question which the author constantly asks of herself as a girl: 'How can I prove that I am not who I am?' (*AWMF*: 43).

Lim's gendered sense of dislocation is exacerbated by the affective and gender economy of her particular family, where she is the only girl among several male siblings. In striking contrast to Soyinka's affectionate narrative of a largely untroubled domestic life, Lim's portrayal of Malacca is coloured by deep personal unhappiness about her relationship with her parents. In describing them as

having 'unwittingly mutilated me' (*AWMF*: 20; compare 303), Lim corroborates
El Saadawi's conviction that female circumcision does not have to be a physical
operation. Lim also anticipates El Saadawi's strong attachment to her father and
acknowledges crucial paternal support for her educational ambitions. Nonetheless, she deplores Baba's unfaithfulness, gambling and violent rages (she is
often thrashed when she disappoints his expectations, locking her into a pattern of
abuse which the author is courageous enough to admit reproducing when she, in
turn, becomes a parent). Baba's violence towards his wife, moreover, leads to the
decisive event in Lim's early life, her mother Emak's abandonment of the family
(when the author was 8) for a new life in Singapore. Lim's ensuing trauma is
never fully healed. Indeed it is exacerbated during one adult visit to Singapore
when Emak insists that Lim call her 'auntie', so as not to put off a new lover. In
the US, the author suffers a breakdown which is connected directly to unresolved
feelings about her mother (*AWMF*: 224–5). Such conflict underwrites Lim's later
restless efforts to 'unbecome' Emak (*AWMF*: 223) as she searches for a more
sustaining 'family' in the United States. This quest embraces – with varying
degrees of satisfaction – volunteer host families, shared student houses, the academic community and the feminist movement – before she finally achieves the
grounding of marriage and motherhood. These, it could be argued, constitute for
Lim her most vital claim to 'being at home' in the US.[40]

Furthermore, in strong contrast to Soyinka's unquestioning assumption of an
essential rootedness and belonging in his birthplace, Lim represents herself as
already displaced in other important ways, before migrating to the United States.
Unlike Abeokuta (where only the temporary presence of Congolese soldiers and a
tiny Hausa quarter disturbs its ethnic homogeneity), Malacca is to a significant
degree the product of a variety of diasporic communities. Friends with names like
De Souza reflect the history of Portuguese colonialism. Lim's grandfather lives on
Heeren St, evoking the subsequent era of Dutch power. British colonialism brings
in its wake not only a new material infrastructure symbolised by the Indo-Gothic
railway hotel where Lim has her liaison with a predatory English lecturer, but
large numbers of Indians and Chinese, creating a far greater degree of cultural
hybridity than in Soyinka's childhood home-town. Lim celebrates this fact in
various ways, not least in her recollections of the striking ethnic diversity of her
lovers and friends. Equally, while she is baptised as a Catholic, she frequents
Hindu temples and her family also observes many Confucian customs and rituals.
Later, she enthusiastically anticipates that independence will dispense with
colonial racial hierarchy and usher in 'a multiracial, multicultural, pluralistic
democracy' (*AWMF*: 175).

However, Lim insists equally on the negative aspects of such hybridity. Her
sense of dislocation while growing up derives substantially from belonging to the
Chinese diaspora which migrated to what is now Malaysia in the wake of Britain
taking control of the peninsula. Her grandfather, a penniless labourer, comes in
pursuit of precisely the kind of life-opportunities that Lim herself will later seek in
America. As a member of the Malay-assimilated *peranakan* fraction of this diaspora, Lim suffers more specific kinds of psychic/affective displacement. Many

Chinese-Malays, especially during periods of nationalist agitation, regarded *per-anakans* disapprovingly as a group which had lost touch with its roots. One of Lim's earliest memories is that 'Chinese-speaking Malayans called me a *"Kelang-kia-kwei"* – or a Tamil devil – because I could not or would not speak Hokkien' (*AWMF*: 23; compare 182). Conversely, Baba insists that English be spoken at home once Emak flees, cutting his daughter off from her maternal Malay. Thus, despite her deficiencies in Hokkien, Lim records, 'The Malay-speakers placed me as an ancestral talker' (*AWMF*: 24). The existential 'confusion' which this liminal linguistic-cultural location engenders is partly reflected in the multiplicity of names Lim is given – Agnes and Jennifer, in addition to Shirley and her Chinese ones (compare Equiano's multiple namings) – which bespeak 'too many identities, too many languages' (*AWMF*: n.p.).

Lim's psychic/cultural dislocation is exacerbated by contact with colonial culture, despite her growing love for the English language, in which she increasingly feels most 'at home'. Whereas Soyinka's childhood experience of colonialism is essentially benevolent, providing new cultural elements to be absorbed relatively unproblematically into his psycho-social repertoire, Lim's exacerbates her *angst* in important respects. This is partly because her exposure to its influence is far more direct and extensive than Soyinka's. While her father buys her British comics and books as a child, the writer's primary engagement with colonialism comes in a series of expatriate-run educational institutions which are sometimes hardly more palatable than Miss Hamer's establishment in *A Daughter of Isis*. While on the one hand welcoming school as a relief from problems at home and appreciating that it represents the best avenue of escape from the single gender 'shape' which her community enforces, Lim is sometimes as damning as Ngugi[41] about the emotional 'damage of colonial education' (*AWMF*: 126). Seduced into longing to be like the privileged British boarders at her convent, she is further alienated from her 'home' culture by 'a pedagogy of terror' (*AWMF*: 105). As curious and independent-minded as El Saadawi, however, Lim bridles increasingly against the conformism and obedience demanded by the nuns, in a relationship which allegorises the struggle for autonomy of her country. The same pattern of conflict is observable during her undergraduate education, where British culture is dangled before students as an impossible object of desire, full communion with which they are in the end denied by virtue of being racially Other.

Yet whereas Abeokuta becomes progressively more hybrid as it is incorporated within the system of globalisation, to the extent that Soyinka bewails the degree of erosion of its traditional culture, the opposite dynamic is observable in Lim's Malacca – causing the writer no less regret. For Lim, the price of Malayan independence is regression towards mono-culturalism. Even as a child, the future author senses that the Chinese diaspora is often regarded by indigenous Malays as at best temporarily resident aliens, if not positively unwelcome outsiders. When decolonisation approaches, the community comes under increasing pressure to prove its right to a place to the soon-to-be-independent nation, enabling Lim's father to begin a new career as translator of attestations to nationality and citizenship rights. Such legal documents count for little. After independence in 1957, increasing violence against those of Chinese origin culminates in the expulsion of Chinese-majority Singapore in 1965 from the Federation and the massacres in mainland Malaya of 13 May 1969. These developments are major factors in enhancing Lim's sense of dislocation, reinforcing – although not precipitating – her decision to 'translate' herself to the United States.

More explicitly than is the case with Soyinka, displacement thus becomes as much a positive as negative condition in Lim's writing, representing an opportunity to escape not only the deteriorating political situation, but the psychic dislocations engendered by Emak's disappearance, the family's increasing poverty, and an initially detested step-mother – as well as to fulfil educational ambitions. This is consistent with a pattern observable earlier in the text. The child Lim keenly feels the pain of eviction from the security of grandfather's house, which represents her most powerful early idea of 'home', and subsequently from Baba's shop-house, a dislocation violent enough to render Malacca a 'foreign town' (*AWMF*: 68). Nonetheless, she quickly begins to associate such displacements with autonomy and liberation: 'I began to value … my home which was not a home' (*AWMF*: 138), precisely because of the uncustomary freedoms it allows her as a teenage girl. To escape her new step-mother, for example, Lim cycles unsupervised ever further from the family dwelling, before graduating to the greater mobility offered by motor-bikes. Later, she is attracted to Iqbal, her first serious lover, because of his 'openness of movement' (*AWMF*: 191), signified above all by his studies in California.

Lim's life-writing differs from Soyinka's not only by virtue of the attention she gives to the motivations leading to her displacement from her home-town but to the process of adjusting to the new milieu in which she finds herself. In certain ways, Lim's migration involves a radical 'translation' of her subjectivity. 'I have become transformed', she announces at the outset of her narrative, reviewing her life at the time of writing (*AWMF*: 20). The psychological as well as physical distance travelled from her culture of origin and the identities enforced there is suggested in Lim's sub-title. These are not the 'memoirs of a Malay(si)an woman', but of an 'Asian American' one. In some ways, her narrative reads like a classic American immigrant narrative of successful assimilation into the melting-pot of popular myth, represented by her marriage to a Jewish liberal professional. Further, their production of an ethnically hybrid child generates stereotypically aspirational daydreams that he may become the country's President. Consonant with such narratives, in which talent and hard work are the primary motors of social integration and success, Lim rises seemingly inexorably from teaching in an obscure Community College in the Bronx, to a professorship at the University of California. Her later accounts of a jet-setting international academic life measure how far Lim has transcended her initial self-image on arrival in the US: 'I was a true immigrant, shabby, unrooted, poor, and perpetually afraid of losing my way' (*AWMF*: 208).

Also typical of such narratives of successful assimilation is Lim's enumeration of the advantages which the US offers in comparison to her country of origin. First, she represents it as more genuinely multi-cultural than a Malaysia which is becoming ever more narrowly reconfigured in the interests of its dominant ethnicity (*AWMF*: 339). This plurality is especially accessible along the axis of gender. Many of the women Lim meets combine in communities inconceivable in an increasingly ethnically divided Malay(si)a, such that 'across these divisions of white middle-class women and myself, for example, or young Chicanas and myself now, a rare yet common ground is visible' (*AWMF*: 233; compare 313). Her first experience of such networking comes when Lim works as a women's dorm counsellor at Brandeis. As she settles into her role, she at last finds relief from the chronic feelings of isolation which characterised her initial period in Boston, finding a 'home' in relationships of mutual care and service. The faculty world Lim later enters also provides further sustaining networks of women, with Lim's turn towards feminism as such being propelled by participation in a summer school led by Nancy Miller.

Yet all this by no means implies either Lim's total assimilation to American culture nor the negation of her Malay(si)an past. After all, barely a third of the text addresses life after arrival in the US. (Intending initially to return to Malaysia as 'the native daughter made good' (*AWMF*: 248) to teach in its universities, Lim decides to settle in the US only after meeting her future husband.) Soon after arriving in America, Lim alludes to her 'other psyche' (*AWMF*: 221), which is rooted in Malaysia. This aspect of her subjectivity is represented in the powerful dreams of 'home' Lim remains prey to and the intensely felt absence of Iqbal. For a while she devours science-fiction, until she realises that: 'All the books were about aliens ... alien languages ... disasters at work in alienness' (*AWMF*: 230). But Lim's sense of estrangement in America never entirely disappears, as is evident from her description of Malay(si)a at the time of writing as 'a parallel universe played out ... in journeys *home* ... and in a continuous undercurrent of feelings directed to people I have known, feared, loved and *deserted* for this American success' (*AWMF*: 20–1, my emphasis).

Thus, while Lim is physically 'translated' to what is in some ways a spectacularly different world, and certainly changes significantly as a result, there are also strong psychic continuities between the two phases of her life and in her identity. In the United States, as much as in Malay(si)a, Lim's characteristic ambivalence derives from her occupation of an 'in-between' position, neither fully belonging, nor wholly an outsider. Thus, on arriving in the US, Lim finds that she must 'play the roles set out for me' (*AWMF*: 209) as surely as in her natal culture. Consequently, while academic life provides the feminist support described above, it is also often no less patriarchal than Malay(si)a, where a junior lectureship for which she is supremely qualified is given instead to an ethnic Malay male. She notes acerbically that (temporary) composition instructors in the US tend to be women, while the full-time literature faculty is as male-dominated as was the case at university in Kuala Lumpur. Rendered 'seriously invisible' by 'institutionalised neglect' (*AWMF*: 217), she can barely fend off another predatory lecturer who advises her that she should get married rather than pursue graduate studies. Even at Brandeis she is sometimes condescended to on the grounds of her ethnicity. Philip Rahv, for example, complains to the aspiring young author that: 'There are no good immigrant writers, they write only sociology. And all this attention to black writers!' (*AWMF*: 212). There is therefore some justice in Lim's occasional explicit comparisons of the US education system to the one she experienced in colonial Malaya (*AWMF*: 272).

Other aspects of American life prove equally alienating. Thus, if Lim is strongly critical of the effects of British colonialism, she is also uneasily aware of the negative influence of US power around the world. She arrives for graduate studies at the height of the Vietnam protests and remains troubled about the geo-political role of her adopted homeland long afterwards, citing American inter-vention in El Salvador as another instance of its malign influence. Further, dis-placement teaches her a good deal more about the sometimes negative consequences of class identity, replicating Behan's trajectory in *Borstal Boy*. Although her grandfather is wealthy and her feckless father leads the family into poverty, Lim has little class-awareness as such while growing up; even her distaste for Ah Peng is largely personal. In America, by contrast, she comes to recognise class as a powerful, if often unacknowledged, presence deforming social relations. From disputes with neighbours in the gentrifying part of Brooklyn where she and Charles buy their first home, to encounters with elderly working-class males able to attend Community College only in retirement, Lim comes to appreciates that gender and race are not the only social fault-lines in her new homeland. Equally, she remains sceptical about the emphasis on individualism in the US. While appreciating that her birth community was often stifling, she recognises that it prevented the atomisation which is the reverse side of the medal of American individualism. Neither social system, in the end, seems fully satisfactory (*AWMF*: 231).

To this extent, it could be argued that patterns of affect and behaviour acquired in her natal culture remain decisive in Lim's identity. *Pace* the author's occasional tendency to construct herself as a multiple and divided being, prey to 'super-fragmentation' (*AWMF*: 239), one might suggest that her ambivalence about 'place' in fact expresses the existence of a consistent '*unmovable* self' (*AWMF*: 20, my italics) throughout both strands of her narrative. As with Soyinka, the continuity of Lim's identity between childhood and adulthood, as well as before and after displacement, is further illustrated in the author's lan-guage-use. In the prologue, she discusses the 'pidgin' which arose in Malaya at the confluence of cultures which constituted the colony during her childhood, generating 'a pattering patois which was our very own' (*AWMF*: 13). While it would be incorrect to describe Lim's autobiographical discourse as 'pidgin', it is certainly characterised by the inflection of the Standard British English learned in colonial institutions with a variety of other languages, ranging from *Bahasa* Malay (for example, *pisang emas, nyonya, pintu pagar*) to both Standard American English (for example, stoop and math) and slang (schleppers, teeter-totter). The sig-nificance of this pattern is complex. On the one hand, one might argue that the Americanisms are evidence of Lim's increasing assimilation to a new identity. Indeed, during one visit to Singapore, a visiting Australian academic thinks of Lim as American and asks her to check idioms in his translation of some stories set in New York. On the other hand, despite Lim's argument that little of the polyglossic features of Maly(si)an culture appear in her memoir,[42] her discourse is sufficiently mixed as to be consistent with the hybrid(ising) cultural dynamics in which she grows up (compare Soyinka). To this extent, one might conclude that Lim remains a 'resident alien' in crucial subjective-affective respects long after acquiring citizenship rights in the U.S.

One might wish to suggest that Lim resolves the dilemma which her language-use reveals about her identity through defining herself as 'Asian American', a newly-emerging category with which she is increasingly taken after reading Maxine Hong Kingston. By means of this term, she can at last 'place Malysia side by side with the United States' (*AWMF*: 334). The lack of hyphen might be deemed to signify a dualistic model of hybridity already encountered in Equiano, in which neither term is dominant, rather than either a more chronic form of disjunctive decentredness or synthesis into a unified new identity of the kind elaborated by Morgan. As Lim suggests elsewhere, however, a further interpretation is possible, whereby her hybrid language expresses a desire for her writing, at least, to be located nowhere specific, but to be seen rather as a form of 'flight from territorialisation',[43] if not her true home.[44] This supports Jeffrey Partridge's argument that instead of embracing either or both of the national-cultural identities available to her, Lim instead ultimately locates herself in relation to a 'transnational aesthetic'.[45] 'How strange to be a poet without a country!' Lim exclaims at one point (*AWMF*: 277–8). More explicitly than *Aké*, therefore, *Among the White Moon Faces* in the end prioritises the productive contradictions of displacement over the security of roots in specific locations, old or new.

Conclusion

The texts discussed in this chapter demonstrate the crucial role that issues of 'place' can play in the constitution of postcolonial subjectivity, irrespective of the gender of the writers concerned. Indeed, the recurrence of the word in titles as diverse as Morgan's *My Place*, Yasmin Alibhai-Brown's *No Place Like Home* (1995) and Said's *Out of Place* (see Chapter 7) suggests that in the postcolonial context auto/biographical Selfhood can scarcely be conceived separately from socio-spatial concerns. Yet as both *Aké* and *Among the White Moon Faces* suggest, feelings of being 'at home' or of displacement can be as much subjective and psychological as a function of the material (dis)location of the Subject. Soyinka experiences some measure of alienation in the places most familiar to him. Conversely, in some measure, Lim comes to feel 'at home' in her apparent homelessness.

The relationship between (dis)location and Selfhood in postcolonial life-writing is therefore often fraught and contested. On the one hand, a secure socio-spatial affiliation is often represented as crucial to security and stability of identity. There is thus an implicit regret throughout *Aké* for the loss of organic relations to the environment which Soyinka grew up in. A similar tone is struck in Nehru's *Autobiography*. On returning to the homeland he has dreamed of so intensely during his years abroad, Nehru experiences 'an exile's feeling'[46] because his country has changed so profoundly in his absence. By contrast, an organic, uninterrupted relation to familiar places can also be the source of deep oppression. Sometimes, this is a consequence of colonialism and its aftermath, at others of indigenous social structures and value-systems. Whether confined to the Reservation (as is the case with some of Morgan's extended family) or Bantustan (some of Magona's relatives in *To My Children's Children*), or traditional female spaces in the village (El Saadawi's experience for much of her childhood) or confined to their homes by outside forces (Suad Amiry, see Chapter 7), innumerable (post)colonial subjects have been involuntarily tied to filiative locations they would rather escape or enlarge. Others, by contrast, are transported to alien locations where they are involuntarily fixed in place, whether through plantation slavery (Equiano and Prince) or colonial imprisonment (Behan and Gandhi), with potentially equally deleterious psychic consequences.

As the latter examples suggest, dislocation is an equally ambivalent predicament in postcolonial life-writing. On the one hand, voluntary displacement is characteristically represented as liberating, for reasons which can be inferred from the preceding discussion. For Claude McKay, for example, displacement opens up a new personal ethic: 'Go, better than stand still, keep going.'[47] This anticipates the 'nomadism' and 'deterritorialisation' widely celebrated as characteristic of (post)colonial and, more particularly, of diasporic, experience.[48] Conversely, voluntary forms of displacement can also prove traumatic, as Nehru's experience attests. The same conflicting pattern can be found in representations of involuntary dislocation. From James's traumatic deportation from the US (on which he is, symptomatically, almost silent, although it is clearly one of the elements in his turn from Marxism to nationalism – and from 'straight' to cultural politics), to the varieties of exile anatomised in Palestinian life-writing (see Chapter 7), involuntary displacement can prove profoundly challenging, if not catastrophic, for a sense of Self. However, even such dreadful experiences are often reconfigured as positive in their consequences for the (post)colonial Subject's identity-formation and sense of personhood. A spectacular instance of this attitude is the providentialism widely expressed in precursor forms of postcolonial life-writing. Like many slave narratives, Equiano ostensibly plots his disastrous start in life in terms of the happy outcome that Christian salvation promises. At the opposite end of the historical spectrum, there is an unexpected echo of this structure of feeling in Said's *Out of Place*, where the pain of exile is transmuted into something enabling, even liberating: 'My search for freedom ... could only have begun because of that rupture, so I have come to think of it as fortunate.'[49] Such examples corroborates Glissant's argument that 'uprooting can work toward identity, and exile can be seen as beneficial'.[50] Yet, as the work of Soyinka and Lim illustrates to different degrees, even when exile is embraced in this positive fashion, it does not necessarily undo what Paquet calls 'a consciousness of lineage in territory as a distinctive marker of individual identity that is coexistent with journey in space [*sic*] and/or consciousness beyond regional space'.[51]

This thematic of subjectivity provides a clear contrast to those discussed in previous chapters in terms of the strategic concern of this monograph with the specificity of postcolonial life-writing. In each of those cases, the sub-genre provides important inflections of the thematics defined by feminist critics as distinctive of western women's life-writing. Nonetheless, it was also observed, there is also considerable overlap between the two sub-genres in all three instances. However, if the thematic of (dis)location appears to at last open up blue water between them in terms of the construction of autobiographical subjectivity, as well as between postcolonial life-writing and the western canon, the strategic issue of its specificity requires investigation of further elements of the sub-genre, notably its forms and styles. In the next two chapters, therefore, I will analyse aspects of these in comparative relation to both women's life-writing and the western canon.

5   Working the borders of genre in postcolonial life-writing

As suggested in the Introduction, autobiography has always proved difficult to classify in anything approaching watertight theoretical terms. Nonetheless, as the existence of the canon suggests, there has been broad agreement in practice about what is and is not included in the genre. Further, as has been seen, Misch's early definition of 'the autobiographical pact' was resurrected and refined by Lejeune towards the end of the second phase of Auto/biography Studies and broadly disseminated during the 1980s in the Anglophone world, where it remains extremely influential. Thus, while lamenting the often slippery variety of their objects of study and debating the hierarchy of sub-forms which constitute their objects of study, for most of its history, critics in the field have operated within parameters consonant with what Derrida describes as the fundamental 'law of genre', namely that 'genres are not to be mixed'.[1] However, as Marcus, Gilmore and Anderson variously suggest, as the third phase of Auto/biography Studies develops, postmodernism poses radical problems for the idea of genre, including autobiography.[2] The same can be claimed of the effects of feminist interventions in the critical field. If, as has been seen, thematics of subjectivity constitute one important focus for its contestations of the cultural politics of the canon and its formation, issues concerning the forms and borders of auto/biography have proved equally fertile.

In the view of many such critics, the conception of autobiography as a properly coherent genre with its own protocols and boundaries rests on three principal premises. First, the text in question must conform to the terms of the 'autobiographical pact'. Second, it must demonstrate the integrity of its Subject's Selfhood. For example, Misch argues that 'from this element of unity proceed the substantial merits of the genre'.[3] Gusdorf concurs, asserting that the autobiographer 'strains toward a complete and coherent expression of his entire destiny'.[4] However, generic integrity is enforced as much by aesthetic consistency as psychological 'continuity'.[5] Thus, according to Olney, the genre has been considered to be properly literary largely insofar as it conforms to the traditional criteria of 'wholeness, harmony, and radiance'.[6] If 'stylistic harmony' is crucial in this regard, this is guaranteed above all by the all-important *convention* of what Gusdorf calls 'fine logical and rational order' in the formal arrangement of the development of the protagonist's subjectivity and identity.[7]

In the view of many feminists, such positions are, once more, clearly gendered, further helping to explain the relative marginalisation of women's life-writing in the critical history of the field. Thus, Estelle Jelinek argues that the qualities of 'harmony and orderliness [and] unidirectionality' prized by male colleagues in securing the aesthetic unity of the genre, rather 'betoken a faith in the continuity of ... their own self-images'.[8] Because of the different nature of their subjectivity and 'the multi-dimensionality of women's socially conditioned roles', according to Jelinek, their life-writing is often 'disconnected, fragmentary, or organised into self-contained units'.[9] However, later critics have expressed concern that such arguments might reinforce patriarchal stereotypes about the 'nature' of femininity. Consequently, they have instead attributed to women's life-writing a programmatic desire to subvert not so much its 'internal' rules of organisation but the 'external' borders which separate it from other genres. Thus, Liz Stanley asserts that a crucial characteristic of women's life-writing is its desire to 'experiment at the boundaries between different writing forms'.[10]

For other critics in turn, this subversiveness extends beyond an exaggeration of the inter-generic 'contaminations' which in fact characterise all genres,[11] to a questioning of the very identity of autobiography as a separate and distinct mode of writing. In these debates, the law of genre is often represented as an instance of 'the law of the father', insofar as the canons which anchor such generic rules were traditionally dominated by male authors, chosen by critics who were also, historically, overwhelmingly male. Consequently, Sidonie Smith, for example, argues that the 'progressive' woman auto/biographer 'refuses to obey the prohibitions of the father's culture'.[12] Gilmore spells out the potential implications of such disobedience in asserting that if 'autobiography itself seems closed to women's self-representation, then women may choose forms other than straightforward, contractually verifiable autobiography for self-representation'.[13] Such claims are supported by the analysis in Chapter 2 of the 'relational Self' promoted in women's life-writing. As has been seen, this perforce erodes the traditional distinction between autobiography and biography which, as noted earlier, Olney argues that every critic in the field should be keen to maintain. As will shortly be seen, similar strategic assaults on the traditional identity of the genre have also been effected by western women writers who erode the boundaries between autobiography on the one hand and, on the other, fiction and History.[14] Comparable arguments have been extended to minoritarian women's life-writing. Torres, for example, claims that it 'tend[s] to mix genres in a manner we have not seen in mainstream autobiographies'.[15] In turn, Lionnet asserts of postcolonial women's life-writing that it is characterised by 'the *métissage*, or braiding, of cultural forms', a strategy which 'help[s] change the form of the genre as well as relations of power in society'.[16]

With a view to complicating the gendered nature of the positions elaborated by such critics, however, in the first two sections of this chapter, I will analyse some ways in which male postcolonial life-writing, too, challenges traditional conceptions of autobiography's generic identity by engagement with the genres of fiction and History. I will then explore postcolonial life-writing's negotiations with a further genre, travel-writing, which has thus far played little part in such discussions about its women's analogues – with a view to differentiating between the two fields of writing in this respect. Once more, Fanon's *Black Skin* provides a template for later postcolonial writers (of both genders) in its renegotiation of generic rules and form. At once 'a clinical study', a tract of political philosophy and 'the sum of the [existential] experiences ... of seven years' of the author's life, its discourse ranges between the modes of scientific analysis, confession and poetry, and between the oral and the literary – all within a structure which is sometimes highly fragmentary and imagistic.[17] This extraordinarily hybrid form, reinforced by its multiplicity of styles, is perhaps the principal reason why *Black Skin* has rarely been studied under the rubric of autobiography, even within Postcolonial Studies. Nonetheless, it clearly anticipates the sometimes radically experimental stylistic properties of 'autobiographics'/'autogynography'/'autography'.

Fiction

The relationship between fiction and autobiography has long been a matter of debate. Thus, while Richard Steele complained in *The Tatler* in 1709 that 'the word *Memoir* is French for a novel', Anatole France defended his use of an alias in his 'autobiographies' on the grounds that it gave him 'a much wider freedom to talk about myself ... The fictitious name [Pierre] did not disguise me.'[18] Within Auto/biography Studies, the boundary between fact and fiction has also been investigated persistently. For example, as far back as Misch, memory has been viewed as a mode of creation, even invention, rather than as something which offers unproblematic access to past 'realities'.[19] The more it is claimed as a *literary* mode of representation in the second phase of the history of the field, moreover, the more foregrounded has been autobiography's reliance on such 'fictive' devices as the 'emplotment' of the protagonist's trajectory in relation to particular moments of crisis (which function as 'dramatic climaxes'), its use of figurative language and self-conscious manipulation of 'narrative voice'. Thus, as Pascal suggests, there is inevitably some measure of conflict between 'design' and 'truth' in canonical autobiography which is generally the work of writers/critics who are highly self-conscious about matters of form.[20] More radical claims have been made in the third phase of Auto/biography Studies, even by liberal-humanist critics. For example, in asserting the right of autobiographers 'to present themselves in whatever form they may find appropriate', Spengemann proposes that texts such as Dickens's *David Copperfield* and even Hawthorne's *Scarlet Letter* should be reclassified as autobiographical.[21]

While many might find Spengemann's argument strained,[22] he is nonetheless correct in attributing an enhanced accommodation of issues surrounding 'fictiveness' within contemporary Auto/biography Studies partly to 'changing ideas about the nature of the self'.[23] In the wake of post-structuralism, moreover, the claim that Selfhood – and reality itself – are always constructed, if only insofar as they are mediated in language, has further eroded older truth claims made on behalf of the genre. Thus, de Man famously concluded in 1979 that: 'The distinction between fiction and autobiography is not an either or polarity but one that it is undecidable.'[24] Such leads have proved productive for some feminist colleagues. For example, Mary Evans asserts that since, from a postmodernist perspective, 'the "whole" person' can only be understood as a 'mythical construct of our society and our social needs', the autobiographical Self which replicates it is necessarily an aesthetic and performative rendition of an ideological fiction.[25]

Nonetheless, the generic identity of autobiography continues to be advocated in large measure on the basis of its empirical rather than aesthetic or psychological truth claims. If Gusdorf argues influentially that 'the truth of facts is subordinate to the truth of the man',[26] simply 'making it up' is widely deemed to disqualify the writer accused of doing so from writing autobiography 'proper' on generic as well as moral grounds. While one should discriminate both wilful lies and subjective conceptions of truth from fiction as such,[27] the latter remains clearly excluded, in the eyes of many critics, by virtue of the terms of Lejeune's 'pact', which insists that the narrative is by and about 'a real person'.[28] Furthermore, the considerable continuing investment in retaining fact/fiction distinctions in relation to the genre can be deduced from sometimes heated controversies over the truth status of particular texts. For example, as Anderson points out, reaction to suggestions that the self-styled Holocaust survivor Binjamin Wilkomirski had invented the narrative recounted in *Fragments* (1995) demonstrated a fear not just that the events described had been thereby diminished, but that autobiography had also been brought into disrepute as a genre.[29] Postcolonial life-writing has not been immune from such controversies, as furores over the veracity of texts ranging from Equiano's *Interesting Narrative* and *The History of Mary Prince* to Nobel Prize-winner Rigoberta Menchú's *I, Rigoberta Menchú* (1983), Said's *Out of Place* (see Chapter 7) and Ishmael Beah's *A Long Way Gone* illustrate.[30]

In the rest of this section, I will explore issues surrounding the fact/fiction border-line in relation to V.S. Naipaul, with particular reference to *Finding the Centre* (1984) and *A Way in the World* (1994). This choice is governed primarily by the fact that these works exemplify the pressure which the deployment of fictional resources places on traditional conceptions of auto/biographical boundaries to a greater degree, perhaps, than any other text considered in this volume. In analysing them, I further aim to complicate arguments about the distinctiveness of women's life-writing in its troubling of this boundary.

One factor underlying the permeability of the fact/fiction distinction in Caribbean life-writing[31] is no doubt the fact that, as Sandra Paquet suggests, the dominant tradition of the genre, in the Anglophone parts of the region at least, has been furnished by creative writers – from Claude McKay and C.L.R. James through Edgar Mittelholzer, Michael Anthony and George Lamming to Naipaul himself and Jamaica Kincaid.[32] However, the explanation seems more complicated than this, since the same holds true in other parts of the postcolonial world. One might frame an alternative line of inquiry with John Thieme's observation that Caribbean autobiographies are relatively thin on the ground (he was writing in 1984) and that where they do exist, they tend to focus primarily on the early part of the protagonist's life. He relates both patterns to the difficulty of producing fully-achieved self-portraits in a culture characterised on the one hand by chronic cultural fragmentation[33] and, on the other, by the imperative in adult life to identify with a collective destiny.[34] While one might question aspects of Thieme's argument, his invocation of social factors seems a useful initial context within which to approach the traffic between fact and fiction in Naipaul's autobiographical writings.

The closest that Naipaul has (thus far) come to writing an autobiography as traditionally understood is, perhaps, his 'Prologue to an Autobiography'. In the Foreword to *Finding the Centre*, in which this was republished simply as the first of 'two narratives' (the sub-title of the text as a whole), however, Naipaul insists that it is 'not an autobiography, a story of a life or deeds done' (*FC*: 9). Instead he prefers the description 'personal narrative' (*FC*: 9). In part, this discrimination is justified on the grounds that the piece is limited to reconsideration of his beginnings as a writer. Nonetheless, it broadens out from this to become, among other things, a tribute to his journalist father who not only encouraged his son's aspirations but himself had ambitions as a writer. (To this extent, it conforms to the pattern elaborated in Chapter 2, being as much a biography as an 'autobiography'.) Inasmuch as his father is so central, it might even be understood as the 'prologue' to the autobiography that Seepersad Naipaul never wrote, despite the younger Naipaul's encouragement. (In this respect, one might also compare 'A Prologue' to Jamaica Kincaid's later, equally fictionalised and apparently oxymoronic, *Autobiography of My Mother*.)

The reasons behind Seepersad's inability to narrate himself as a Subject are disquieting and affecting in equal measure and shed light on Naipaul's own 'refusal' of autobiography as conventionally understood and, more specifically, its traditional investment in fact/fiction distinctions. This failure is structurally linked in the text to the moment when Naipaul's father suffers a nervous breakdown. According to his mother, from whom the younger Naipaul gets the story, Seepersad 'looked in the mirror one day and couldn't see himself. And he began to scream'[35] (*FC*: 70). On one level, the breakdown is attributed to personal circumstances, notably the older Naipaul's career problems and increasingly unsuccessful efforts to either individuate himself within, or free himself from, his oppressive extended family. However, behind this personal dimension to his father's existential void, Naipaul implies the influence of a much wider predicament of cultural 'vacancy' (*FC*: 64) which afflicts every Caribbean subject, including any would-be autobiographer (*FC*: 9, 28). In essence, this is a function of the artificial and fragmented nature of the *New* World of which Trinidad forms part (and which C.L.R. James addressed in a quite different way, as seen in Chapter 2).

A Way in the World insists that the overwhelmingly constructed nature of the Caribbean as a consequence of colonialism extends even to its 'natural' environment (compare Soyinka's treatment of landscape in *Akê*). Thus, on a trip to the uninhabited north-easternmost tip of the island, the unnamed first-person narrator (henceforth 'V.S. Naipaul' to preserve the element of undecidability in that narrator's identity, which also has crucial implications for the text's generic identity) remarks on some rare remnants of indigenous vegetation. These contrast with the imported 'coconut, mango, breadfruit, bamboo' covering the rest of the territory.[36] The artificial character of the human environment of the Caribbean is equally striking, and is represented as a consequence of the loss of its 'original' inhabitants, a cultural/historical rupture provoked by the extirpation of Trinidad's aboriginal cultures. Moreover, even the later Spanish period in Trinidad's history is largely 'burnt away' (a recurrent phrase) or exists overseas, notably in the archives of Venezuela and Seville (with limited, and by implication, inferior *copies* in Trinidad). Such 'absences' are in equal measure responsible for the lack of 'reality' (*WW*: 209–11) which confounds the quest to ground Caribbean identity.

The wave of ill-synthesised migrations from Africa, India, the South Seas and China (symbolised in the tree species Naipaul identifies), as well as Europe, out of which the modern island society has emerged, fails to fill this void. With no foundational culture of his/her own, the 'floating' Trinidadian Subject is, moreover, hard-pressed to anchor a sense of Selfhood in relation to any of his/her available cultures of origin. While brought up as a Hindu, 'V.S. Naipaul' remarks recurrently on the debased understanding of traditional religion which characterises his community.[37] A similar dislocation characterises the Black population, large sections of which, in the narrator's eyes, invest in an essentially mythical Africa to ground their identity (compare *FC*: 51–3). The Trinidadian Subject is therefore suspended between dying or invented traditions, on the one hand, and, on the other, a colonial modernity which alike have their origins elsewhere, thereby requiring 'foreign witness' (*WW*: 77) to validate 'Caribbeanness'. This conflicting matrix of identifications makes 'finding the (psychic) centre' both an urgent and impossible existential task which can all too easily lead to the kind of crisis experienced by Seepersad. The blankness he sees reflected in the mirror symbolises a wider 'lack' in Trinidadian self-image which pre-empts traditional conceptions of 'sovereign' autobiographical personhood. This parlous existential predicament also helps explain the younger Naipaul's experimental mode of writing the Self in *A Way in the World*, insofar as he seeks not so much to capture 'presence' but its lack. More particularly, it underwrites his predilection for negotiating his own sense of fracture (*WW*: 73), even 'nonentity' (*FC*: 34) by means of a fragmented, and mutually destabilising, mixture of fiction and non-fiction.

Such inter-generic negotiation is anticipated by *In a Free State* (1971) where (seemingly) non-fictional autobiographical fragments provide the prologue and epilogue to three fictional pieces, with which they share an interest in the themes of travel, displacement and cultural re/dislocation which characterise so much of the writer's later *œuvre*. In this instance, Naipaul's distribution of non-fiction and fiction appears to retain some confidence in the separability of the two. But on closer inspection, even here the division is less clear-cut than one might suppose. This is largely because one cannot be sure that prologue and epilogue are, indeed, non-fictional. Anticipating his subsequent auto/biographical writing, Naipaul scrupulously evades the terms of Lejeune's 'pact' by refusing to let their narrating 'I' (or 'I's, since there can be no assurance even that the first-person narrator in these parts of the book is one and the same) be named – either by 'himself' or an interlocutor.[38]

However, such generic undecidability is markedly enhanced in *A Way*, beginning with the very identification of the work. Published in Britain with the sub-title 'a Sequence', a descriptor with no specific generic indicators, it was simultaneously published in the United States with the sub-title 'A Novel' (it is hard to believe that this would have been done without Naipaul's authorisation). Even the British paperback, however, also describes it as 'fiction' (on the back-cover of the Minerva edition). The problem of generic identity is also more acute than in *In a Free State* partly because the apparently autobiographical sections are now distributed piecemeal among the seemingly non-autobiographical ones. The table of contents reinforces this epistemological uncertainty, with one 'autobiographical' section described as 'History' and three others, despite being more ostensibly 'historical', each sub-titled '*an unwritten story*'. Moreover, in *A Way*, the two categories each play on the distinction between them which is in theory preserved in the earlier text. For example, the traffic between fiction and non-fiction continues *within* the opening 'autobiographical' narrative, 'An Inheritance', which is described as a '*Prelude*'. This invites comparison with Wordsworth's poem not just as a meditation on the 'growth of an artist's mind', but as a highly artificial *literary construct*. Consequently, as Stephanie Jones comments, 'The book's fusion – or corruption – of these given genres [confuses] hard definitions of fact and fiction.'[39]

The concept of 'fact' comes under severe pressure for other reasons. If one compares the fourth apparently autobiographical section of *A Way*, 'On the Run', with the travel piece 'The Crocodiles of Yamossoukrou', the second 'personal narrative' in *Finding the Centre*, one finds certain 'facts' in the earlier piece heavily (cavalierly?) amended. The 'Phyllis' of 'On the Run' is clearly based on the 'Andrée' of the former work, now amalgamated with aspects of her friend 'Arlette'. 'Phyllis' is now given a husband, the refugee Keita, a 'character' who is quite unrelated to either woman in the earlier narrative. Moreover, in the final 'autobiographical' section of *A Way*, 'Home Again', much of the fate of 'Blair' is clearly simply invented. 'V.S. Naipaul' refers to 'the version of his death I carried in my imagination' and conceives of it in terms of 'some Edgar Allan Poe story' (*WW*: 367), ending with 'a fanciful picture of the ceremonial return of Blair's body to Trinidad' (*WW*: 369). Such moments perhaps substantiate 'V.S. Naipaul's' conviction that memory is essentially a creative act (*WW*: 30), but they also encourage the idea that fact and fiction segue into each other in this text not so much in a 'sequence', but in an epistemologically dizzying, tail-chasing 'whirligig' of 'revolving doors' of the kind de Man describes.[40]

In *A Way*, 'fact' is further compromised in a quite different way. While 'V.S. Naipaul' draws heavily in the text on archival investigation, much of it apparently executed in person, the three sections of the 'sequence' which address the history of the New World are presented as treatments for plays or films. The point seems to be not simply that much of Trinidad's past can now only be imagined, or that archives are comprised simply of verbal and therefore partly fictive artefacts, or that history has to be narrativised and to that extent also begins to merge into the domain of the fictive. It is a reminder that the 'real' history of the New World has been shaped by fable (*WW*: 210) to an extraordinary extent, from Walter Raleigh's feverish imaginings of El Dorado to Francisco Miranda's Enlightenment dream of a just new society – quasi-Orientalist fantasies which have their analogue in contemporary revolutionary projects of the kind described in 'New Clothes'.

A Way thus proposes that Caribbean subjectivity is chronically suspended between the 'real' and the fictive, domains which cannot, in any case, be easily isolated from each other or distinguished in themselves. As a consequence, the traditional homology proposed (for much of the history of Auto/biography Studies) between unity of genre and unity of autobiographical Self breaks down.[41] Equally, Naipaul's work calls into question Lejeune's fundamental premise that autobiography is defined by being by and about the same 'real' person. Despite my invocation of de Man, these deviations from the rules of genre do not derive, however, simply from abstract philosophical conundrums which might find in Naipaul evidence of typically postmodern and Eurocentric epistemological doubts. Rather, they respond to the concrete historical-cultural predicament of parts of the New World as Naipaul sees it. Indeed, to the extent that the traffic between fact and fiction in his autobiographical writings *anticipates* such experiments in Caribbean women life-writers like Michelle Cliff and Jamaica Kincaid, gender may not be, as claimed by Lionnet and Gilmore, the prime factor in respect of this aspect of their 'autobiographics'.[42] Instead, explanations are perhaps more convincingly sought by contextualising all three writers' work within material and psychic problematics entailed by their Caribbean culture of origin.

However, while the troubling of borderlines between fiction and autobiography may be particularly evident in Caribbean life-writing, it can also be found in other parts of the postcolonial world, though not always for directly comparable reasons (space constraints prevent me from pursuing this argument on the present occasion). Notable examples range from the series of autobiographical texts produced by Mulk Raj Anand, beginning with *Seven Summers* (1968), through Nawal El Saadawi's *Memoirs of a Woman Doctor* (1957) and Hanif Kureishi's *Intimacy* (1998).[43] As the example of El Saadawi suggests, all this is not to deny that gender plays some role in such interrogations of the genre as traditionally understood. In the next chapter there is another striking example of the diverse motivations behind such experimentations in Assia Djebar's *Fantasia* (1985, subtitled in French editions 'a novel'), which demonstrates how gender can also play its part in such generic self-attributions. Equally, as will also be seen in the next chapter, Sara Suleri's description of *Meatless Days* as 'these quirky little tales'[44] suggests a comparably gendered desire to trouble the distinctions which Lejeune and others draw between autobiography and fiction.

History

If Naipaul 'works' the traditional boundary between autobiography and fiction, he also, as has been seen, troubles the borderline between the former genre and historiography. There has been intense debate about the latter relationship in Auto/biography Studies, which offers a divided view of this conjunction. From its beginnings, some have seen it as a close and productive one. Thus, for Misch, as 'personal history', autobiography exists at one end of a spectrum which encompasses more public forms of History and to some extent provides their foundations; he therefore approvingly quotes Herder's dictum that 'a Library of Writers on Themselves' would form an excellent 'contribution to the history of mankind'.[45] In the second phase of the field, Gusdorf described the autobiographer as the 'historian of himself', who locates his account of 'private motives' in relation to 'the objective course of events'.[46] At the cusp of its third period, Weintraub once more insisted that autobiography is, in these respects, at least, 'an historical genre'.[47]

Conversely, however, Marcus suggests that since its inception Auto/biography Studies has also expended considerable effort on 'the project of "rescuing" autobiography from incorporation into history and history-writing'.[48] Throughout its existence, critics have insisted that History focuses on collective experience, often in time-frames which exceed individual life-spans, while autobiography is regarded as the record of more private domains of self-reflexive analysis and feeling. Thus, Misch in fact relegates sub-genres like memoir to second-class status within the hierarchy of autobiographical modes because their authors are 'merely observers of the events and activities of which they write'.[49] Similarly, Gusdorf deprecates the fact that memoir 'is limited almost entirely to the public sector of existence' and Weintraub distinguishes sharply between the *res gestae* of the Emperor Augustus and the 'ideal type' of Augustine's *Confessions* which focuses primarily on 'character, personality, self-conception'.[50] Equally, Olney describes as 'naïve' the idea that an autobiography can approach the condition of an 'objective historical account'.[51]

Historical Studies has been equally divided about the connection between the two discourses. According to Misch, historians have long used autobiography in their researches, a tendency which became entrenched in the nineteenth century when the genre 'acquired a fixed place among the sources of ... social history'.[52] Modern historians have been rather more sceptical. Indeed, Gandhi speaks for many such figures, ironically, when he complains of the 'inadequacy of all autobiography as history'.[53] Such attitudes are apparent even among some of those seeking to promote new kinds of History 'from below' (this movement seeks to make traditionally marginalised groups – what Swindells calls the 'silenced voices of the past'[54] – more prominent as historical agents). Thus, Jerry White complains that 'the autobiographical mode reinforces a superficial historical consciousness and by doing so actually distorts reality.' Since autobiography is full of 'immanent biases and distortions', it lacks sufficient 'critical understanding' to explain the larger historical forces which shape individual lives.[55]

Feminist Historical Studies has taken a rather different view. In aiming to expose the traditionally gendered nature of History,[56] many women historians, according to Sue Morgan, embrace the task not just of 'democratising the vision of who [but] *what* constitutes historical discourse'.[57] Three aspects of this initiative are especially germane to present discussion. First is the strategic erosion of established distinctions between the public/political and private/personal spheres, such that the former becomes 'deprivileged as the main arena of authentic historical activity'.[58] Second is the critique of the supposed 'objectivity' of History such that it is seen instead as 'a self-aware reconstruction of the past circumscribed by the subject position, theoretical intent and historical/political context of the writer'.[59] Finally, feminist History questions the traditional primacy of archival material because it disproportionately reflects the power and interests (and legacies) of the dominant gender. Instead it stresses the importance of sources such as 'oral testimonies', as a means of correcting all three biases in traditional (male) historiography.[60]

Feminist Auto/biography critics have widely seconded the objectives and methods of their historian colleagues, proposing that women's life-writing should be considered not just as legitimate historical evidence but also as a form of (counter-) History.[61] Such arguments have been extended to western minoritarian women's life-writing, whose subjects have also traditionally been marginalised within mainstream History if not excluded from it altogether.[62] Thus, Anne Goldman proposes that ethnic American women's life-writing reconceptualises traditional relations between History and 'personal life history' such that the former becomes 'the twin to life history, not the master narrative engineered to supplant it'.[63] The same has been argued for some strands of postcolonial women's life-writing, notably the sub-genre of *testimonio*.[64] For example, Longley argues that Australian Aboriginal women's writing provides 'a primary historical record' which urges 'a revision of *all* Australian history to incorporate crucial Aboriginal histories'[65] (an argument confirmed in relation to Morgan in Chapter 1).

The convergence of History and postcolonial life-writing will be investigated in the rest of this section with particular reference to Nirad Chaudhuri's *The Autobiography of an Unknown Indian* (1951). The choice is governed primarily by the fact that it exemplifies the pressure which History puts on traditional conceptions of autobiographical boundaries to the same degree, perhaps, as is the turn to fiction of writers like Naipaul. To this extent, it also offers particularly appropriate evidence to reconsider some of the claims made by certain feminist critics about the generically subversive role of History within women's life-writing.

An initial impression of Chaudhuri's *Autobiography* might suggest that the generic affiliation claimed in the title is perversely inappropriate. The ostensibly autobiographical portion of the book does not begin until a quarter of the way into the work. It is seemingly unconscionably delayed by detailed preliminary investigation of the social environment in which Chaudhuri's first twelve years are to pass. This first quarter of the text is therefore aptly described as 'more an exercise in descriptive ethnology than autobiography' (*AUI*: 129). Equally, the text does not end with any summary of the self-understanding arrived at by the close of the relatively short period of life (twenty-five years) on which it concentrates (compare James's 'Epilogue and Apotheosis'). Rather it closes with a lengthy chapter entitled 'An Essay on the Course of Indian History', in which the narrator is reduced to no more than a speck against the 'large historical perspectives'

(*AUI*: 513) elaborated there. Further, even within the more personal narrative sandwiched between these respective exercises in ethnography and historical reflection, there is a clear departure from the terms of Lejeune's 'autobiographical pact' insofar as the first-person narrative voice takes the plural form 'we' as often as the singular 'I' – whether in relation to Chaudhuri's family, Bengalis or Indians more generally. Despite this first-person voice, moreover, the text often appears to aspire to the 'objectivity' more commonly associated with traditional History than autobiography. Thus, while Chaudhuri apparently reproduces verbatim his youthful essay on 'The Objective Method in History' only as a yardstick by which to measure his later deviation as an historian from its prescriptions, *The Autobiography* ends with an affirmation that the conclusions drawn 'stand clear of subjective and passing clouds' (*AUI*: 513). Consonant with the relative marginalisation of autobiographical matter, in turn, there is little insight into the development of Chaudhuri's affective life (compare James). Close relations often remain unindividualised by name and it is not until three-quarters of the way into the text that we are introduced to a personal friend of any importance, apparently confirming feminist claims about the monadic nature of male autobiographical subjectivity.

Yet Chaudhuri partly redeems his text as autobiography – a term he uses insistently to describe it (*AUI*: 22, 129, 198, for example) – precisely through extensive attention to those aspects of his formation which explain how he became 'endowed with the consciousness of history' (*AUI*: 268).[66] This is represented as the most important aspect of his development as a self-reflective being, attention to which is traditionally conceived as one of the key demands of the genre. *The Autobiography* therefore provides a detailed conspectus of Chaudhuri's historical studies.[67] Two works encountered at university are especially important in understanding how his own text might also be read as History. The first is J.R. Green's *Short History of the English People* (1874), which has more recently been claimed as one inspiration for contemporary western 'history from below'.[68] Indeed, Chaudhuri's text anticipates many features of such historiography, not only in his focus on the 'lives of the obscure' (most obviously he represents himself as 'an unknown Indian') but also in both his stress on his specific geo-cultural (and class) 'situatedness' (see also Chapter 4) as an historian and his conception of appropriate source material. Eschewing the (colonial) archive which Naipaul favours, he draws instead on the indigenous resources of individuals' memory (his own, pre-eminently, which is constantly cross-checked against that of relatives), family, clan and village *oral* history (*AUI*: 15, 85, 132), material culture (consider his descriptions of the evolution of family houses) and folk culture. To this extent, Chaudhuri's intention is clearly in part to write a 'History of the *Bengali/Indian* People', using a – for the time – highly unusual methodology partly elaborated in response to *local* conditions, both sociological and historiographical.

The second key figure is Edward Gibbon, first cited as early as the Preface to *The Autobiography*, whose magisterial *Decline and Fall of the Roman Empire* (1776–88) is in many respects the polar opposite of Green's work in its conception of History. Insofar as Chaudhuri's text is 'history from below', it provides an implicit critique of the latter's lack of interest in social history, let alone 'the common man'. Instead, Gibbon's preoccupation is with 'great men' (overwhelmingly western) represented through a 'drum and trumpet' focus on war and politics. Nonetheless, Gibbon's historiography clearly significantly influences his successor's, most obviously in terms of the latter's 'thematics of decline'. Thus, Chaudhuri pays close attention to the decay of his class, the East Bengal squirearchy which is progressively and unwillingly urbanised as the nineteenth century progresses. These themes are subordinated to discussion of much grander kinds of failure, however, including the decline not just of Britain as a great imperial power comparable to Rome but of the West as a whole, which is depicted in Spenglerian terms (*AUI*: 405). The idea of decline receives its most extensive elaboration, however, in relation to modern Indian civilisation which, according to Chaudhuri, reached its high point in the 'Indian Renaissance' of the last half of the nineteenth century. Bengali humanism, *An Autobiography* argues, achieved its gains 'mainly based on the formula of a synthesis of the values of the East and the West' (*AUI*: 182; compare 231). By the time of Indian independence, however, this great cultural revolution has, in Chaudhuri's eyes, dissipated into the 'decadence' (*AUI*: 364) of a chauvinist variety of nationalism (compare Behan) which is not dissimilar from the Nazism so recently defeated in the Second World War. The bitterest fruit of this particularism is what might be called 'partitionism', which is expressed not simply in the erection of new political borders which sunder Chaudhuri's beloved birthplace from independent India, but an increasingly communalist mentality within the new rump nation (compare Lim's account of independent Malaysia).

Nonetheless, Chaudhuri's thematics of decline exceed Gibbon's remit by virtue of the self-consciously *situated* character of Chaudhuri's account. Thus, a considerable portion of the *Autobiography* is devoted to a personal narrative of Chaudhuri's own gradual disaffection with modern Indian nationalism, set within a memoir of key events and public figures in twentieth-century Indian history to which the writer was sometimes directly linked (for example, for a while he was secretary to the brother of S.C. Bhose, who led the Japanese-armed Indian National Army against the British). Further, there are clearly private dimensions to Chaudhuri's 'thematics of decline'. These include the collapse of his mother's mental health and Chaudhuri's own failure to become a professional historian. 'Plucked' from the MA, he spends much of his adult life in a variety of dispiriting occupations, from private secretary to jobbing journalist.

In offering a personal as well as traditionally Historical account of the 'thematics of decline', Chaudhuri is evidently influenced by a different text of Gibbon's. Among the many 'autobiographical masterpieces' (*AUI*: 129) cited in *The Autobiography*, Gibbon's is described as 'a great favourite' (*AUI*: 359). Unfinished in six drafts on the historian's death, Gibbon's *Autobiography*, edited and published in 1796, became one of the most widely admired examples of the genre in the nineteenth century. Gibbon's account of his intellectual development is similarly overshadowed by premonitions of apocalyptic civilisational decline. The specific reason, in Gibbon's case, was the French Revolution, watched with increasing alarm from Lausanne while Gibbon was working on his autobiography and which engendered a comparable revolution in his political sympathies to Chaudhuri's. From Chaudhuri's later perspective, the overthrow of the *ancien régime* has obvious parallels with the end of the British Empire; and Gibbon's personal testimony of revolutionary fanaticism provides a model for the narrativisation of Chaudhuri's own experience of the chauvinism of twentieth-century Hindu revivalism.

Thus, while Indian history is the principal theme of *The Autobiography*, the author nonetheless gives himself considerable discursive space. From this angle, Chaudhuri's 'testimony' can legitimately be seen 'as a contribution to contemporary history' (*AUI*: vii). In explaining that the relationship is indeed conjunctive rather than disjunctive, the author offers perhaps the most breath-taking claim about the autobiographer's representativity in all of postcolonial life-writing. Unashamedly echoing Louis XIV's claim that '*l'état, c'est moi*', Chaudhuri asserts that, for all his untypicality, '*l'Inde, c'est moi*' (*AUI*: 470). The conjunction he claims further allows him to boldly reverse the perspectival positioning of History and autobiography as traditionally conceived. The autobiographical elements are often presented in conformity to the objectivity advocated by historiographers like Ranke, or from what Chaudhuri calls a position of 'estrangement' (*AUI*: 261). Conversely, not only is history personalised in *An Autobiography*, but the *style* of History is foregrounded, in conformity with Gibbon's insistence that 'style is the image of character'.[69] In praising Green's discourse, Chaudhuri stresses its 'Keats-like delicacy' (*AUI*: 334). If a self-conscious artistic 'delicacy' (the range and variety of his diction being particularly remarkable) is one hallmark of Chaudhuri's own style, so is the inter-subjective, empathetic, Keatsian 'negative capability' which characterises so many of his engagements with the historical personages encountered in his narrative.

To this extent, Chaudhuri's text mounts a critique of generic 'partitionism' which resonates with his broader hostility to a variety of divisive particularisms within contemporary India. It thereby constitutes a direct challenge to the form as well as the perspectives of contemporary nationalist historiography, or what Chaudhuri terms – with a contemptuous irony worthy of Gibbon – 'the Clio of the Bazaars' (*AUI*: 357). Above all, Chaudhuri accuses such work of the cardinal sin of forgetfulness, specifically in relation to the contributions made by both Muslims and the British to Indian culture. In one of his most heartfelt declamations, the author asserts that at a time 'when most of my fellow-students and teachers appeared to think that history existed only for the sake of exalting Indian nationalism' (*AUI*: 342), 'historical' as well as moral rectitude required him to honour the contribution of non-Hindu communities to his country.

The Autobiography thus offers not just an accommodation between the seemingly antithetical historiographical methods of Green and Gibbon but a broader negotiation between the discourses of History and autobiography. Nonetheless, Chaudhuri's generic experimentations might be understood to be framed through recourse to western templates, supporting Ruvani Ranasinha's judgement that he exemplifies 'the process of affiliation [to the West] in an extreme form'.[70] To this extent, he might thereby also be understood as conforming to Gusdorf's argument about the non-western life-writer's inability to escape the terms of colonial modernity. However, according to Chaudhuri, synthesis is a constitutive element not just of Bengal Renaissance humanism which, as its name implies, modelled itself on western precedents, but of traditional Hinduism itself (compare Soyinka's childhood *Aké*). It is this which distinguishes it from the narrow, exclusionary forms of contemporary Hindu revivalism which, ironically, make the latter little more than a simple *imitation* of the grosser forms of European nationalism. For example, Chaudhuri claims that 'Hinduism, as we have known it during historical times, has always been an admixture of foreign … and indigenous' (*AUI*: 204). Elsewhere he insists: '"Synthesis" was our magic word. This tendency was reinforced in us … by our belief that the Hindu outlook on life was "synthetic"' (*AUI*: 336). To this extent, Chaudhuri's experimental traffic between traditionally distinct genres is at least as much an affirmation of (post)colonial difference as 'a derivative discourse',[71] or what Naipaul called an unparalleled example of 'the penetration of the Indian mind by the West'.[72] In this respect, it is also significant that, paradoxical as it may seem, *The Autobiography* supports the argument of Chapter 2 that postcolonial subjectivity is characteristically constructed *between* individual and collective historical experience. If Naipaul undoes the homology traditionally proposed between unity of genre and unity of autobiographical Selfhood, Chaudhuri undoes the equivalent homology between unity of genre and the singularity of that Selfhood, not just through his use of the first person plural, but in his (C.L.R.) Jamesian attention to the social grounds from which individuals and their personalities emerge.

This troubling of borderlines between History and autobiography is widely observable across the range of texts studied in this monograph. Some even describe themselves (partly) as Histories, notable examples being James's *Beyond a Boundary* and Mary Seacole's *Wonderful Adventures* (see next section).[73] Moreover, even when such authors disclaim expertise as historians, they often demonstrate a clear understanding of what is at stake in historiography, as is the case with Claude McKay.[74] Their engagements are not, however, necessarily consonant with traditional forms of History but rather reflect a range of emphases and techniques more commonly associated with what Samuel calls 'people's history' or 'history from below'. Thus, while several figures work to challenge the dominant historiography of (neo-)colonialism (Gandhi, James, Soyinka, Morgan, Djebar, Allende, Behan), others provide a critique of nationalist élite historiography (McKay, Behan again, El Saadawi, Suleri, Djebar).

Insofar as these two branches of historiography are largely the preserve of male writers, moreover, the women life-writers concerned provide specifically gendered counter-narratives which seek to write subaltern women, in particular, back into hegemonic versions of History. Nonetheless, to the extent that the inter-generic traffic I have described in Chaudhuri's autobiographical writings offers parallels to those of western and postcolonial women life-writers alike, gender is clearly not the only explanation for the experimental hybridisation of auto/biography and History in this context. Instead, it is equally likely to be found by contextualising all such writers' work within both the traditionally anti-individualist ethos of their

cultures of origin and their efforts to rewrite the received terms of histc
to open it up to a range of traditionally marginalised Subjects which includes,
is not confined to, women.

Travel-writing

The preceding two sections of this chapter offered two examples of ways in which
the borders of autobiography are 'worked' in postcolonial life-writing in a manner
comparable to western women's life-writing. To try and distinguish between the
sub-fields in relation to this strategy, therefore, I will now explore a third inter-
generic conjunction, the axis between autobiography and travel-writing. As suggested earlier, this relationship has not been the subject of detailed investigation
among feminists who have sought to reconstitute Auto/biography Studies from a
gendered perspective,[75] perhaps because the mainstream critical tradition has
historically declared travel-writing outside its purview.[76] However, the two genres
have clear affinities. Like autobiography, according to Patrick Holland and
Graham Huggan, travel-writing is often animated by the desire to achieve self-
understanding.[77] Both genres also traditionally involve personal quests, whether
literal or metaphorical (the trope of life as a journey of exploration is a staple of
autobiography), usually narrated in the first person.

Nonetheless, there are important differences, too. Insofar as travel-writing
expresses the quest for self-understanding, this is characteristically pursued in
terms of an investigation of Self in *alien* surroundings. Moreover, too much self-
reflection entails the danger of 'immobilising' the traveller's journey and narrative
momentum, as well as potentially diminishing proper attention to those alien
surroundings. As these competing priorities might suggest, travel-writing exists
along a continuum between an outer- and inner-directed narrative 'I'/eye. Holland and Huggan illustrate this difference of emphasis through comparison of two
leading contemporary exponents of the genre, Bruce Chatwin and Redmond
O'Hanlon. They argue that: 'In Chatwin's narratives the traveller is primarily an
observer, hiding behind the eccentricities of the characters he observes; in
O'Hanlon's, the traveller himself is the greatest eccentric.'[78] To the extent that
the narrator is self-effacing, on Chatwinian lines, travel-writing might, indeed, be
seen as having 'an *anti*autobiographical aspect'.[79]

It is perhaps unsurprising, therefore, that mainstream Auto/biography Studies
has been neglectful of the genre, particularly in view of the fact that travel as a
dynamic in the formation of personhood plays little part in itself within canonical
autobiography (with the limited exception of Rousseau's *Confessions*). By contrast,
postcolonial life-writing engages to a very significant degree with both travel and
its effect on the constitution of subjectivity, not least because of the substantial
psychic and affective implications of (dis)location (see Chapter 4). Many of the
texts considered in my text conform to this pattern, involving most conceivable
motives for – and modes of – travel. Some of the life-writers already mentioned
spend long periods travelling (Equiano, for example, passes more than ten years
at sea,[80] McKay many months wandering in Europe, Naipaul equivalent periods

gathering material). Others journey abroad to live there temporarily (Gandhi passes several years in South Africa, as Nehru and Behan do in Britain and El Saadawi in the United States) or permanently (Said, Emecheta), whether voluntarily or not. Others undertake crucial journeys of 'return' either within their homeland (Morgan, Magona, Amiry) or back to it from abroad (Lim, Said).[81] As also indicated in Chapter 4, others, by contrast, bewail the inability to travel in certain circumstances (Said, Amiry, El Saadawi), seeing this as a constriction on their personal development or even a threat to their identity.

The remainder of this section will focus on Mary Seacole's *The Wonderful Adventures of Mrs Seacole in Many Lands* (1857), which provides a particularly interesting example of the conjunctions between autobiography and travel-writing for a number of reasons. These include the author's gender (it was very rare for women of any ethnicity to travel so widely and write about it in the nineteenth century); her 'in-between' ethnicity (she was born of a Jamaican mother and 'Scotch' father); the early date of composition compared with the other texts considered in this chapter; and the purpose and nature of her travels. Above all, Seacole anticipates the interest in the inter-relationship between travel and the quest for identity which characterises a good deal of subsequent postcolonial writing.

To this end, Seacole self-consciously manipulates the conventions of autobiography and travel-writing both in concert with and against each other, in a manner parallel to the experimentations of Naipual and Chaudhuri with the respective genres just considered. The very first sentence of her text appears to promise autobiography (if not a novel): 'I was born in the town of Kingston, in the island of Jamaica, some time in the present century' (*WA*: 11). This is the seemingly unproblematic opening gambit of a Subject desiring to initiate 'the story of [her] life' (*WA*: 128). Perhaps not coincidentally (Seacole was already in her thirties before Emancipation was proclaimed in Jamaica), it is also consonant with the conventions of slave narrative, echoing the opening of *The History of Mary Prince*, for example. Such a beginning is certainly unusual in travel-writing, though this kind of information might emerge later in the narrative. However, the very next sentence of *Wonderful Adventures* sets limits to the extent of autobiographical matter which will be divulged: 'As a female, and a widow, I may be well excused giving the precise date of this important event' (*WA*: 11). This anticipates a teasing pattern of self-censorship which frustrates the reader's desire for material that might be expected in an autobiography. Thus, her shadowy husband's rapidly diminishing role is perhaps symbolised in the way his name contracts from 'Mr Seacole' to 'Mr S'. Perhaps most intriguing in this respect is 'the little girl' (also Mary) who accompanies Mrs Seacole throughout her travels to Central America and thence to the Crimea. The reader might suspect that the girl is, in fact, Seacole's daughter – and remain baffled by her unwillingness to clarify the relationship. *Wonderful Adventures* subverts the conventions of autobiography in a number of other ways. For example, the title appears to promise a view of the subject from the outside, if not an actual biography. Significantly, when Seacole begins to get to know another nurse in the Crimea, she describes them as exchanging 'biographies' (*WA:* 82). This emphasis is reinforced by Seacole's persistent citation of testimonials and references from others, shifting her text towards 'biography' insofar as she deploys them primarily to 'let another voice speak for me' (*WA:* 96) rather than to vindicate herself.[82]

However, such refusals of aspects of autobiographical convention do not necessarily confirm the text's identity unambiguously as travel-writing. For example, in contravention of its norms, this 'female Ulysses' (*WA:* 11) does not return to her point of departure; rather, like Equiano, she settles finally in England. Moreover, while one sees little of Seacole in Jamaica, the birth-place to which she journeys back intermittently during her early sojourns in Central America, and while most of the action takes place 'abroad', Seacole is curiously selective in the range of travel experience she shares. There is little on her initial trips to London, less on her voyages to other Anglophone Caribbean islands and the barest mention of trips to the more exotic locations of Haiti and Cuba. These are no sooner alluded to than dropped without explanation: 'But I hasten onward with my narrative' (*WA:* 14). This clearly suggests that the description of 'alien surroundings' which constitutes conventionally the principal object of traditional travel-writing is not the prime concern of her text.[83]

While Seacole's refusal to describe her 'first impressions of London' (*WA:* 13) might be understandable, given the metropolitan location of her target audience, comparable omissions are less explicable. En route to the Crimea, for example, Seacole explicitly disavows what is expected of a travel-writer: 'I am not going to risk the danger of wearying the reader with a long account of the voyage to Constantinople, already worn thread-bare by book-making tourists' (*WA:* 76). As her ship crosses the bay of Trafalgar, she complains of being woken at 'an unreasonable hour … and expected to be duly impressed' (*WA:* 76). The ironical reference to 'book-making tourists' might suggest that Seacole is, paradoxically, deploying a standard trope of the genre, presenting herself as a disillusioned (because belated) kind of anti-travel writer precisely in order to reinforce the authority of her accounts of alien surroundings when she does provide them. The grumpy persona she sometimes adopts in both Panama and Turkey – 'I do not think that Constantinople impressed me so much as I had expected' (*WA:* 78) – anticipates the jaundiced narrators of more recent postcolonial (and other) travel-writing, including Naipaul's *An Area of Darkness* and Caryl Phillips's *The European Tribe.* Yet in the end, Seacole's reticence seems to have more to do with a genuine fear of boring her readers, implying that they are not expecting travel-writing as conventionally understood any more than she intends to provide it.

Nonetheless, *Wonderful Adventures* certainly conjoins both genres in pursuit of its author's quest to achieve greater self-understanding.[84] Seacole is especially preoccupied by issues surrounding her ethnic/national affiliations, a problematic sharpened by the wide range of ethnicities and nationalities with which her travels bring her into contact. Indeed, this preoccupation is announced in the first voyage described in any detail before her Panama travels. During her early visit to London, Seacole and her companion are assailed by street urchins who make fun of their 'colour'. The narrator laughs the episode off in a gesture which might be understood as designed to flatter the target audience of a book written to re-establish her fortunes after the disasters of the Crimea (compare Equiano's 'scrupulously delicate' manipulation of his readers' self-image). Nonetheless, it is clearly significant in being the first time that she recalls her identity being publicly brought into question.

That this issue still plagues her is suggested at the very beginning of the text, where Seacole describes herself as 'Creole'. This descriptor is deeply ambiguous: as Sarah Salih has demonstrated,[85] it then referred variously to both 'whites' and 'blacks' born in the Caribbean and, in Seacole's use, to mixtures between the two races. While she defiantly rejects the demeaning alternative term 'mulatto', the apparent confidence of the affirmation 'I am a Creole' (*WA*: 11) thus conceals an apparently unstable foundation for identity in national/ethnic terms. This becomes further evident not only in her ambivalent account of stereotypes about Creoles, but in the slippery meanings of 'home' in the first chapter. On the one hand, Seacole recalls that 'I never followed with my gaze the stately ships homeward bound [to England] without longing to be in them and see the blue hills of Jamaica fade into the distance' (*WA*: 13). Conversely, two paragraphs later, she describes how, after her first two trips to London (where she stays three years in total), 'I again started homeward' (*WA*: 13) to Jamaica. Her self-identifications *within* Jamaica appear to be equally fluid (or contradictory) into adulthood. On the one hand, she is seen as a fit wife for the respectable Mr Seacole (in real life, supposedly, Admiral Nelson's godson[86]). On the other, the British colonial class from which her husband (and father) comes is described unambiguously as comprised of 'strangers' and 'foreigners' (*WA*: 58–9).

These twin aspects of Seacole's national/ethnic identity pull her in different directions during her travels. At times, she proudly affirms her identification with 'Blackness', not least in Panama where she is complimented patronisingly by a 'benevolent' Yankee who praises her in spite of her 'colour'. Her stinging response not only contradicts her objective status as 'an unprotected female' (*WA*: 40; compare 78) but as a member of a putatively inferior race. Equally, she consistently takes the side of Panama's blacks against its (overwhelmingly American) white population, for example, when she supports the local *alcalde*'s decision to free a female slave accompanying an American woman in transit to California. And she is scarcely persuaded to give up her berth on the ship taking her back to Jamaica from Navy Bay, even when 'little Mary' is spat upon by the white American child.

If she reserves her strongest criticism for the United States, Seacole can also be a stern critic of the racial politics of imperial Britain from the perspective of a raced subaltern – despite her evident self-interest in flattering its *amour propre*. Like Equiano, she reminds her target audience unambiguously of past misdemeanours towards 'those poor mortals whom you enslaved' (*WA*: 21). Perhaps the most disillusioning moment in her whole travels comes when she is rebuffed in her attempts to find work in the Crimea through official channels in London: 'Was it possible that American prejudices against colour had some root here?' (*WA*: 73). The critique of Britain's racially-based conception of its superiority is extended in

Seacole's role as an 'historian' of the Crimean war (*WA*: 128; compare the previous section). In this respect, *Wonderful Adventures* provides an at times deeply disobliging picture of imperial incompetence. For example, she stresses that the British army fails completely in its assault on the Redan in Sebastopol and that the situation is saved only by a French counter-attack. Indeed, there could barely be a more biting denunciation of one period of British military inactivity, which she ascribes to the temporary absence of her patron, the *Times* war correspondent, W.H. Russell (*WA*: 139).

Nonetheless, while never disavowing her 'black' identity, and while sometimes ironical about or directly critical of 'civilised England' (*WA*: 45), Seacole's travels often prompt an equally strong articulation of her affiliation to Britishness. For example, in both Panama and the Crimea, she calls her establishment 'The British Hotel'. In Panama, she confesses to having 'a prejudice against *our* cousins across the Atlantic' (*WA*: 21; my emphasis), the pronominal shift aligning her with her target audience against American racism. However, while such sentiments are understandable, given her own direct experience of slavery, at times, Seacole's affirmation of Britishness is itself expressed in worryingly imperialist terms (compare Equiana). In Panama, she excoriates the local population (with the exception of the escaped black slaves from North America, to whom she attributes what saving graces New Granada can boast) for their idleness, cowardliness and dishonesty. Once in Turkey, moreover, she indulges in Orientalist stereotypes about the dirt, disorder and despotism of the non-western world – while reserving an imperially 'primitivist' admiration for the North African *zouaves* in the French army, on account of their unquestionable 'manliness'. This pattern is reinforced by Seacole's hierarchisation of European ethnicities. Greeks, Maltese and Spanish are all stereotyped mercilessly as inferior groups to the British, French and, interestingly, the Russians (perhaps not only on account of their courage but because they make no comment on her 'complexion'). One particularly interesting example is 'Jew Johnny' (with characteristic 'British' ineptitude, Seacole finds his real name is too complicated to master). He is constructed as the traveller's 'faithfullest servant' (*WA*: 84), a trope which recurs in colonial literature from Aphra Behn to Kipling and Conrad. To this extent, Seacole appears to use travel-writing in normative ways for the time.

Seacole's complex matrix of self-identifications is reflected in the ambivalent cultural politics of *Wonderful Adventures* as travel-writing. To some extent, the text operates counter-discursively. For example, her journey is not from the centre to the periphery and back but largely *between* peripheries (Jamaica, Panama, the Crimea) through a centre (London) which is, however, not given significant discursive space. Insofar as the metropolis does appear, moreover, it is constructed in terms of a somewhat disobliging counter-ethnography which emphasises the ironical tone of terms such as 'civilised' in Seacole's descriptions. However, while its gendered perspective is certainly unusual, like many of the most famous travelogues of the nineteenth century, to some extent *Wonderful Adventures* constructs Seacole in the image of male imperial explorers. For example, in both her ethnographic rendering of the 'manners and customs' of Amerindians and 'promontory' descriptions of the local landscape as she prospects for gold in Panama, Seacole approximates closely to the 'capitalist vanguard' model of nineteenth-century European travel-writing analysed by Mary Louise Pratt.[87] Indeed, in Said's *Orientalism*, on which Pratt draws, such work is assigned a major role in constructing the contemporary non-West in ways which enable and legitimise imperialism.[88]

Seacole's autobiographical negotiation between Britishness and her 'black' identity remains equally ambiguous. On the one hand, *Wonderful Adventures* offers a mobile and plural model of personhood which varies with location and situational requirements. In this reading, 'Creole' stands for a comfortable kind of hybridity or 'in-between' position *vis-à-vis* the different races of her parents. Consonant with this interpretation, Salih argues that once arrived in the Crimea, Seacole's preoccupation with questions of national/ethnic affiliation gives way to self-identification in terms of gender.[89] But there is strong evidence against this reading, not only in Seacole's repeated references to her origins and 'complexion' in the Crimea but, above all, when the war ends and the time comes to leave. Seacole clearly laments that she had 'no home to go to' (*WA*: 164). At this moment, as at other times, her elaboration of 'travelling subjectivity' expresses a liminal sense of identity which is the source of considerable anxiety. As with her rebuff in London, which reduces her temporarily not just to tears but to *immobility*, she can take no interest in the bustle of departure, identifying instead with those fixed forever in the cemeteries near Spring Hill.

While this incident once more suggests the propensity of the hybrid, in Rushdie's terms, to 'fall between two stools' (compare Lim) rather than to 'straddle cultures' (compare Equiano), Seacole's predicament is by no means unproductive and only very rarely compromises her agency. Indeed, Seacole anticipates the paradigm of subjectivity represented in travel-writing by O'Hanlon which, Holland and Huggan argue, is 'less concerned with recuperating, or reinventing a single self than with following the trajectory of a series of selves in transit'.[90] Equally, parallel to the challenges offered by Naipaul and Chaudhuri to traditional conceptions of autobiographical subjectivity, Seacole interrogates the generic convention that such texts end with the establishment of a stable, complete and 'sovereign' Self. To this extent, she produces a generically hybrid (or formally 'Creole') text which at once reaffirms and troubles the conventions and boundaries of both canonical autobiography and the (imperial) travel-writing of her time – from the gendered as well as 'raced' perspective of what she describes, foreshadowing Chaudhuri, as 'an unknown Creole woman' (*WA*: 70). Such a text might best be described neither as autobiography nor as travel-writing but as what Pratt calls 'autoethnography', an enabling, counter-discursive practice of self-representation characterised by 'partial collaboration with and appropriation of the idioms of the conqueror'.[91] If there is nothing to compare with this in western women's life-writing, the same pattern is observable in other texts considered in this monograph, albeit to a lesser degree. As has been seen, Equiano uses travel to provide both autobiographical material, an 'insider' ethnography of his West African community and an at times highly disobliging counter-ethnography of the West. Gandhi's travels generate a similarly complexly layered narrarive project, as do Lim's.

Conclusion

While the three genres under consideration in this chapter have been considered separately for analytical purposes, it is important to note that they sometimes occur together and, indeed, in combination with other genres. Thus, Chaudhuri's later considerable body of auto/biographical work, for example, could equally be studied under the rubric of travel-writing by 'a nomad of the industrial age, wandering from pasture to pasture' (*AUI*: 262). Conversely, Mary Seacole designates herself as 'the historian of Spring Hill' (*WA*: 128), a title also conferred in the Preface to her text by the noted *Times* reporter of the conflict, W.H. Russell. As such, her work might therefore be considered alongside – and in opposition to – mainstream historiography of the Crimean War. Equally, the second 'personal narrative' in V.S. Naipaul's *Finding the Centre* could easily have been analysed within the framework of travel-writing and much of his *A Way in the World*, as noted earlier, as a mode of historiography. At times, the degree of such inter-generic traffic threatens to undo altogether the rules and borders of auto-biography as conventionally understood. Thus, of Chaudhuri's text, one critic comments huffily that it is no more than 'a book of erratic [Historical] essays'.[92] The decision to publish *A Way in the World* with the sub-title 'a novel' (in the US, at least) also suggests a wilful refusal to adhere to the rules of autobiography as traditionally conceived. Similar inferences might be drawn from the title of Seacole's text, which could as well be shelved in the travel as autobiography section of a bookshop. Furthermore, as has been seen, such 'working' of generic boundaries has important implications for hegemonic conceptions of autobiographical subjectivity as 'real', singular and unified/'sovereign'. While there is not space to consider the relationship between travel and the Body in detail, travel certainly foregrounds issues of embodiment, in relation to diet, physical comfort and health. Further, as Seacole's early visit to London indicates, estrangement from 'home' also enforces the bodily/cultural differences represented by 'colour', with sometimes powerful consequences for self-image – an experience corroborated by Fanon's painful encounter with the white child on a train.

This pattern apparently overturns Gusdorf's argument about the inherently imitative nature of non-western life-writing *vis-à-vis* the canon. Equally, these formal attributes require reconsideration of some of the claims made about the specificities of western women's life-writing. Conversely, however, the fact that a comparable pattern of inter-generic traffic occurs in such work, in respect of fiction and History, if not travel-writing, should make one circumspect about over-emphasising the formal distinctiveness of postcolonial life-writing in this regard. Moreover, insofar as travel-writing is, belatedly, being considered as an auto-biographical form, at least by western women critics *outside* Auto/biography Studies,[93] it is probably only a matter of time before it, too, is adduced within feminist inflections of the critical field as further evidence of the experimental nature of women's life-writing. As has been suggested, there are sometimes important differences in the socio-cultural explanations for each sub-field's engagements with fiction and History and significant variations in the ways these genres are deployed. Nonetheless, insofar as each of the three genres under discussion here might themselves be deemed western cultural forms, Gusdorf's argument about the secondary and imitative nature of non-western life-writing cannot as yet be fully refuted. This strategic objective, together with the subsidiary objective of distinguishing women's and postcolonial life-writing at the stylistic level, therefore, demands investigation of further aspects of form, which will be the task of the next chapter.

6 Non-western narrative resources in postcolonial life-writing

Given constraints of space, this is not the appropriate place to debate in detail whether the genres considered in the last chapter have long-established, independent equivalents in the non-West. In any case, the texts under consideration in this monograph show little evidence of drawing on such putative equivalents, for example, the fiction of Murasaki Shikubu (*The Tale of Genji*), the historiography of Ibn Khaldun (*The Book of Evidence*) or the travel-writing of Ibn Battuta (*The Journey*). A more immediately productive approach to defining the formal distinctiveness of postcolonial life-writing may lie instead in attention to other aspects of its narrative articulation. It has long been observed of postcolonial literature generally that when it uses genres – and even languages – which clearly derive from the West, it can nonetheless often be distinguished from its metropolitan counterparts by virtue of a consistent deployment of non-western narrative resources and linguistic elements within those imposed/inherited cultural forms.[1] The same phenomenon of hybridisation will now be explored within postcolonial life-writing more specifically. The more this process can be demonstrated to be at work, the more difficult it is to sustain Gusdorf's argument about the simply imitative and secondary nature of non-western auto/biographical writing. Equally, it should allow clear water to emerge at last between postcolonial life-writing and western women's auto/biography at the level of form. While it has long been claimed both that western women use language in specific ways and that they have – or aspire to – writing styles which are *sui generis*,[2] at present, they enjoy neither a language, nor – *pace* critics like Elaine Showalter – a repertoire of cultural texts entirely of their own in the way that aspects of the language and narrative traditions drawn on by Soyinka, for example, are the property of the Yoruba people to which he belongs.

Some critical work has already been done from this angle, both on life-writing considered in this book and elsewhere. One important example is Gandhi's *Autobiography* which, as was seen in the Introduction, Gusdorf adduces as prime evidence of the 'mimic' nature of non-western autobiographical writing. Both Pilar Casamada and Javed Majeed demonstrate the influence on Gandhi's writing of a range of indigenous Indian texts, notably the *Bhagavad Gita* and *Ramayana*; these, Majeed argues, provide 'regulative psychobiographies' in terms of which Gandhi constructs autobiographical Selfhood. Indeed, he concludes that 'Indian-derived notions of text and performance' outweigh the influence of western templates in *An Autobiography* (as he argues they also do in comparable work by Nehru and Iqbal).[3] Drawing on such analysis, one might even infer that the 'experiments' to which Gandhi's sub-title alludes extend from abstruse philosophical issues of 'truth' to exploration of the possibilities of culturally-specific conceptions of autobiographical form. This would certainly account for the author's explicit disavowal that he is using the genre as conventionally understood in the West.

Indian autobiography in English has proved an equally rich field of investigation in this respect, squarely contradicting G.N. Devy's splenetic claim that it 'has not inherited anything from the rich Indian heritage'.[4] As the last chapter argued, Chaudhuri argues that 'synthesis' is emblematic of Indian tradition. Further, as suggested in the Introduction, Shirley Lim makes a similar case to Majeed in respect of Kamala Das's *My Story* (1976), arguing that the author's Self-conception is plotted in terms of the contrastive psychobiographic models represented in Hindu tradition by Kali and Krishna respectively. To this extent, Das demonstrates 'the ideological interpenetrations of the Hindu worldview with a feminist, although not necessarily wholly Westernized text'.[5] Secular forms of traditional narrative have proved equally productive as a template for life-writing in the sub-continent. For example, Ganeswar Mishra claims of Prafulla Mohanti's *My Village, My Life* (1973), that the author 'retains in his work much of the folk narrative form' typical of his region of India.[6]

Devy further claims that 'a genuinely Indian autobiography can be written in Indian languages alone',[7] implying that (post)colonial Selfhood must be articulated in an indigenous mother tongue to be authentic (compare the inferences to be drawn from Ngugi's discussion of language noted in the introduction). However, in the first place, this ignores the predicament of those postcolonial subjects who have no choice but to write in English. As Jamaica Kincaid comments: 'Isn't it odd that the only language I have in which to speak of this crime [colonialism] is the language of the criminal who committed the crime?'[8] Beyond the Caribbean, other factors sometimes enforced the use of English. Thus, Bharati Mukherjee comments that: 'I was born into a class that did not live in its native language.'[9] Further, Devy ignores the fact that English has been increasingly recognised since Independence as one *Indian* language among others – especially in the South of the sub-continent (a situation widely paralleled in other parts of the decolonised world). In this regard, it bears some comparison with Urdu, the language which developed through hybridisation by Hindi of the Persian which Mughal conquest imposed on India in the (western) early Modern period.

Salman Rushdie recognises that in the eyes of many, work in English 'will never be more than a post-colonial anomaly, the bastard child of Empire, sired on India by the departing British'.[10] Nonetheless he asserts (contentiously) that English-language literature in India is 'proving to be a stronger and more important body of work than most of what has been produced in the sixteen official languages of India, the so-called "vernacular languages"'.[11] Rushdie defends the use of English as a literary medium not simply because of the quality of work produced in it, or the number of English-speakers in the sub-continent,[12] or the fact that its lack of a regional base actually makes it more 'Indian' than a language like Tamil. In English, he claims, 'we can find ... a reflection of other struggles taking place in the real world, struggles between cultures and within ourselves and the influences at work upon our societies.'[13] However, Rushdie also argues that 'we can't simply use the language the way the British did ... it needs remaking for our own purposes.'[14] Such ideas have long been anticipated among postcolonial writers. As Achebe argued half a century ago, English could already by the 1950s be considered a 'world language', available to all who wished to use it, insofar as it was prepared to pay the price of 'submission to many different kinds of use'.[15] The trajectory of the English language's 'submission' in postcolonial life-writing more specifically has already been studied by several critics. As has been seen, Robert Fraser has asserted of Soyinka's indigenisation of Standard English in *Aké*, that the linguistic norm is not English, but Yoruba. And Gillian Whitlock draws similar conclusions from studying the 'Arablish' of Salam Pax's *The Baghdad Blog*.[16]

In the rest of this chapter, I propose to look at two further examples of the subgenre which use non-western narrative resources and are also characterised by linguistic experimentation and hybridisation. My strategic aim is to demonstrate formal properties which distinguish postcolonial life-writing from both its canonical and western women's analogues. Once more, Fanon provides a useful point of reference for these discussions. A Caribbean Subject like Kincaid, Fanon had only French and Creole, itself a heavily hybridised, language, to choose between for *Black Skin*. He certainly recognises the huge capital which accrues to the colonial subject by virtue of 'his mastery of the French language';[17] conversely, anticipating Ngugi, he also acknowledges that to speak a language 'is to take on a world, a culture'.[18] Nonetheless, he sees little future in attempting to produce a Creole literature in the Caribbean, partly because of the opprobrium the language attracts in both white colonial and metropolitan culture. Further, he suggests that Creole too closely resembles the 'pidgin-nigger' spoken by colonialists themselves.[19] Therefore, to make the colonised 'talk pidgin is to fasten him to the effigy of him, to snare him, to imprison him, the eternal victim of an essence, of an *appearance* for which he is not responsible'.[20]

Yet, on occasion, Fanon does draw on 'dialect', for example, using untranslated diction like '*toubab*', or uses 'a local figure of speech'.[21] Equally, his articulation of metropolitan standard French is often highly 'deviant'. The French editor of *Black Skin* was constantly obliged to ask for clarification of its phrasing and diction. Describing Fanon's language as 'most unsettling', Francis Jeanson also describes a letter in which his author asserts that 'once liberated from its conventions, language was for him the ultimate resource'.[22] *Black Skin* also foreshadows debates over the use of non-western narrative resources in later postcolonial life-writing. It complains that: 'The folklore of Martinique is meagre, and few children in Fort-de-France know the stories of "Compé Lapin," twin brother of the Br'er Rabbit of Louisiana's Uncle Remus.'[23] Yet if Fanon does not draw extensively on what he represents as a heritage withering under the pressure of policies of colonial assimilation, a burden perhaps felt more heavily in the French Empire than the

British, he nonetheless has recourse to 'the oral tradition of the plantation', notably in the opening pages of the text and those passages which are highly interpellative, whether of himself or his audience.[24] In both these respects, then, Fanon anticipates the attitudes and strategies of later postcolonial life-writers.

Assia Djebar, *Fantasia: An Algerian Cavalcade* (1985)

Fantasia (1985) is a complex articulation of aspects of Djebar's life, the historiography of colonialism in Algeria (compare Chaudhuri) and a collective auto/biography of a broad range of predominantly indigenous women from the French invasion of 1830 to the 1980s. More particularly, the author seeks to understand the process of her own identity-formation in relation to recent (post)colonial history and the experiences of the generation of women (including relatives) who participated in the War of Independence (1954–62). In the Algerian context, however, the access of women to auto/biography is fraught. According to Djebar, even relatively class-privileged and well-educated females have to negotiate 'two absolute rules' of traditional culture: 'one, never talk about yourself: and two, if you must, always do it "anonymously".' As for speaking anonymously, she goes on exasperatedly, 'one must *never* use the first person'.[25] This suggests that in the eyes of the majority of Algerian society, no less than in El Saadawi's Egypt, auto/biography is a solecism as potentially serious for women as appearing in certain contexts without a veil.

The weight of this prohibition has profoundly influenced Djebar's career. Perhaps most obviously, it motivated her use of a *nom de plume*.[26] Born Fatma Imalhayère, her pseudonym signifies 'she who consoles' (in Berber-inflected 'dialect') + 'intransigence' (in standard Arabic).[27] This collocation of apparently conflicting meanings *and* languages reflects a pattern of dualities in Djebar's work which speaks to the 'interior warfare'[28] she has sometimes experienced in relation to her identity (compare the young C.L.R. James). But while a *nom de plume* provided Djebar with sufficient sense of security to embark on writing fiction, a radical enough move for an Algerian woman in the 1950s, it soon threw up intractable problems. Coming to realise that 'for a woman to write, inevitably meant to write about oneself',[29] Djebar attempted a more confessional register in her fourth novel, *Les Alouettes Naïves* (1967). However, the effort proved so traumatic that she published nothing further for many years, ploughing her energy into film instead. She has explained this long silence partly in terms of a frustrated quest for autobiographical modes appropriate to her particular cultural predicament (*WoA*: 168–9).[30]

The choice of linguistic medium and narrative form posed particular difficulties. Educated in French-medium institutions from primary level, Djebar describes herself as 'writing classical Arabic poorly, loving and suffering in my mother's dialect'.[31] Apart from limited competence in its written forms, classical Arabic entailed other complications. As the official medium of government and law, Djebar sees it as complicit in the cultural/political marginalisation of Algeria's Berber-speakers, the section of society she identifies most closely with.

Further, as both the instrument of the (technically) secular Algerian state *and* a badge of the Islamist opposition movement of the 1980s (and since), the standard forms of Arabic are also implicated in the oppression of women. In *Women of Algiers in their Apartment* (1980), Djebar therefore draws an important distinction between standard Arabic and what she calls 'colloquial Arabic ... feminine Arabic ... underground Arabic' (*WoA*: 1). Indeed, two decades on, standard Arabic seems to her 'more and more a masculine language'.[32]

Aside from her greater familiarity with its written forms and its 'neutrality' in the cultural/political conflict between Arabic and 'dialect', French offers Djebar other clear advantages as an auto/biographer. These include the possibility not only of more easily preserving her anonymity among potentially hostile monophone local constituencies but also greater scope to address issues of sexuality and desire, both positive and negative. For example, Djebar considers that rape can be discussed frankly in French, whereas it is sanitised by euphemism in local languages.[33] Like Ngugi, Djebar is nonetheless troubled by certain implications of writing in the language of the recent colonising power, notably possible complicity in reaffirming its project of acculturation. Above all, she fears that her translations into French of the testimony of ex-combatants of the War of Independence will result in new kinds of effacement, comparable to their veiling (and silencing) in conservative Islamic society. This anxiety is expressed in an apology to one interviewee: 'I have captured your voice; disguised it with my French without clothing it. I barely brush the shadow of your footsteps!' (*F*: 142).

Like many postcolonial writers, Djebar partly mitigates her concerns by reworking the standard forms of the colonisers' language, in the manner that Achebe and Rushdie advocate. As early as 1968, she was arguing that it was the duty of the North African writer to 'arabise' French; more recently, she has described her French as 'deviating slightly'[34] from the norm (compare Fanon). The most obvious sign of such 'deviation' in *Fantasia* is the frequent incorporation of Arabic and 'dialect' diction. In the original French edition, no glossary of such words is provided (in contrast to the Heinemann translation for the Anglophone world – which is, however, far from comprehensive). As a result, the average western reader is reminded of the material differences of the world Djebar describes, while any quasi-colonial pretension to total mastery of its culture is frustrated (compare the effect of Soyinka's partial translations of Yoruba).

The choice of narrative form is equally problematic. Like many writers considered in this text, Djebar betrays unease with autobiography as traditionally understood. Thus, she describes *Fantasia* as no more than a 'preparation' for an autobiography than a fully achieved example of it[35] (compare the implications of Naipaul's 'Prologue to an Autobiography'). One might infer that her unease with the genre derives from similar reasons to those informing her disquiet about using French, namely that it is the cultural form of an imposed and alien culture. However, Djebar's citations of both Augustine and Ibn Khaldun (*F*: 47, 111) suggest that she also attaches herself to what she regards – in an implicit riposte to Gusdorf and Pascal – as a long non-western tradition of Self-representation.[36] Like many other postcolonial life-writers, moreover, Djebar addresses these anxieties in part by experimenting with the conventions of the genre, notably by inflecting it, sometimes radically, with non-western narrative resources.

Perhaps the principal example is Djebar's importations into her work of aspects of the musical traditions of the *Maghreb*, which she researched extensively in the period during which she ceased to write. Such interests are reflected thematically throughout 'the Algerian Quartet'. For instance, in *Women of Algiers*, Sarah works at an institute of musicology. Here she studies 'the *haoufis* of Tlemcen, women's songs of time gone by' (*WoA*: 16; the gendering of this popular musical form is important, and is re-emphasised later when it is glossed as 'a kind of popular, feminine poetry that is sung' (*WoA:* 154)). Similarly the unidentified first-person narrator[37] of *So Vast the Prison* (1995; the title is taken from a traditional Berber song[38]) conducts research in indigenous music and is particularly fond of 'the popular laments of Abou Madyan, the saint of Béjaia'.[39]

When she returned to writing, Djebar began to incorporate musical terms and structures derived from her researches. In *Fantasia*, the influence of local musical forms is particularly pronounced. The most significant model is the *nouba*, the conventions of which Djebar had already drawn on extensively in her film *La Nouba des Femmes du Mont Chenoua* (1978; the first feature film by an Algerian woman).[40] According to Tony Langlois, this (now) characteristically *maghreb*ian form belongs to the repertory 'known collectively as *andalouse*',[41] which was brought to North Africa as a result of the expulsion of Muslims from Spain between the thirteenth and fifteenth centuries. Pre-eminent in prestige among the various forms of the *andalouse*, the *nouba* is composed of 'five sections of introductory pieces, overtures, song series, solos and finales, arranged in a traditional sequence of rhythmic patterns'.[42] Although, strictly speaking, the term for a specific musical form, the *nouba* has acquired other connotations which bear upon its deployment in *Fantasia*. In the first place, it has come to signify 'public celebration' in the vernacular (*WoA*: 199). This communal dimension is further emphasised by its etymology, which, according to Réda Bensmaïa, derives from the Arabic *nowba*, meaning 'taking turns'.[43]

Understood in these various ways, the *nouba* offered means of unblocking Djebar's impasse after *Les Alouettes Naïves*.[44] Most obviously, perhaps, by virtue of the 'lengthy narrative songs sung by a single performer',[45] which are a feature of the *nouba*, Djebar is in theory licensed to include her own 'solitary song' (*F*: 217) while still ostensibly respecting cultural tradition. The same holds true of the ex-combatant women whom she interviews. Moreover, insofar as their individual contributions both aggregate and seemingly seep into each other (distinguishing who is speaking within the different 'movements' of the sub-sections entitled 'Voice' and 'A Woman's Voice' is sometimes difficult), their combined voices equate to another feature of the *nouba*, the 'chorus'. In this capacity, the women provide a communal commentary on the tragedy of contemporary Algeria.

The impress of the *nouba* is further apparent in the structure of *Fantasia*. One might argue that the three Parts into which the text is divided correspond to the 'three rhythms' according to which the form is traditionally arranged.[46] But its influence is perhaps paramount in Part Three, the five 'movements' of which conform to the pattern described by Langlois. With the exception of the fifth, which is composed of two, each 'movement' is in turn split into six sub-sections. These are distributed evenly between autobiographical reflections, the testimony of ex-combatants, and authorial commentaries on the implications of that testimony for Djebar herself, the women themselves and modern Algeria more broadly. The effect is at once rigorously precise and seemingly improvisatory, fragmentary and accumulative, so that distinct – though not necessarily harmonious – patterns of 'character', tone, 'voice' and theme emerge out of the interplay both between each sub-section within a given 'movement' and across the 'movements' which comprise the 'suite' as a whole. This arrangement appears to be deliberately anti-syntagmatic, in that the 'voices' in any particular 'movement' could be switched to their corresponding position in other 'movements' with little loss of coherence. The same applies to Djebar's self-reflections, which have the air of arising spontaneously out of successive interviews, which could themselves be fairly arbitrarily switched around the text.

Insofar as these sections are not ordered chronologically, this aspect of her text clearly conflicts with the conventions of mainstream western autobiography, which emphasises the progressive development of the personality concerned. Indeed, the 'Fifth movement' of Part Three ends with a sentence which is a direct echo of that with which Part One begins. This recursive, anti-linear trajectory is further evident in relation to the accounts of the ex-combatants' experience which in many respects seems to repeat that of their nineteenth-century forebears, described in Parts One and Two of the text. This powerfully suggests the stasis inflicted on Algeria by the long (anti-)history of colonialism. Further, while the idea of a 'Finale' conventionally signifies closure, this expectation is flatly contradicted (compare James's anti-epilogue). Not only is *Tzarl-rit* glossed with quite incompatible definitions (*F*: 222), but the late introduction here of a wholly new protagonist (the nineteenth-century French political exile Pauline Rolland) suggests a desire at once to return to the text's beginnings and to open out to new thematics – in particular the possibility of transnational alliances between marginalised women.

Within these complex formal arrangements, Djebar pursues her inquiries into identity in relation to herself, Algerian women as a social group and, indeed, the modern nation to which they belong. In respect of herself, as Jane Hiddleston ably argues, Djebar 'shuttles between a series of provisional identity constructions and a more uneasy sense of the impenetrability of singular existence, and this sense is heightened in turn by the chaotic mass of influences that drift around the intractable core'.[47] Such ideas could be extended to other axes of self-identification, however. At the collective level, what emerges is the internally differentiated nature of Algerian women as a group. While the ex-combatants have much in common – as indicated by the anonymising titles which frame their testimonies – their experience of both the War of Independence and its aftermath is often highly particularised. If Djebar refuses to sublate such differences under the sign of 'Woman', still less does she invoke the unifying category of 'national identity' to smooth over such differences. It is clear that while such women played a vital role in the anti-colonial struggle, their participation has been marginalised – to some extent during the war, but more especially since – by a variety of patri-archal belief-systems, both secular and religious. If modern Algeria has been torn apart by ideology and history (compare El Saadawi's account of Egypt), Djebar implies that its wounds cannot be sutured without fundamental changes to ensure the greater equality of women as agents within the national culture.

In all three areas, then, Djebar can be understood as trying 'to grasp the traces of some ruptures' of identity (*WoA*: 1; compare Naipaul), rather than offering some falsely consoling resolution of them. This pattern is reinforced by the text's own lack of resolved or integrated identity at a number of levels. Rather than confining itself to any single genre, individual autobiography co-exists with col-lective auto/biography, historiography and fiction in a manner which is mutually interruptive (compare Chapter 5). Equally, oral and written and literary and musical forms are juxtaposed rather than synthesised. Such disjunction is evident even in Djebar's deployment of musicological templates. Thus, her adaptation of the *nouba* operates mainly in relation to the second half of the text. In seeking a term which also embraces the material in Parts One and Two, however, Djebar selects the term *fantasia*, a term which ostensibly indicates a wish to identify her text primarily in relation to a western musicological model. This might suggest that, despite their many affinities,[48] the text is conceived in a strikingly different way to Djebar's earlier film *La Nouba*.

Christopher Field describes the *fantasia* as a 'composition whose form and invention spring solely from the fantasy and skill of the author … its formal and stylistic characteristics may consequently vary widely from free, improvisatory types to strictly contrapuntal and more or less standard sectional forms'.[49] In the first instance, therefore, Djebar's title perhaps intends in the first instance to foreground the *individual*, autobiographical aspects of the book by stressing the creative subjectivity of its author, as against the communal focus and connotations of the *nouba*. It also suggests a greater acknowledgement of the cultural influences of the West than her film. More specifically, Djebar cites Beethoven's experiments in the genre. His Opus 27 Sonatas are sub-titled *quasi* [like/almost/more or less] *una fantasia* (*F*: 111). This suggests, however, that they are not *fully* representative of the genre but perhaps even subversive of it. This is corroborated in two prin-cipal ways, each of which also bears on Djebar's deployment of the form. To begin with, as Field suggests, with Beethoven, 'the term is associated for the first time with the idea of large-scale unification of multi-movement works'.[50] Perhaps more radical still was Beethoven's introduction of the voice, since traditionally an 'essential of the fantasia is its freedom from words'.[51] Thus, Beethoven 'broke most strikingly with tradition by introducing a chorus into a form that had been instrumentally conceived for some 300 years'.[52]

If Djebar is to this extent drawing on a western template, then it is with one which is itself transgressive and revisionary, albeit of western tradition. Consonant with this, she in turn challenges Beethoven's revision of the form in two main ways. First, as was argued earlier, her text does *not* move definitively towards 'large-scale unification' of its disparate 'multi-movement' parts, whether within

Part Three or the text as a whole. Second, Djebar introduces not only the idea of a 'chorus' but, insofar as her 'voices' are in the first instance those of individuals, the 'solo'. Absent from Beethoven's *fantasias*, this is, as has also been seen, a characteristic element of the *nouba*. However, if this suggests a desire on Djebar's part to 'interrupt' the *fantasia* by bringing it into conjunction with an Algerian musical form, the converse is also true. One explanation for Djebar's 'interruption' of the conventional *nouba* is her perception of the immobilising rigidity of Algerian tradition, which has particularly negative consequences for women (compare El Saadawi). 'Masculine' cultural forms like the *nouba* are not immune from this conservatism and may even exacerbate it. Thus, Hadi Bougherara comments on the 'rigid and austere protocol' of a form largely unchanged since its emergence in ninth-century Andalusia, and Mahmoud Guettat sees it as tending to the 'sclerotic' by the second half of the twentieth century.[53] Consequently, when Sarah stumbles upon a singer performing *al fresco* in *Women of Algiers*, she is startled by his unwonted willingness to experiment with 'the Andalusian song, unchangeable when others sang it' (*WoA*: 26).

Arguably, then, Djebar seeks to 'stretch' the form of the *nouba* just as much as the *fantasia*. Like the singer whom Sarah encounters, she employs it 'without following traditional modulations' (*WoA*: 26). For one thing, Djebar 'translates' the *nouba* into literary terms; for another, in doing so, she is not entirely faithful to the established form. For example, Part Three of *Fantasia* is, strictly speaking, composed of six rather than five 'movements'. And, as has been seen, the 'mood' of the *Tzarl-rit* is deeply ambiguous, in contradiction of the all-important unity of mood traditionally assumed to characterise the *nouba*.[54] Further, while the 'solo' is a constituent element of the form, Djebar's use of it for detailed auto/biographical self-expression is unprecedented. However, perhaps the most significant innovation is Djebar's adaptation of what is traditionally an exclusively masculine and class-specific performative form. Historically the composers, singers and orchestra were made up entirely of men and it was generally performed for wealthy patrons to express ordinary women's experience. To this extent, Djebar is self-consciously interrupting the gender economy which distinguishes the *nouba* from the *haoufi* and which traditionally accords the former greater prestige.[55]

However, a further twist in this complex of cultural (self-)identifications is that the term *fantasia* also occurs in one of the colonial texts Djebar engages with most, Eugène Fromentin's *Une Année dans Le Sahel* (1858), which provides the epigraph for her text. In the course of his Algerian travels, Fromentin stumbled on an example of 'the ravishing spectacle of what is called [*qu'on appelle*] an arab *fantasia*'.[56] Djebar's translator, Dorothy Blair, asserts unequivocally that her title is 'derived from the Arabic *fantaziya* [meaning ostentation]'.[57] If *fantasia* had, indeed, already passed into Arabic (in the way that, conversely, the word 'algebra', for example, has passed into English), this suggests a tail-chasing process of mutual hybridisation or appropriation which helps illuminate the unresolved 'traces' which complicate the cultural identity of both Djebar and her text.[58] Fromentin's usage is certainly much more specific in purview than the western musical term would suggest, meaning something like a local fair, composed of 'a riding festival, followed by a night-time dance with Homeric feasts'.[59] The equestrian spectacle, more precisely, signifies a display of martial skills, designed to 'compensate the veterans who no longer make war, or the young people who have never done so'.[60] If Fromentin nonetheless plays on the conjunction between *fantasia* in its western sense (at one point he uses the term 'prelude' to describe the opening of the festival[61]) and its Arabised equivalent, *fantaziya*, perhaps Djebar does, too. Her text may be seeking not just to adapt the conventions of the *fantasia* as a western musical form but thereby to 'stage' qualities of 'cavalcade' corresponding to Fromentin's description of the Hadjout festival. From this perspective, the gathering 'movements' in Part Three of her text are perhaps analogous to successive waves of riders showing off their skills, accompanied (and interrupted) by individual singing and communal celebrations.

In contrast to Fromentin, however, for whom the festival stages only token resistance in the form of a commodified spectacle (at least for alien observers like himself), Djebar's conception of *fantasia/fantaziya* is directly linked to the project of cultural decolonisation, which she describes as still unachieved.[62] Its attainment involves, first, the resuscitation or reinvigoration of local cultural forms, including the *fantaziya* and *nouba* (according to Guettat, the tradition was actually in danger of disappearing by the time of Algerian independence[63]). The second involves a critique of colonial cultural forms and systems of representation. Thus, Djebar clearly deprecates the 'Orientalist' tradition, perhaps most obviously in her critique of the 'superficial Orient' (*WoA*:137) constructed in Delacroix's celebrated painting, 'Women of Algiers in their Apartment' – the title of which she (re-) appropriated for the first text in the 'Algerian quartet'.

Nonetheless, while Djebar clearly intends *Fantasia* to be counter-discursive in this respect, it would be wrong to understand the text as an act of 'nativist' disavowal – whether of western *fantasia* and autobiography, or the wider metropolitan culture these genres seemingly derive from. Not only is Djebar indebted to French culture for giving her a language and forms to write in/against, but she is clearly influenced by a range of very specific western precedents. For example, her reworking of Delacroix has parallels with Picasso's, on which she comments approvingly. If the latter restores movement to the immobilised bodies in Delacroix's canvas (*WoA*: 149), Djebar's work can be understood as recuperating their silenced voices. Metropolitan *writers* have provided equally productive models for her. Thus, she observes of the work of Marguerite Duras, with which her own has sometimes been compared: 'I am touched by this disembodied voice that is on the verge of self-decentring' (*WoA*: 182). Further, she even expresses gratitude to 'Orientalists' like Fromentin (*F*: 226) himself, for providing templates for her text.[64] Indeed, several of the features which Donadey detects in Djebar's 'arabisation' of French are, in fact, anticipated by Fromentin.[65]

The title of Djebar's text therefore involves such complex significations in terms of the author's relations to both western and 'indigenous' culture that one could argue that both its author's cultural identity and its own are thrust into a dizzying *aporia* or *mise en abyme*. If *fantasia* is a term which has been rearticulated into Arabic as *fantaziya* before being 'retranslated' by Fromentin, this does not thereby efface

the western-derived connotations of the term. However, the origins of those connotations, in turn, do not, in Djebar's view, compromise its appropriateness for
the (re)affirmation of a local identity nor, more specifically, one which pursues the
anti-colonial struggle by cultural means. This explains Djebar's wariness of cultural 'nativism', the extreme (and usually *masculinist*) nationalist argument that all
foreign influences must be extirpated if an indigenous culture is to be resurrected
or constructed (compare Behan and El Saadawi). As one element of the *andalouse*,
the *nouba*'s cultural purity is already compromised by the Spanish (and Jewish)
influences at its origins. A national culture built on these and other (notably
Turkish) imported forms cannot, therefore, ground its members' identities in any
foundational way.

Djebar insists paradoxically that *Fantasia* is 'openly autobiographical'.[66] Nonetheless, the text poses a radical challenge to the conventions of western autobiography. For example, her use of a pseudonym flouts the conditions of
Lejeune's 'pact' (of which she is well aware),[67] quite as much as Naipaul's (see
Chapter 5). Equally, her attempt to recuperate the silenced voices of female ex-
combatants erodes the boundary between autobiography and biography (see
Chapter 2). Further, she 'works the borders' of the form by incorporating historiography wholesale, in the manner of Chaudhuri (see Chapter 5). In turn, the
paratactic structure of *Fantasia* rejects the coherent, linear progression of mainstream western autobiography. More broadly, the multiplicitous nature of the
'traces' of Djebar's (and Algeria's) identity undermines the traditional unity of
Selfhood and text, as well as 'nation'. Such ideas are compromised above all by
Djebar's ambiguous existential and cultural positioning between French and
Algerian cultures, which are shown to have already hybridised each other to a
considerable degree by the time she began to write.

Sara Suleri, *Meatless Days: A Memoir* (1989)

In *Boys Will Be Boys* (2003), Sara Suleri Goodyear's 'elegy' for her father,[68] the
author describes an occasion when her younger siblings acquired a pair of pet
rabbits. To Suleri's chagrin, both turned out to be male, so that 'we never had a
bunch of baby rabbits hopping round the garden: a regret for me, who even then
was obsessed with things small'.[69] The 'obsession' with scale is more broadly
conceived in Suleri's earlier auto/biographical text, *Meatless Days* (1989), on which
this section of the chapter will focus. Here, the idea of 'the unswerving truths of
size' (*MD*: 73) is explored in relation to topics as diverse as the (diminishing)
dimensions of Pakistan and the giant proportions of Tom, who makes Suleri feel
Lilliputian (*MD*: 79). However, scale is also an issue in relation to *Meatless Days*
itself, which could justifiably be described as an auto/biographical 'miniature' –
certainly when compared with the sprawling works of, for example, Montaigne,
Gandhi or Isabel Allende. The concept of 'miniature' has important implications,
not least because it is one of the ways through which a (partly) postcolonial
identity is asserted – in relation both to *Meatless Days* and to Suleri's constitution
as an auto/biographical Subject.[70]

In repeatedly invoking (and enacting) ideas of 'miniaturism', *Meatless Days* can be linked to two 'indigenous' cultural forms in particular. The first is the heritage of Mughal painting, which is alluded to during Suleri's meditation on the run-up to Independence in 1947. For Muslims especially, she suggests, the prospect of Partition required the realignment of 'spatial perspective with something of the maniacal neatness of a Mughal miniaturist' (*MD*: 74). One can fairly assume that Suleri was well acquainted with such work. The main museum in Lahore (the capital of the Mughal empire under Akbar from 1585 to 1598), to which she refers on more than one occasion (*MD*: 55, 153), boasts an important collection of 'miniatures'.[71] The genre appears to provide a template for *Meatless Days* partly because it offers a strong tradition of portraiture (amply represented in the Lahore Museum collection). Alongside images of individuals, the Mughals commissioned a considerable amount of group portraiture, of the kind *Meatless Days* also attempts. While certainly rarer, the tradition also includes notable instances of self-portraiture, a further aspect of Suleri's text.[72]

In a short discussion like this it is impossible to adequately summarise the stylistic qualities of the genre over its centuries of evolution and diversification. Developed out of a history of book illustration, Mughal 'miniatures' were often no more than a few inches square, even once they had developed into a free-standing cultural form. Despite this, their density of signification is often remarkable. Mir Sayyid Ali, the greatest painter at Akbar's court, described his conception of 'miniature' thus: 'In every grain [of rice] a hundred ass-loads are contained; a whole world can be encompassed easily within a single heart.'[73] One painting in the Lahore Museum, entitled 'The Construction of a Palace', illustrates something of Ali's ambitious aim. With its grand subject-matter and ample cast, its epic quality is enhanced rather than diminished by its drastic compression,[74] which is achieved through what Som Verma describes as the genre's distinctive emphasis on accurate detail and precision of execution.[75] Indeed, given its dimensions, the abundance of subject-matter in Mughal painting is often astonishing, confirming Milo Beach's argument that 'attention to descriptive detail [often] extends far beyond narrative necessity'.[76]

One could argue that in her own auto/biographical 'miniature', Suleri achieves similar feats of compression. Within less than two hundred pages, she manages to distil a complex self-portrait, the group biography of a (large and diverse) family *and* a considerable range of Pakistani history (compare Djebar). This is accomplished in part by a similar 'exquisite precision' (*MD*: 29) of descriptive detail, for example, in the account of Irfan's childhood accident with boiling water: 'He clutched at his groin, and everywhere he touched, the skin slid off, so that between his fingers his penis easily unsheathed, a blanched and fiery grape' (*MD*: 11). Time and again, in a few beautifully exact brush-strokes, Suleri constructs dramatic scenes in which not only event but character is anatomised with a sometimes cruel sharpness and insight. Compression is enhanced by other techniques discernible in Mughal 'miniature'. Comparable with its allegorical iconography, for example, *Meatless Days* figures the decline of Pakistan through consistent parallels with the disintegration and dispersal of Suleri's family – and vice versa (compare Chaudhuri).

As Suleri's allusion to Mughal painting suggests, it offers lessons not just about scale, but perspective. In the essentially two-dimensional arrangement of 'The Construction of a Palace', no hierarchy of 'background' and 'foreground' orders the visual 'reading' of the work. Consequently, as Milo Beach asserts, 'no single detail or episode dominates. Visual interest is evenly distributed over the entire surface of the work.'[77] Equally, the lack of perspective in such work means that the eye is not led to 'read' its parts in any particular order, nor is any vantage point especially favoured. Comparable claims might be made about *Meatless Days*. In contrast to traditional autobiography, it does not 'foreground' the progressive development of a privileged Self, in relation to which events and other persons are arranged as 'background'. Instead, narrative attention is 'evenly distributed' between Suleri herself, family members and the seemingly inexorable degeneration of the new nation. Nor is the text organised round moments of crisis, on which the 'plot' turns, of the kind one finds in Augustine's or Rousseau's *Confessions*. The deaths of Mairi and Ifat and Suleri are clearly critical but they have already happened when the narrative opens and do not dominate the text in terms of the narrative space they are accorded. Equally, with the possible exception of the 'framing' chapters, Suleri's 'tales' could be read in any order without materially affecting their meaning (compare the paratactic structure of *Fantasia*). In *Boys*, Suleri confesses that 'my instincts have never led me to chronology' (*B*: 38). This is reflected not only in the recursive temporality of *Meatless Days*, but in the fact the chapter primarily devoted to Suleri's mother (who died first) comes after Ifat's.

Suleri's allusion in *Boys* to 'Mughal-like curlicues of great intricacy' (*B*: 35) suggests other ways in which her earlier text might be compared to the tradition of 'miniature'. Under Akbar and Shah Jehan, in particular, Mughal painting was characterised by 'dazzling ornamentation',[78] a description which could just as well be applied to the profusion of metaphors, metonyms and conceits in *Meatless Days*. In relation to her first bereavement, for example, Suleri muses: 'It reminds me that I am glad to have washed my hands of my sister Ifat's death and can think of her now as a house I once rented but which is presently inhabited by people I do not know' (*MD*: 42). Such startling figurative language in part accounts for the semantic density of the text. Further, the idea of 'curlicues of great intricacy' applies to Suleri's syntax. This sometimes strains under the pressure of containing the dissemination of images, yet through that straining multiplies connotation:

> So Tom's story can never begin back yonder, in his neck of the woods: it has to be here, with travel-ache already over, when I have washed my hands of sequence and can glance at its swarming tiny autonomies in order to hiss, *'Down, wantons, down.'*
>
> (*MD*: 76)

The unusual semantic compression of Suleri's writing perhaps derives equally from a second and perhaps more important non-western narrative model discernible in *Meatless Days*. This is the *ghazal*, often considered to be the pre-eminent form in classical Urdu literature, which D.J. Matthews and Christopher Shackle describe as 'a short love-poem in which the two halves of the first couplet and the second line of the remaining couplets rhyme'.[79] Suleri demonstrates close familiarity with the tradition, alluding to recent exponents of the form like Iqbal (*MD*: 121, 184) and Faiz (*B*: 50, 57). *Boys* regularly quotes their *ghazals* in the original (among those of other poets – and other Urdu poetical forms) as epigraphs to its chapters. However, Suleri reserves her greatest admiration for Ghālib – the *nom de plume* of Mirza Asadullah Beg Khan (1797–1869), widely regarded as the finest *ghazal* poet in Urdu. In a rapturous account of her discovery of Ghālib, Suleri describes him as 'the master poet' (*MD*: 99; compare 82) and he is similarly praised in *Boys* (114, for example). Ghālib's work certainly seems to inspire some of the most distinctive qualities of *Meatless Days*.

It is not difficult to find reasons for Suleri's affinity with Ghālib. He, too, wrote a memoir, *Dastambu* ('A Posy of Flowers') which Ralph Russell argues was conceived 'primarily as a literary work'[80] (and another possible template for *Meatless Days*). In it, Ghālib expresses a number of preoccupations which concern Suleri, too, including some regret for not having a child.[81] Both writers are extremely liberal in matters of religion[82] and share what Aijaz Ahmad calls a 'psychology of ambivalences'[83] towards the cultures that most influence them. Thus, Ghālib expresses a love–hate relationship with both Mughal culture and the British *raj*; Suleri is comparably equivocal in relation to Pakistan, Britain and the United States in turn. Further, Ghālib considered himself to be living in an era of continuous political crisis, culminating in the dissolution of Mughal rule after 'the Mutiny' of 1857. A similar sense of living under the shadow of recurrent political upheaval is evident in *Meatless Days* (compare Chaudhuri in Chapter 5 and Amiry in Chapter 7). As Suleri's description of Pakistan as a country 'where history is synonymous with grief' (*MD*: 19) suggests, for both writers, public and private griefs intertwine. The often elegiac tone of Suleri's text has its analogue in Ahmad's description of Ghālib's work as 'a poetry of losses and consequent grief'.[84] Conversely, however, Russell remarks on the latter's 'sense of humour which was his main shield against the afflictions of life'.[85] Suleri herself stresses her predecessor's 'mischievous' qualities (*MD*: 99), which provide a precedent for her own sometimes 'nervously comic' (*MD*: 27) tone. For example, when Ifat dies, she is buried in the space which Suleri's father planned one day to occupy. 'Children take over everything', the author observes, with her trademark laconic wit (*MD*: 18).

The *ghazal* has much in common with the tradition of 'miniature' painting. It, too, derived originally from Persia (Ghālib wrote with equal facility in Persian) and for a long period was also associated primarily with the court (the poet was for a time advisor to the last Mughal emperor, Bahadur Shah, 'on matters of versification'[86]). In terms of style and technique, the *ghazal* is another art-form in which issues of scale are crucial. While, in theory, there is no limit to the number of couplets, Russell states that a *ghazal* 'rarely comprises less than five couplets or more than twelve'.[87] The longest of Ghālib's poems in the Matthews and Shackle anthology is sixteen couplets, with several composed only of two. In what Ahmad calls 'so small a [poetic] unit',[88] economy and concentration of meaning are at a premium. Consequently, Ghālib's work is always highly condensed, in a manner which Suleri imitates. Further, the influence of the *ghazal* would help explain the fragmented structure of *Meatless Days*. Ahmad suggests that the form can be highly discontinuous at the thematic level:

> The *ghazal* is a poem made up of couplets, each couplet wholly independent of any other in meaning and complete in itself as a unit of thought, emotion and communication. No two couplets have to be related to each other in any way whatever except formally ... and yet they can be parts of a single poem.[89]

Consequently, Russell argues, the *ghazal*'s 'close unity of form' can stand 'in startling contrast with a complete disunity of content'.[90]

One might argue that like the *ghazal*, *Meatless Days* is composed of what, as has been seen, Suleri calls 'tiny autonomies' (*MD*: 76). The first narrative, 'Excellent Things in Women', was conceived and published independently[91] and the remaining chapters stand as almost equally self-sufficient entities. Within each one, moreover, thematic transitions are often abrupt, even sometimes startling (see, for example, the sequencing of paragraphs on 34–6, 38, 73–6, 101–2). Suleri comments ruefully on her 'merely indifferent talent for construction' (*MD*: 73; compare 79). But as a comment about her disjunctive portrait of Tom suggests, this apparent artlessness is quite deliberate: 'Perhaps I should have been able to bring those bits together, but such a narrative was not available to me, not after what I knew of storytelling' (*MD*: 37). In any case, despite the tendency of *ghazal* to fragmentary structure, Adrienne Rich detects a 'gathering, cumulative' effect in Ghālib's poems.[92] This is also true of *Meatless Days*, both within and between the different chapters. Such an effect is evident at both the level of theme (reconstituting the vanished family past, the decline of Pakistan) and that of image and motif. For example, 'meatless days' at first seems to signify simply the days of the week chosen by Pakistan's early rulers to conserve the national supply of livestock. The signification of this leitmotif becomes expanded and complicated by a process of association in later chapters. For example, Nuz describes meat as something 'you bury in your body' (*MD*: 33). Later, in a dream, Suleri figures her mother as 'hunks of meat' (*MD*: 44) and slips one of her mother's bones under her tongue. Through this linkage of meat–burial–mother, the title of Suleri's text perhaps comes to figure the (endless) period of mourning occasioned by the disappearance of her mother and sister.

Meatless Days corresponds in other important ways to the conventions of *ghazal*. Ahmad claims of the form that 'personality [is] kept rigorously out of the poetic substance'.[93] This sheds light on the relatively detached, even impersonal, narrative voice which Suleri employs, whether describing a simple meal with her sister in the United States or her deepest griefs, for example the deaths of Ifat or her first paramour, T.K. (*MD*: 43, 62). Dadi, by contrast, is condemned for excessive and self-dramatising lamentation for her daughter-in-law's death (*MD*: 16). However, while the impersonality of the *ghazal* might suggest that it cannot be described as a properly autobiographical form, it is nonetheless common for poets like Ghālib not only to use the first-person in their *ghazal*s, but to apostrophise themselves (usually by their pen-name) in the last couplet of their poems.[94] It is perhaps no coincidence, therefore, that Suleri reserves perhaps the most confessional and self-revealing section of *Meatless Days*, 'Saving Daylight', for the conclusion of her text, a link reinforced by the attention she draws there to the stage-name adopted in her acting days (*MD*: 179).

Reinforcing Suleri's characteristic detachment as an auto/biographical persona is her resolute intellectualism, again anticipated by Ghālib. Ahmad emphasises his 'extremes of verbal ingenuity and obscurity' while Matthews and Shackle draw attention to the 'verbal brilliance and rhetorical tricks' which subtend his 'growing tendency towards obscurity and allusiveness'.[95] Such comments could apply equally well to Suleri. The elusiveness of both writers' work is primarily a function of their tendency to abstraction. At one point, Suleri describes Ghālib's language as being like 'geometry' and praises his 'mathematical ingenuity' (*MD*: 99). According to Ahmad, his poetry typifies the Urdu tradition by always moving *away* from concreteness: 'Meaning is not expressed or stated; it is signified.'[96] Suleri argues comparably that 'revelation must be a hiding' (*MD*: 176) – and perhaps, one might infer, vice versa. One demonstration of this comes in her account of things which made her mother squeamish: 'Chopping up animals for God was one. She could not locate the metaphor and was uneasy when obeisance played such a truant to the metaphoric realm' (*MD*: 4). Conversely, however, Matthews and Shackle highlight Ghālib's often 'idiomatic use of language'.[97] This also has parallels in Suleri's work, without necessarily making it any less defamiliarising, or challenging for her readers: 'In Pakistan, of course, there is no spring but only a rapid elision from winter into summer, which is analogous to the absence of a recognizable loneliness from the behaviour of that climate' (*MD*: 6).

Despite these signs of the influence on *Meatless Days* of both the heritage of Mughal 'miniatures' and the *ghazal*, it would be incorrect to infer that Suleri simply reaffirms either cultural practice as templates for her own writing. Instead, one might argue that she reconfigures both from a gendered perspective (compare Djebar's reconceptualisation of the *nouba*). Both artistic traditions were largely the work of men. Verma suggests that there were few women painters in the Mughal ateliers.[98] Neither anthology by Ahmad or Matthews and Shackle includes women writers. Nor are representations of women in either form unproblematic from a contemporary gendered perspective. In *ghazal*s, women are all too often figured as nightingales or roses rather than fully human beings.[99] Conversely, as Beach comments of Mughal portraiture, 'studies of particular women are almost unknown'.[100] Several of the female portraits in the Lahore Museum have flat, featureless, or decoratively abstract backgrounds, enhancing the idealised quality of their subjects. If, as Suleri claims, metaphorically at least, 'there are no women in the third world' (*MD*: 20),[101] this is partly the responsibility of cultural traditions like the *ghazal* and Mughal 'miniatures'. In place of the types such work characteristically offers, Suleri paints highly individualised portraits of real women 'living inside history' (*MD*: 34).

However, as is the case with Djebar, the provenance of *Meatless Days* at the level of narrative form is not exclusively non-western.[102] The text clearly expresses Suleri's weariness with being made to perform as an 'otherness machine' (*MD*: 105). Instead, she presents herself as, culturally speaking, a 'two-faced thing' with 'ambidextrous eyes' (*MD*: 77, 92). This is particularly apposite in relation to her conception of herself as a woman writer. In the absence of an indigenous 'female tradition' to look back to in Mughal miniature and the *ghazal* alike, Suleri appears to draw particular inspiration from two figures in western culture. The first is Jane Austen, a great favourite of Suleri's (Welsh) mother, who for many years worked as a lecturer in English literature in Lahore.[103] Aside from a shared preoccupation with the (often stifling) condition of women in their respective cultures, and a predilection for narrative irony, both writers share a fascination with 'scale'. Austen famously described her writing as 'the little bit (two inches wide) of ivory on which I work with so fine a brush'.[104] This suggests that Suleri may have learned as much from Austen as from indigenous cultural traditions about the scale of her canvas and the corresponding virtues of precision and economy of narrative description (although Austen's works are characteristically much longer than Suleri's).

Equally important to Suleri's feminist writing project is Virginia Woolf. In one conversation, her half-sister Nuz invokes *To the Lighthouse* (1928) for the insight it offers for their own home life (*MD*: 153). Suleri's large and sometimes chaotic family, dominated by an egocentric father, and held together primarily by a deeply sympathetic, self-effacing and enigmatic mother, has obvious parallels with the Ramsays. Mothers and children die off-stage in each text, exposing the 'terrible dependencies' (*MD*: 151) of bereft patriarchs. There is even a direct, parodic, echo of Mr Ramsay's failure to get beyond the letter 'R' in his philosophical systemising (*MD*: 23). Both families progressively disintegrate against the background of war and ensuing political and social changes. Within this reconfiguration of elements of Woolf's text, Suleri's role perhaps most closely approximates to the artist Lily Briscoe. Just as one of the central themes of *To the Lighthouse* is Lily's production of a portrait of Mrs Ramsay (a mother-figure to Lily), so *Meatless Days* is at one level a portrait of Mairi Suleri. In *Boys*, the earlier text is described as 'largely an elegy for her' (*B*: 16). And just as Lily seeks to preserve her personal independence from importuning men, so Suleri finally decides to leave her homeland to escape the pressure to marry (*B*: 45).

The parallels between Suleri and Woolf extend to issues of form, *To the Lighthouse* being as recursive and fragmentary in structure as *Meatless Days*. In both texts, coherence is to a considerable degree the effect of leitmotif. The narrative perspective in *To the Lighthouse* is often equally impersonal and multi-perspectival. It might be argued further that Suleri's difficult syntax is as much the product of a Woolf-like struggle with the 'male sentence', as of the author's desire to inflect the coloniser's language from a postcolonial standpoint. One imagines that the author of *A Room of One's Own* (1928) would approve the assertion of the female author of *Meatless Days* that to be 'engulfed by grammar after all is a tricky prospect, and a voice deserves to declare its control in any way it can, asserting in the end it is an inventive thing' (*MD*: 155). Equally, the often-remarked-upon 'poetic' style of Woolf's prose has obvious parallels in Suleri's.

As this might suggest, western poetry is another important axis to consider in terms of Suleri's self-identifications. As an adolescent, one of Suleri's favourite writers was Wallace Stevens (*B*: 119), whose affinities with Ghālib, notably his abstraction, playfulness and wit, are remarked on by Ahmad.[105] Another important intertext is Wordsworth, on whom Suleri wrote part of her doctoral dissertation. His poem 'We are Seven' (alluded to in *B*: 120), in which the 'maid' stubbornly insists that she retains her full complement of siblings, though two lie buried in the church-yard, resonates poignantly with Suleri's project. (Counting her half-sister Nuz who also dies prematurely and her adopted sister Shahida, there are also seven Suleri siblings.) Such inter-texts, together with the influence of Ghālib, underwrite one of Suleri's most radical challenges to autobiography as conventionally understood. Lejeune's 'pact' insists that it is a *prose* genre, a position seconded by critics such as Spengemann, who specifically excludes 'lyric poetry' from the genre, despite his claim that the supreme impulse and form of autobiography is 'poetic self-expression'.[106]

In *Boys*, Suleri laments that '*we* Orientals all look alike to the rest of the world' (*B*: 87; my emphasis).[107] The deployment of non-western narrative resources within her auto/biographical writing can be seen to respond to this perception in a complex way. To some extent, at least, it reaffirms the partly postcolonial difference of Suleri's identity, by distinguishing her narrativisation of the auto/biographical from its mainstream western counterparts. But this is perhaps subordinate to her more urgent task, which is to do justice to the human complexity and individuality of those she writes about, especially women. In doing so, like Djebar, Suleri redeems her subjects from the condition of the anonymous or typical, to which they are so often consigned in both 'indigenous' and colonial patriarchal traditions of representation.

Conclusion

This discussion indicates that postcolonial life-writing sometimes draws heavily on indigenous narrative resources and hybridises to a significant degree the standard forms of metropolitan languages handed down by colonialism. While the two examples considered above are both by contemporary women life-writers (to provide a balance to the preponderance of male texts discussed earlier in this volume), this pattern is established very early in the women's tradition. Thus, *The History of Mary Prince* (1831) corroborates the assertion that it 'was taken down from Mary's own lips'.[108] Not only does the structure of the narrative reflect the sometimes digressive structure of *orature*, but the text also incorporates Creole into its narrative discourse.[109] The same pattern of linguistic hybridisation is easily found in male writing, as has been seen. Constraints of space preclude more detailed discussion of other kinds of indigenous narrative resources, notably those supplied by the oral tradition, which has only been touched on here. In texts as diverse as Sindiwe Magona's *To My Children's Children* (1990) and Isabel Allende's *Paula* (1995), this particular resource plays a crucial role in the narrative construction of subjectivity.[110]

Such templates have important implications for the thematics of postcolonial subjectivity. Not only do they 'indigenise' the individual identities concerned, sometimes making them geo-culturally, even ethnically, specific, they also at times invoke quite different conceptions of Selfhood to what is normative in the West. As Lionnet suggests, hybridisation of language undermines the traditional western model of unified subjectivity by foregrounding 'the double consciousness of the postcolonial, bilingual, and bicultural writer'.[111] *Orature*, by contrast, is intrinsically a dialogical form, emphasising the relationality of personhood in a performative way. Certain aspects of non-western form also imply a sometimes radically different relationship of autobiographical subjectivity to temporality. The recursive character of some such work (both that influenced by *orature*, as well as Djebar and Suleri, for example) suggests less a preoccupation with the development of the Subject in historical linear time than with its 'location' in a variety of discursive and material relationships and positions (compare Chapter 4). Like Suleri, Bharati Mukherjee draws on the Mughal tradition of painting,[112] which particularly emphasises the spatial relations of its Subjects; like Suleri, Isabel Allende references the traditions of fresco, with similar implications for the constitution of auto/biographical subjectivity.[113] This desire to conceive autobiographical identity in spatial rather than temporal terms is, however, neither gender-distinctive nor historically-specific. As has been seen, it extends from Equiano's image of the chequer-board to Morgan's of the jigsaw puzzle as metaphors of Self.

However, one should not assume that a refusal to draw on indigenous narrative forms, or the use of standard English in postcolonial life-writing, is necessarily evidence to support Gusdorf's strategic claims about the secondary and imitative nature of non-western life-writing. As Fanon suggests, in certain contexts, at least, and in certain periods, 'indigenous' resources are far harder to access than in others. Thus, in the French Caribbean, which he describes as having experienced 'the death and burial of its local cultural originality'[114] (in a chapter symptomatically entitled 'The Negro and Language'), the life-writer, at least in Fanon's predicament, is represented as being obliged to use what colonial culture made available: 'It was only with the appearance of Aimé Césaire that the acceptance of negritude and the statement of its claims began to be perceptible.'[115] If the situation Fanon describes threatens to render the Caribbean life-writer, linguistically speaking, 'a complete replica of the white man',[116] the operationality of racial discourse is nonetheless often stymied by perfect replication of the coloniser's language. Even without discounting the pressures to conform to publishers' demands and expectations (the Europhone arms of which industry are overwhelmingly located in the West),[117] this may shed a more sympathetic light on figures like Naipaul. Instead of seeing his lapidarily (or, depending on one's point of view, sometimes stiltedly) correct English as evidence simply of abject assimilation to the norms and values of the standard forms of metropolitan culture, it is possible – theoretically at least – to argue that he is enacting Rushdie's conviction that: 'To conquer English may be to complete the process of making ourselves free.'[118] Equally, in the context of Doran's threats against Equiano for talking 'too much English' (*IN*: 94), the 'white' discourse of *The Interesting Narrative* can be seen as defying the expectation that its author should discourse in what Fanon calls 'pidgin-nigger'. And, as Lyn Innes suggests, Seacole's emphasis on 'correct' expression of the Queen's English turns the tables on many of those who consider themselves her racial/cultural superiors, precisely by emphasising their own 'broken English'.[119]

7 Political Self-representation in postcolonial life-writing

Attempts to constitute autobiography as a *literary* mode in the first two phases of Auto/biography Studies were governed by the predominant systems of aesthetic criticism, from genre theory itself to New Criticism. In contrast to a nascent Marxist literary criticism, these generally divorced literature 'proper' from politics, which was deemed to threaten the instrumentalisation of a supposedly autonomous and sacrosanct aesthetic sphere. For Auto/biography Studies, the effects of these emphases were profound. As was seen in Chapter 5, Misch hierarchised autobiographical forms according to their inverse proportion 'worldly' preoccupations.[1] Despite claiming that autobiography expresses a concern which has been of good use in colonialism, Gusdorf also draws a distinction between canonical 'masterpieces' and the memoirs of 'heads of government or generals, ministers of state', largely on the basis that the latter aim simply to provide 'posthumous *propaganda* for posterity'.[2] As seen in the previous chapter, for Spengemann, writing at the beginning of the third phase of Auto/biography Studies, 'poetic self-expression' represents the supreme development of the genre after successive stages of historical self-exploration and philosophical self-scrutiny.[3] Such criteria shed further light on the exclusion of women's life-writing from the canon and its marginalisation within traditional Auto/biography Studies. As Sauling Wong suggests, the traditional privileging of the private/personal over the public/political domains is inimical to the sub-genre's preoccupation with a variety of woman-centred engagements of instrumental kinds.[4]

As a result of these emphases in mainstream Auto/biography Studies, some feminists regard canonical autobiography as a conservative form with what Evans calls 'a deep commitment' to prevailing social orders.[5] However, others strongly disagree. Swindells, for example, suggests that even in the canon, 'the autobiographer's voice is often … oppositional, heretical or radical'.[6] Consequently, many colleagues have insisted that auto/biography has progressive political potential. At the opposite extreme to Evans, Whitlock claims that the genre is 'fundamental to the struggle among individuals and groups, to the constant creation of what it means to be human and the rights that fall from that'.[7] Feminist Auto/biography Studies has identified the political purchase of women's life-writing, more specifically, in a number of areas. First, it emphasises the agency involved in appropriation of this hitherto privileged and exclusive cultural form, which thereby offers women the opportunity to transform themselves from objects of representation to Subjects of self-representation.[8] However, mindful that an unthinking insertion in this traditionally patriarchal genre might constitute the co-option – if not deformation – of the subjectivity of women, Gilmore locates their resistant agency above all in experimentations with established rules of the genre, as discussed in Chapter 5.[9]

From this perspective, issues of women's discursive representation and location in patriarchal cultures are inevitably political and contemporary women's life-writing is thereby willy-nilly connected to the public sphere.[10] As Chapter 4 suggested, one should not underestimate the importance of finding new discursive locations for hitherto marginalised auto/biographical Subjects, or the critique of patriarchal representations which arises from their investment. Nonetheless, one needs to draw a distinction between the *cultural* politics of contemporary western women's life-writing and more concrete political programmes and mobilisations. Thus, whereas Sidonie Smith celebrates the emergence of new 'standpoint epistemologies' which the experimental nature of contemporary women's life-writing makes available,[11] Maroula Joannou has analysed Suffragette auto/biography as a specific instrument in early twentieth-century agitation for votes for women.[12] Such emphases impact upon established conceptions of autobiographical form in sometimes unexpected ways. For example, according to Lejeune, autobiography is defined by its *retrospective* gaze. By contrast, life-writing which embraces the kind of politics represented by Suffragism looks forward as much as it does to the past, to a future where its aspirations will be realised.[13] In turn, similar arguments have been made in relation to both western minoritarian and postcolonial women's life-writing.[14]

Once again, Fanon's *Black Skin* anticipates many claims about the political potential of the genre. On the one hand, it persistently seeks new *discursive* positions in the postcolonial context to release the colonised from their psycho-affective sense of 'crushing objecthood'.[15] To this end, Fanon seeks forms of 'recognition' which will fully acknowledge both his own humanity and that of those he speaks for. But this is not a passive process of 'bondsman' waiting for the 'master' to become enlightened. Fanon's discursive politics segue into a demand for more concrete forms of action by virtue of his perception that, faced with a recalcitrant 'master', the colonised must 'fight for his freedom'.[16] There is thus a clear continuity between this aspect of Fanon's auto/biographical work and the call for armed revolution against the colonial polity in *The Wretched of the Earth*. In this respect, *Black Skin* is 'future-oriented' in the manner discussed above. Indeed, Fanon insists that both his personal 'disalienation' and its collective equivalent will only be achieved by a refusal to accept the present as 'definitive'.[17]

In the rest of this chapter, I will explore some of these issues in relation to two examples of Palestinian life-writing. This raises important conceptual problems in relation to the critical frameworks employed in this text. Most obviously, the case of Palestine reminds one graphically that much of the world is not yet post-colonial, even in the technical sense of being formally independent. Indeed, in many respects – according to the evidence of Palestine life-writing – Palestine is a classic (as well as, in some senses, unique) example of ongoing 'settler colonialism' in which are visible many of the ideologies and techniques of conquest and repression which characterised earlier phases of western imperialism. This includes the wholesale theft of the indigenous population's natural resources (notably, in the case of the Occupied Territories, Palestinians' best agricultural land and water; compare 'settler' Kenya, South Africa or Australia); the violent political repression of that population, including systematic assassination of its political leaders (and targeted violence against outsiders attempting to alleviate the suffering of ordinary Palestinians[18]); the denial of basic human rights to the subjugated;[19] the physical redistribution of the population, notably by means of the 'apartheid (separation)' wall and 'defence' infrastructure,[20] and the transfer of large numbers of the invaders' population into the conquered territories, a practice forbidden in international law by the fourth Geneva Convention (1949), which Israel signed up to in 1951.[21]

Palestine and Palestinian life-writing, more specifically, are under-developed fields of inquiry within both Postcolonial and Auto/biography Studies. While Israel–Palestine is occasionally fleetingly alluded to as a site of colonial contestation within the former field,[22] it is little short of astonishing that so little subsequent critical work has built on the foundations provided by Said's *The Question of Palestine* (1979), published more than a generation ago. If I may myself be autobiographical for a moment at this late stage of my book, I too have been responsible in allowing Palestine and the cultural-political issues it raises to remain largely invisible in my field,[23] principally because of what I now regard as unfounded anxieties about being misunderstood as anti-Semitic, a change which the Zionist lobby seeks programmatically to confuse with legitimate criticism of Israel as a colonial polity. What follows is therefore in part an attempt to remedy the defects of my earlier (minor) contributions to defining the contours of Postcolonial Studies. Ironically, perhaps, the situation is marginally better in Auto/biography Studies. The past twenty years or so have witnessed several engagements with life-writing by Palestinian women. Stanton's *Female Autograph* initiated this project by including a short commentary on one example of such work, which was reproduced in her collection of essays.[24] As indicated in the Introduction, Janet Gunn provides a substantial discussion of Leila Khaled and, more recently, Whitlock analyses 'Saoud's' *Burned Alive* in the context of her important discussion of 'tainted testimony'.[25]

Perhaps more ironically still, postcolonial life-writing itself has contributed to the general occlusion of Palestinian concerns. The process begins with Fanon's *Black Skin*, which is heavily indebted to Sartre's *Anti-Semite and Jew* (1946) and other anti-anti-Semitic writings for its anatomy of the psychopathologies of (post) colonialism. Like Césaire, Fanon constructs his conception of the colonial predicament of the Black man partly by analogy to the traditional position of Jews in European society, a strategy structured by deep sympathy for the appalling fate which that eventually entailed in the Second World War. Conversely, *Black Skin* demonstrates an already well-developed interest in the Arab, both in metropolitan France ('with his hunted look, suspicious, on the run'[26]) and elsewhere, identifications which were to famously lead Fanon to participate in the armed struggle for Algerian independence. Despite this, and his solidarity with other colonised peoples, including the Vietnamese, *Black Skin* makes no mention of Palestine's indigenous inhabitants, nor of the price they paid for the establishment of the Jewish State. Instead, he approvingly anticipates the emergence of a new kind of Jew in Israel.[27]

If this founding text of Postcolonial Studies allows its sympathy with (post-) Holocaust Jewry to over-ride any acknowledgement of the renewed colonial predicament of many Palestinians after the collapse of the British Mandate, later postcolonial life-writing at times explicitly endorses Zionist mythography. The prime example in this monograph is *Among the White Moon Faces*, which records Shirley Lim's argument with her nominally Muslim boyfriend Iqbal about the significance of the June 1967 War, when Israel launched a surprise simultaneous attack on a number of its neighbours and occupied East Jerusalem, the West Bank and Gaza. While contentiously claimed as a pre-emptive war (illegal under international law[28]), the Israelis used the occasion to prosecute their strategic ambitions – stymied in the conflict of 1947–48 – of conquering all that remained of former Mandate Palestine.

Lim's grasp of events so far from Malaysia is clearly shaky (for example, she describes the conflict as 'the Seven Days' War'[29] – adding an extra twenty-four hours to Arab resistance to Israel's *Blitzkrieg*). Rather than seeing it as an act of Israeli aggression, as Iqbal suggests is the case, Lim comments: 'I was convinced that the efforts to destroy the Jewish date [*sic*] were anti-Semitic and historically related to the Holocaust.'[30] As she readily admits, however, her emotional identification with Israel owes less to an understanding of what was actually at stake in the region than to her own ethnic-cultural position in Malaysia: 'The hostility I felt at his criticism of Israel was strangely personal, as if it threatened my own being.'[31] As Chapter 4 suggested, even as a member of the highly-assimilated *peranakan* diaspora, Lim feels under increasing pressure within a Muslim-Malay-dominated society which will eventually carry out its own pogroms against her community – events with implicit parallels to those leading up to the Holocaust.

Yet the fundamental incoherence of Lim's stance on Israel–Palestine is evident in the disconnection between the last sentence quoted and what immediately follows: 'The prospect of studying with Irving Howe at Brandeis appealed to me as a strenuous counter-Americanism to Iqbal's Berkeley laissez faire.'[32] It is impossible to disentangle this. Brandeis, while 'a college that was homogeneously Anglo American and Jewish [*sic*]',[33] is here linked to 'counter-Americanism'. Asymmetrically, 'Berkeley laissez faire' (whatever that means) becomes associated with anti-Semitism, on no stronger grounds, apparently, than Iqbal's years of study there. Perhaps more significantly, Lim makes no retrospective adjustment to her interpretation as a jejune MA student of the Israel–Palestine problem. A number of explanations for this offer themselves (though all must remain speculative), including a continuing conviction of the rightness of her original position, her marriage to a (secular) Jew by whom she falls pregnant, formation in academic life in Brandeis or her life-long location within what has remained a predominantly pro-Israel US academy.

Palestinian life-writing can thus be understood in the first instance as an attempt to mitigate the invisibility of Palestinians in accounts as diverse as Fanon's and Lim's, as well as across postcolonial literature[34] and swathes of western regimes of representation. Since 1948 – and more particularly since 1967 – the sub-genre has flourished in direct proportion to Israel's ever-tightening stranglehold on Palestinian lives and resources. One might even argue that it has become the major branch of contemporary Palestinian literature, at least in the eyes of those in the West. This is no doubt partly because there is a greater demand for it there than for Palestinian fiction or poetry. Many Palestinian life-writers, including Amiry,[35] also write in English with an eye on international audiences because therein lies the only possibility of influencing the international public sphere to bring pressure on Israel to give up its territorial gains of 1967 and to redress the depredations it has inflicted on Palestinians since 1948.

Indeed, as the analysis below will demonstrate, the claims made in Palestinian life-writing for Fanonian forms of recognition are often negotiated at the most basic existential level, below the radar of debates about basic individual rights, let alone collective emancipation. For example, Ghada Karmi records how, even by the early 1950s, 'When people asked me where I came from and I answered, "Palestine," they would respond with, "Did you say Pakistan?"'[36] Equally, many of Edward Said's American friends 'assumed that being Palestinian was the equivalent of something mythological like a unicorn'.[37] It is out of this predicament of being a 'non-person',[38] that Palestinian life-writing so often emerges in the first instance. Further, it characteristically reflects the bitter truth of Nietzsche's dictum that 'we become conscious of ourselves only after certain injuries have been inflicted'.[39]

Edward Said, *Out of Place* (1999)

A preliminary reading might suggest that Said's text itself seems 'out of place' alongside the substantial critical and political engagements with issues of colonialism – and its effects in Palestine more specifically – on which his public profile largely rests. It offers no sustained critique of post-1948 Israel–Palestine, nor any practical programme for nation-building of the kind encountered in the life-writing of Gandhi or C.L.R. James, for example. Instead, *Out of Place* can be read as a seemingly unexceptional, even rather traditional, example of literary autobiography written by an intellectual located since the age of 15 in the West and conversant with the conventions of the genre as it developed there – in which the political dimensions of the idea of 'self-representation' are also, as has been seen, generally 'out of place'. As Tobias Döring reminds us,[40] Said's debut academic monograph was *Joseph Conrad and the Fiction of Autobiography* (1966), a text in which he demonstrates familiarity with canonical western autobiographical texts like Rousseau's *Confessions* and Newman's *Apologia*. Conforming to Said's description of such work, his own text might be interpreted initially as primarily 'a chronicle of states of mind … an attempt to render the individual energy of one's life'.[41] Much of the 'energy' of Said's memoir is devoted to exploring ideas around being 'out of place', as his subject-formation unfolds, in what appear to be essentially existential and psychological terms.

A good example of the seemingly non-political meanings of being 'out of place' is the author's uncomfortable relationship with his body, an element of auto-biographical identity whose importance was calibrated in Chapter 3. In contrast to the material analysed there, however, Said's body does not allegorise issues in the public domain through its inscription with specifically ethnic or national sig-nifications. Rather, it bears primarily moral meanings once the author discovers that, for his father, Body and character are interchangeable (*OP*: 50). Wadie's attempt to mould the latter aspect of his son's identity is often pursued through attention to the child's supposed physical shortcomings. Through a process of 'virile bullying' (*OP*: 56), which encompasses work on posture, canings, regimes of exercise and a humiliating system of surveillance to inhibit masturbation, the boy is conditioned to 'proper' manliness as Wadie understands it. Rather than strengthening Said's sense of Self, however, such measures make him 'even more awkward and uncertain', not only of his moral but physical identity (*OP*: 67). As this suggests, the writer's early feeling of being 'out of place' can in large measure be attributed to a particular family's inter-personal dynamics (compare Lim). The insecurity engendered by the recurrent tension between son and mother, for example, is not linked directly to Hilda's experience of, or attitude towards, colonialism – whether British, American or Israeli – but arises from an ambivalent personality which is, seemingly, inconsistently sensitive to the child's emotional needs.

The apparently self-absorbed (even, at times, self-pitying) focus on the travails of a misunderstood prodigy is perhaps what led one reviewer to describe *Out of Place* as 'a mostly apolitical childhood narrative',[42] an interpretation Said himself has seemed to legitimise. In 'Between Worlds', for example, he describes the text as 'a memoir of my early – that is, pre-political life'.[43] However, in the Preface to *Out of Place*, Said acknowledges that 'my political writings about the Palestinian situation … must surely have fed into this memoir surreptitiously' (*OP*: xiii). At the very least, *Out of Place* anatomises the affective ground from which the adult Said's political engagements grow. Thus, family relationships which seem to con-stitute a rigorously private space of identity-formation are connected, in the first instance, by metaphorical association, with the varieties of colonialism by which Said will later become so preoccupied. For example, the kind of violent discipline, which Said receives from his father is paralleled in the British-run GPS (Giza Preparatory School), which provides his 'first extended contact with colonial authority' (*OP*: 42). Elsewhere, the author describes his relationship with his mother as like a 'colony to a metropole' (*OP*: 60). Many of the principal factors which contribute to Said's sense of being 'out of place', however, derive more obviously and directly from the colonial milieu in which he grows up. One illustration of this is Said's chronic discomfort about his name, the most basic marker of identity. Christened after the Prince of Wales, son of the 'King-Emperor' George

V, 'Edward' (the name is often placed in inverted commas, as if constantly pro-visional, if not under the threat of erasure) co-exists uneasily with the Arab family name (the genealogy of which Said is in any case radically uncertain about, given that his paternal grandfather's surname is Ibrahim). A motif of the early part of the text is Said's coveting of the apparently solid identities conferred by more 'natural' names. For example, at GPS, one trigger of his sense of exclusion is a conviction that, in contrast to his own, the 'enviably authentic names' of the English children who predominate there 'were just *right*' (*OP*: 39, 42).

The tension between the influences of the West and the pull of 'indigenous' identifications which this exemplifies is familiar from many texts studied in this monograph. As in *Aké*, *Among the White Moon Faces* and *Fantasia*, for example, it is particularly evident in the issue of language. Said attributes his 'primal instability' (*OP*: 4) in part to the fact that he is unsure whether English or Arabic is his mother tongue. Hilda speaks both to him during infancy, peppering each with diction from the other. Symptomatically, Said's tongue becomes one of the bodily/moral organs with which his parents become most concerned (*OP*: 68). Even when he appears to have resolved the dilemma, it returns to haunt him. Thus, having decided that Arabic is indeed his 'mother tongue' (*OP*: 82), he feels bound to conceal this fact in order to press his claims to belonging at CSAC (Cairo School for American Children). The effects of Said's western education, furthermore, tend towards the disorientation experienced by Lim and Djebar than the enthusiastic hybridity of Soyinka. Thrown off-balance by these conflicting (self-)identifications, the child Said yearns for a stable identity of the kind dis-cussed in Chapter 1, wishing that 'we could have been all-Arab, or all-European and American, or all-Orthodox Christian, or all-Muslim, or all-Egyptian, and so on' (*OP*: 5). To a considerable degree, *Out of Place* is the narrative of how Said learns to overcome his need for such a singular and rooted identity and, more specifically, to appreciate that being Palestinian need exclude none of these identities.

The link between the apparently exclusively personal sphere of experience on which Said primarily focuses and the formation of his later political persona is also evident in the growing theme of rebellion as the text unfolds. Growing into adolescence, Said becomes increasingly aware of a turbulent 'underground' Self (*OP*: 284) which is largely repressed at home and derided at school. Initially, the author 'derived no strength, only embarrassment and discomfort' (*OP*: 90) from what his family name represents. Gradually, however, this aspect of his identity is accommodated. As Bryan Turner suggests: '"Said" is "Edward's"' Other, the person for whom *Out of Place* provides a journey of discovery and recovery.'[44] This process is plotted in terms of a progressive revaluation of that marginalised side of himself. Indeed, it comes to provide the grounds for resistance ('under-ground' connoting the kind of guerrilla strategy which characterises his rebellion) to the parental regime which seeks to turn him into the mimic Englishman 'Edward', meekly accepting his place in 'a mock little European group' (*OP*: 75). It also anchors his revolt against the system of colonial discipline associated par-ticularly with the aptly-named Victoria College in Cairo. Forbidden to speak anything but English there, 'Said' increasingly asserts himself as a refractory presence: 'What I had formerly hidden at CSAC became a proud insurrectionary gesture' which pits the author 'against a wounded colonial power' (*OP*: 184, 186).

This 'underground Self', first coded ethnically as an 'Arab identity' (*OP*: 90), is slowly reconceptualised as a specifically Palestinian one. Progress towards the goal of national identification is slow and uneven. As one would expect of a young child, at the outset of the text, issues of ethnic affiliation are not much on Said's mind. Of his mother, for example, he comments: 'I hadn't then any idea ... who, in a national sense of the phrase, she was' (*OP*: 5). The author's slow political awakening also owes something to one of the defining initial characteristics of the family home, its exclusion of political debate. Thus, even the Second World War barely impinges: 'The political, to say nothing of the military, meanings of our situation, were beyond me at age six and a half' (*OP*: 26). The arrival of Palestinian refugees in Cairo after the *nakba* is initially represented as a problem which does not hugely concern the immediate family, although Wadie provides employment for some of them. Celebrating his twelfth birthday in Jerusalem in November 1947, Said still has little idea about 'our conflict with the Zionists and the British' (*OP*: 107). Moreover, when the family leaves Palestine for the last time the following month, there is no hint of coercion, although serious violence had by this time already erupted. Indeed, during July 1948, as the *nakba* reaches its climax, the Saids are found on a luxury liner en route to New York (where Wadie is bound for medical treatment), seemingly oblivious to events in their homeland. Once arrived in America to study, it is therefore little surprise that the adolescent Said is initially not much preoccupied by the fate of the people with whom he comes to identify most passionately in later life.

Nonetheless, the seeds of Said's future national identifications are sown early in his life. As waves of Palestinian refugees arrive in Cairo after 1948, Said's aunt Nabiha takes responsibility for their welfare and she discusses their plight on visits to the Saids. Later, Said looks back on her commitment as a crucial stage in the reorientation of his identity. While 'a scarcely conscious, essentially unknowing witness' (*OP*: 114) of the effects of the *nakba*, Said slowly overcomes his parents' prohibition on discussing the events. Increasingly irritated by what he discovers in the US about Truman's support for Zionism, Said is radicalised by the Suez war of 1956 (despite the destruction of the family business during the Egyptian nationalist riots of 1952) and takes his first tentative steps as a political essayist on behalf of the Arab cause. The Six-Day War proves decisive in his trajectory towards new (self-)identifications: 'I was no longer the same person after 1967; the shock of that war drove me back to where it had all started ... I subsequently entered the newly transformed Middle Eastern landscape as part of the Palestinian movement' (*OP*: 293). Thus, as well as being an account of the formation of a gifted artistic and critical temperament, *Out of Place* is also clearly the narrative enactment of Said's 'growing sense of Palestinian identity' (*OP*: 195). To this extent, the text is consonant with the many postcolonial writings, fictional as well as non-fictional, which plot the formation of the individual protagonist in allegorical relation to the emergence of collective national aspirations to an independent identity.

Arguably, the indirectness of Said's approach to the Israel–Palestine problem in fact enhances the political charge of *Out of Place*. It is in the 'curiously unremarkable' (*OP*: 20), even banal, detail of diurnal existence described so fully (even, at times, tediously, for example the interminable summer holiday in Ramallah), that the western reader gains some measure of the scale of what has been lost by so many Palestinians through the willed effort of Zionism. It is in this sense, too, that Said can claim the kind of representativeness discussed in Chapter 2. Despite his minority religious confession, his privileged class position, the fact that he inherited his father's US citizenship, the family's voluntary removal to Cairo in 1929 (well before the establishment of the Jewish State), and his exceptional cultural capital and celebrity in the West, Said's experience of rupture is only too typical of his people, even if it is also less dramatic in origin than that of the hundreds of thousands who were ethnically cleansed at the point of a bayonet. Alon Confino comments, in an otherwise perceptive article, that 'Said is the only person who is represented as out of place, with the exception of Palestinian refugees.'[45] If this is a criticism, it is to miss the whole point of *Out of Place* as a representative narrative of the material and affective experience of exile of a people.

The claim that Said's memoir is 'mostly apolitical' is further contradicted by attempts to discredit the narrative. The most notorious of these was offered by Justus Weiner, an American Jew who emigrated to Israel and 'settled' in Jerusalem in 1981 and, at the time of writing his piece, worked for the Israeli state.[46] Weiner's response to Said's earlier fragmentary accounts of his life (his piece actually anticipates *Out of Place*[47]), published in the far-right organ *Commentary* (which had already defamed Said as 'the Professor of Terror' in 1989[48]), is articulated in essentially the same terms which have shaped much Zionist discourse about Palestinians. By basing his critique on the assertion that Said was never a 'proper' resident of Jerusalem, Weiner seeks to 'empty' the city of one more Palestinian with claims to belonging there (one thing Weiner does not contest is that Jerusalem was Said's place of birth). He thereby attempts to perform something like a discursive equivalent of the ethnic cleansing of the capital of Mandate Palestine which began in 1947–48 (Said's cousins are driven out of West Jerusalem one by one) and which has gained renewed momentum since the Israeli conquest of East Jerusalem in 1967, to make room for the likes of Weiner. The result is that the proportion of Arab inhabitants of Jerusalem has fallen catastrophically in the past four decades, as the Jewish State seeks to make the capital it claims correspondingly Jewish. Thus, on his return visit Said can barely recognise the Talbiyah where he spent parts of his childhood at his aunt's home.

Despite the pain clearly expressed in such episodes, several critics have commented on Said's refusal to simply bewail the past. In this regard, *Out of Place* is consonant with remarks he makes in *Reflections on Exile*: 'What has been left behind may either be mourned, or it can be used to provide a different set of lenses.'[49] In counterpoint to the sense of loss implied in Said's 'crippling sense of estrangement'[50] (not only in America but sometimes in Egypt, too), *Out of Place* constructs a space from which a new category 'Palestinian' can emerge in a willed act of resistance to 'a condition legislated to deny dignity – to deny an identity'[51] to those like himself. To this extent, the experience of Said reconfigures the *nakba* into something much more positive and enabling. Equally, as Chapter 1 argued, Said's search for a Palestinian identity is premised on a critique of traditional ideas of the 'solid' or sovereign Self. While some might see Said's conception of subjectivity as too postmodern to provide a sufficiently stable basis either for Palestinian identity to ground itself, or for political action in its name, it could be argued conversely that the writer enlarges the possibility of solidarity by affirming hybridity and multiplicity as the 'essence' of the category 'Palestinian' (compare Chaudhuri's conception of 'Indianness'). In this sense it is counterposed against both the 'extraordinary homogenizing power of American life' (*OP*: 233) and the racial discourses of Zionism, on the one hand, and, on the other, by implication at least, the singularisation of identity represented by Egyptian nationalism (compare El Saadawi) which emerged in part as a reaction to the establishment of the state of Israel. Prior to this event, Said suggests, the Levant – from Lebanon to Egypt – was an extraordinarily diverse and variegated inter-weaving of cultures, *including* Jewish ones (compare El Saadawi and Djebar). Indeed, in Said's own case, it is remarkable how important Jewish intellectuals, notably Auerbach and Adorno, are to his self-conception as a spokesperson for the Palestinian cause.

To this extent, Said insists that 'Palestinian' is a contingent identity. The theme of the fictions of genealogical filiation is announced in the very first sentence of the text: 'All families invent their parents and children, give each of them a story, character, fate, and even a language' (*OP*: 3). Later we see Wadie energetically engaged in the 'practice of self-making' (*OP*: 10), a description which applies equally to the Self constructed in *Out of Place*. Later, Said comments on the 'contrived' nature of each 'regulated prerehearsed scene, which we performed' (*OP*: 75–6) in the family films his father takes, creating different versions of 'Edward'. The text suggests that similar processes apply for nations and peoples, with Khalil Raad's photos, 'arranged' with an 'even more demanding rigor' than his father's, providing the 'richest archival resource' (*OP*: 76–7) for future generations of Palestinians to anchor their identity within. Later, Said refers to Khalil Beidas, whose novels 'contributed to the *construction* of a Palestinian national identity, particularly in its encounter with the incoming Zionist settlers' (*OP*: 114; my emphasis).

Thus, the photographs which illustrate *Out of Place* perhaps work in a more complex way than Döring suggests. While lending documentary 'authority'[52] to Said's personal narrative of his heritage, the pictures also suggest that Palestinian identity is something enacted, not given or simply there to be recorded. The example of the young Said and his sister Rosy in Palestinian dress, taken in Jerusalem in 1941, a photograph on which Döring does not comment, is a good example of this emphasis. The portrait is clearly posed, in an artfully arranged set (the blank backcloth strongly suggests it was taken in a studio) replete with ethnic signifiers, as a (parentally-guided) *performance* of affiliation rather than being simply a mechanical reproduction of filiation. This is all the more obvious given its juxtaposition on the same page with the relatively naturalistic photo of the two children in westernised attire on their Egyptian apartment terrace. Such a plastic and multiplicitous conception of Palestinian selfhood remains true to the spirit of the plurality of identities, ethnic and religious, which historically constituted Palestine. Said's version of national allegory is clear, as *Out of Place* thereby promotes not just a conception of autobiographical Self in which this variety of identities 'require no reconciling, no harmonizing' (*OP*: 295; compare Chapter 1) but, by implication, also imagines a Palestinian polity based on the same dynamic principles.

Much has been made of Said's emphasis on the importance of being 'out of place' in order to perform 'secular' intellectual work (compare Chapter 4), both in this memoir and earlier writings, notably *Representations of the Intellectual* (1994). This has led Turner to claim that *Out of Place* is primarily an allegory of the conditions desirable for the modern intellectual to operate effectively, if not, as Confino claims, a 'parable for the modern, or postmodern condition'.[53] In a text which lays such stress on plurality of identity, these interpretations are certainly legitimate and they further reinforce another key lesson of Said's criticism, that the meanings of texts depend in part on when, where and by whom they are read. Within the context of this monograph, however, Said's attachment to being 'out of place' primarily represents the performance of political solidarity and affiliation (see Chapter 2). For Said cannot claim to have solved 'the enigma of arrival' – or to have found any secure kind of 'home' (contrast Lim) – as long as the vast majority of his fellow-nationals remain in exile or under a brutal and illegal military Occupation.

Suad Amiry, *Sharon and My Mother-in Law: Ramallah Diaries* (2003–4)

There are many convergences between Said's text and Amiry's. For example, both were explicitly written 'as a form of therapy'[54] to mitigate traumatic events (in Said's case, the diagnosis of leukaemia, in Amiry's the Israeli re-invasion of Ramallah, in 2001–2). In each, furthermore, trauma is expressed partly in the theme of sleep/lessness. If Said's chronic insomnia is connected only implicitly to the fate of Palestine since 1948, Amiry's hypersomnia is linked directly with the recent history of her nation. Sleep proves a particularly useful way to kill time during the curfews which are such a regular feature of the illegal Occupation by Israel since 1967 of what remained of the former British Mandate. (This rump is theoretically comprised of modern-day east Jerusalem, the West Bank and – though it features only marginally in *Sharon* – Gaza, all of which fell under either Jordanian or Egyptian control after 1948: the rash of illegal settlements peopled by nearly 450,000 'settlers', most either Zionist or religious fundamentalists, has severely diminished this territory).[55] If the motif of sleep/lessness reinforces the thesis of Chapter 3 about the somatic effects of psycho-social realities, both texts also reaffirm the argument of Chapter 4 concerning the role played by issues of (dis)location in postcolonial subjectivity. Thus, both authors undertake a pilgrimage to their ancestral family home in what is now Israel, although in Amiry's case the experience is so painful that the attempt is aborted. Like Said, Amiry speaks for and to (sometimes critically) the collective to which their authors belong. This is consonant with the engagement of both writers at a high level in Palestinian politics. Said served on the Palestinian National Council, while *Sharon* both alludes to Amiry's involvement in aborted 1990 peace negotiations in Washington and describes her appearance on a *CBS* current affairs programme, to explain to a US audience the effects on Palestinians of the 'apartheid (separation)' wall. At the same time, Said's and Amiry's texts demonstrate their atypicality as Palestinians in certain respects, both authors being academics from wealthy backgrounds (Amiry's mother even insists on weekly grocery deliveries to Amman from her home city of Damascus!), as well as secular and leftist.

However, there are also important differences between *Out of Place* and *Sharon* which derive in the first instance from the different life-experiences of each writer. While, as has been seen, Said was born in Jerusalem and belonged to an already voluntarily expatriated family, Amiry was born outside Palestine, as a consequence of her family's expulsion from Jaffa during the 1948 ethnic cleansings.[56] Equally, while she also studied in the West, Amiry returned to the illegally Occupied territories to help rebuild Palestinian society, partly through lecturing in the Architecture Faculty at Birzeit University and partly through work for RIWAQ, an organisation dedicated to the conservation of what remains of Palestine's architectural heritage. In contrast to Said's account of the psychological and cultural consequences of exile far from Palestine, Amiry is thereby able to offer a vividly material account of everyday life in the West Bank under the jackboot of Occupation.

In the fashion of *testimonio*, *Sharon* pulls no punches in detailing the mechanisms by which Israel seeks to subjugate the West Bank and prosecute its aim of making a Palestinian state an impossibility (*SMM*: 194) by creating apartheid-style *Bantustans* separated by endless checkpoints (over 300 at the time Amiry was writing, in an area the size of Greater London). To use the title of one of Assia Djebar's autobiographical works, the region has been transformed into 'so vast a prison' and Amiry's account of incarceration during endless curfews (at one point the West Bank is under lock-down for 36 consecutive days) invites comparison with texts like Behan's *Borstal Boy* (see Chapter 2), Soyinka's *The Man Died* (1972) or Ngugi's *Detained* (1981) as examples of postcolonial prison autobiography. The casual brutalities of Occupation are often most tellingly revealed in passing details – references to the gratuitous shooting of a horse by a vindictive Israeli soldier, a premature birth induced by spiteful delay of the mother at a checkpoint, the looting and vandalism during Israeli raids on private homes, the belated issue of out-of-date gas-masks by the military authorities to Palestinians when the region becomes vulnerable to Saddam's rockets. The illegal Occupation deforms every aspect of life, notably through the system of permits determining nationality, residency, travel, even marriage rights, which inevitably recall the 'pass' laws of apartheid-era South Africa. Amiry's experience of the injustices and humiliations which this regime engenders includes being turned back from her own wedding party when an Israeli (woman) soldier tears up her permit to travel, leaving her husband stranded on the other side of the Jordan (Israel generally forbids Palestinians marrying Palestinians-in-exile from bringing their spouses to live on Israeli-controlled land).

Ultimately, as *Sharon* repeatedly demonstrates, the illegal Occupation rests on brute force. A colleague is badly beaten by the Israeli army for allegedly encouraging a demonstration and a policeman acquaintance is shot in (the back of) the head by Israeli soldiers. Amiry visits the hospital in Ramallah where Jad is presumed to lie only to find a mass pit dug for 29 victims of the first two days of the 2001 re-invasion, whom the Occupation army will allow neither to be restored to their families nor buried in the cemetery. Amiry is herself often in fear of her life and actually comes under fire when approaching Nablus to assess the damage done to the town's architecture during an Israeli blitz. The affective consequences of such oppression are potentially devastating, even for someone as relatively empowered as Amiry. The seemingly inevitable internalisation of these material realities is expressed in her constant struggle against 'the mental and psychological barriers, checkpoints and separation walls I had personally built in and around myself and my life, in besieged Ramallah' (*SMM*: 189). Fittingly the text ends with a visit to the zoo in Qalqiliah, which becomes a potent metaphor for the general predicament of Palestinians under Occupation.

Amiry's account further differs from Said's because of her gender. *Sharon*'s critique of the illegal Occupation from a female perspective opens up a Palestinian women's sphere of experience largely absent from *Out of Place*. For example, the brief lifting of curfew involves a riotous (and poignantly hilarious) rush through the supermarket to buy enough to last until the next time women are allowed out to forage for their families. The particular vulnerability of women during the re-invasion becomes further apparent in Amiry's accounts of the predicament of her widowed mother-in-law and her own parlous situation during her husband Salim's absences. This suggests that Occupation is experienced differently according to gender. Stranded in her apartment immediately next to Arafat's compound, Um Salim is simply too vulnerable to be left alone to the mercy of the Israeli army, despite the danger that her property will be ransacked. Braving the encircling Israeli tanks and trigger-happy squaddies, Amiry steels herself to bring her mother-in-law safely to her own home.

As this episode suggests, *Sharon* also demonstrates how Amiry's gender opens avenues of resistance denied to male Palestinians, who can move around even less easily in such circumstances. Indeed, many of Amiry's acts of subversion take place in the absence of Salim, who is occasionally represented as being more respectful towards the Occupation forces (perhaps unsurprisingly, given that one in four of all Palestinian males have at some time in their life been imprisoned by the invaders). The illegal Occupation is represented not only as racist but deeply patriarchal. Thus, Amiry speculates that she is not at first summoned to sign the anti-PLO statement required of male academic colleagues because 'being a woman helped me not to be taken seriously' (*SMM*: 29). Nonetheless Israeli patriarchy offers Amiry numerous opportunities to express a resistant agency. The very first page of the text describes her uncooperative attitude towards security officers at Lod airport. Insisting that she has simply been to Britain to go dancing, because the innocent truth that she was visiting friends would entail hours of intrusive interrogation, Amiry is threatened with arrest. She responds by threatening to make a scene in an arrivals hall full of unthinking foreign tourists 'coming to enjoy the sun and beautiful, relaxing shores of Israel' (*SMM*: 10). On another occasion she convinces Captain Rafi to hand over her ID card by threatening to throw a hysterical fit in his office. Nonetheless, despite these illustrations of one of 'the weak points' (*SMM*: 29) of the Occupation regime, Amiry reminds her readers that Palestinian women (and children) often pay the ultimate price for Israel's territorial ambitions. While en route to rescue Um Salim, she unnerves herself by remembering one woman shot dead by Occupation forces as she was leaving Ramallah hospital and another in Bethlehem shot in cold blood as she opened her door to Israeli soldiers.

Exceptionally effective as Amiry is at evoking the crushing burdens under which Palestinians have to live as the result of the illegal Occupation, like Said, she is by no means an unreflecting nationalist. Indeed, it is remarkable how often her humanity and common sense over-ride what one might assume to be the 'politically correct' line among Palestinian activists towards the history of ethnic cleansing, deportation and Occupation suffered by their people. For example, her memories of childhood visits to Jerusalem revolve not around iconic symbols of its Arab identity like the Dome of the Rock, but Zalatimo's ice-cream parlour. Equally, her mournful anticipation of the visit to the family home in Jaffa is interrupted by anxieties as to whether her guide, the newly-met Salim, will still find her attractive. Further, Amiry frankly admits the strain which solidarity with her mother-in-law entails while Salim is away. Just as Israel (re-)invades Ramallah, so the frail, forgetful and fastidious Um Salim ends by 'occupying' Amiry's home, adding a new level of inconvenience and disruption to the military Occupation.

Amiry also admits discomfort with certain political commitments demanded of her. For example, she eventually agrees to sign the document disavowing the PLO in order to be allowed to remain in the Occupied Territories with her husband. This might be regarded initially as evidence of Amiry's self-interest over-riding more pressing considerations, or even complicity with Israel. However, her confession is not only a symptom of honesty but reveals the limitations of certain male forms of resistance. By refusing to concede to Israeli blackmail (which in any case makes the signing of such documents morally meaningless), certain of her fellow-academics find themselves expelled from their homeland and thereby prevented from helping their people. Amiry also expresses impatience with the political (non-)process being conducted by male colleagues, notably in the Palestinian Authority run by Yasser Arafat (compare Said's *OP*: 214). At one point she even speculates whether he and Sharon are colluding to prevent much-needed reform of the Authority (*SMM*: 180). On occasion, indeed, the policies of the Palestinian Authority and Occupation regime are shown to mirror each other (*SMM*: 107). Further, Amiry makes no bones about recognising the existence of 'progressive Israelis' (*SMM*: 192), one of whom helps get her work published. To this extent, while it is well aware of the role played by Israeli women conscripts in the oppression of Palestinians, *Sharon* also reiterates Shirley Lim's arguments about the potential of solidarity between women of different ethnicities to transcend narrow racial and national categorisations of belonging (see Chapter 4).

At times, moreover, Amiry turns a disobliging eye on Palestinian society more generally. While acknowledging the role of blackmail, bribery and coercion as powerful strategies of Occupation, she is clearly disappointed by the degree of collaboration evident among certain Palestinians. Immediate neighbours, including Rami and Um Zahi, collude with the invaders simply out of spite towards their community, or for personal gain. Amiry also decries the divisive effects of the Palestinian gender economy, relations within which are sometimes tellingly compared to the unequal relationship between Israelis and Palestinians. Dr Hisham appears to typify the chauvinism of many West Bank males, such that the demonstration organised on International Women's Day is directed as much at Palestinian men as the male Israeli soldiers who intervene so brutally to suppress it. Amiry comments with biting irony: 'It is the *one day* when it is difficult to define who the enemy is. It is also the *one day* when Palestinian men see Israeli soldiers beat up and shoot at Palestinian women but won't do much about it' (*SMM*: 92–3). The issue of gender inequality feeds into Amiry's disquiet about the religious radicalisation of Palestinian society. While she is willing to identify herself as Muslim for strategic purposes, for example, to convince the stricken Israeli whom she drives to hospital that even Muslims might be human (*SMM*: 114), Amiry is dismayed when Um Zahi adopts the *hijab* as the price of reconciliation with her collaborationist husband.

Formally, too, *Out of Place* and *Sharon* differ significantly. As suggested in the previous section, in some ways Said's text can be construed as a classical example of intellectual autobiography. By comparison, Amiry prefers a form moulded equally by the well-established conventions of the diary/journal and the distinctively contemporary mode of email (her Preface describes how the original material was partly reorganised for the British edition). Rather than focusing primarily on the writer's formation as an individual (although one learns a good deal about her background, personality, feelings and emerging attitudes), *Sharon* is more interested in testifying to the realities of life in illegally Occupied Palestine. Drawing on these forms, Amiry accrues the benefits of an immediacy and spontaneity (particularly evident in those entries in the present tense) which lend eyewitness authority to her reportage. One of her themes is 'breaking news' (*SMM*: 145) and the slippage between the journal form and journalism itself is especially marked in her discourse.

Auto/biography Studies has traditionally patronised the diary and journal as secondary modes (partly because they are considered to be particularly 'female').[57] However, consonant with her connections to Palestinian writers like Emile Habibi and Raja Shehadeh[58] and familiarity with other Arab authors as diverse as the medieval poet Antar and Amiry's contemporary, Fatema Mernissi[59] – as well as western authors, notably Kafka (*SMM*: 24) – *Sharon* is more

subtle and self-conscious than one might anticipate from a journal/email corre-
spondence conducted under such difficult circumstances. Thus, the seeming dis-
organisation of the text in 'spatial' terms (the entries sometimes jump abruptly
from place to place) contrives to reflect the geographical dislocations historically
enforced on Palestinians. The temporal disjunctions work equally effectively. The
dates of entries move backwards and forwards, sometimes in dramatic transitions.
While also dramatising the disruptiveness of the illegal Occupation, this arrangement further serves to remind how little has changed in the more than forty years
since Israel's initial invasion of the West Bank, in pursuit of its ambition to own
all of Mandate Palestine (and, sometimes, more[60]). In a sense, then, it does not
matter in what order one reads the narrative (compare Djebar and Suleri), since
the patterns of public events and private life repeat themselves *ad nauseam* under
Occupation. Further, the forms which Amiry employs could be argued to lend
themselves to the project of cultural/political resistance in a more specific sense,
by circumventing the regime of censorship which subtends the Occupation. A
diary can be hidden with relative ease, thus escaping Israeli incursions into the
home and email can similarly elude such searches (as well as physical restrictions
imposed on Palestinians), although it is by no means invulnerable to electronic
surveillance and interference.

Also contrastive to *Out of Place* is Amiry's devastating use of the weapon of humour
as a mode both of self-defence and offence. Tonally, Said's text is comprised in
equal measure of willed optimism and melancholy, which is partly the effect, no
doubt, of the medical diagnosis which provided its immediate stimulus. By contrast *Sharon* is a consistently funny book, despite its sometimes horrendous content.
From the bathetic conjunction in the title, *Sharon and My Mother-in-Law* announces
its characteristically satirical register. Amiry has a brilliant eye for farce, not only
the black farce to which everyday life under Occupation is so often reduced, but
for the often 'absurd' mechanisms of oppression themselves. One instance is
Amiry's attempt to get her dog vaccinated. Alienated by the sexist Palestinian vet
in Ramallah, she seeks help from a sympathetically represented female Israeli in
the illegal settlement of 'Atarvut', one of a ring of fortified suburbs designed to
cut the whole of Jerusalem off from what remains of Palestinian territory. Nura's
documentation, her owner discovers to her chagrin, gives her dog greater freedom of movement under Occupation than she enjoys herself. Another example
occurs when her obstinate mother-in-law dithers over what colour dresses to take
with her as the clock ticks rapidly towards the next curfew and trigger-happy
Israeli squaddies gather outside. Finally, there is the hilarious imagined conversation with George Bush, in which the characteristic obtuseness of the most
fanatically pro-Israel US President in recent history is brilliantly mocked.

Such aspects of the text contribute to what one might call Amiry's innovative
construction of a 'Palestinian Absurd'. Like Beckett's *Waiting for Godot*, the Palestinians wait interminably in *Sharon* for deliverance. The two-part structure of
Amiry's text, in which 'nothing happens twice', is a further parallel with Beckett's
play. The temporal circularity and thematic repetitions of Amiry's text, and its
often inconsequential reported conversational exchanges, offer further points of

comparison, as does the emphasis on solidarity and endurance in the face of an incomprehensibly arbitrary, unjust and absurd predicament. The 'legal illegals' (*SMM*: 33; these include Amiry, initially at least) described early in the text perhaps inevitably invokes the unsurpassed example of Israeli legal double-think, the category of 'present absentees' – in other words those who should have (been) disappeared during the ethnic cleansings of 1948 onwards but unaccountably were/did not and remain within Israel with minimal legal status or rights.[61] However, as with better-known examples of the 'Absurd' mode, humour tends to reinforce the seriousness of what is being written about, making *Sharon* a 'tragicomedy' (*SMM*: 81). The British 'Absurdist' Harold Pinter (in recent years a noted advocate of Palestinian rights) has said of *The Caretaker*, one of his early 'comedies of menace' – and a text which itself revolves around the theme of 'occupation' – that: '[It] is funny, up to a point. Beyond that point, it ceases to be funny and it is because of that point that I wrote it.'[62] The same is true of *Sharon*, where the 'absurdity of the situation' (*SMM*: 114) in no way diminishes the horror of the endless cycles of Israeli land-grabs, assassinations, arrests, curfews and economic strangulation. These are, after all, 'war diaries' (*SMM*: ix) in the manner of Victor Klemperer and as such attest to experiences of fear, violence and disruption – as well as steadfastness and optimism – which are unimaginable for most modern western civilians.

In its mixture of tragedy and sometimes farcical comedy, its resolutely honest eye for both human virtue and foible, including Amiry's own, its commitment to a better future and its ultimate refusal to allow its author's soul to be 'occupied', *Sharon* at times invites comparison with Kafka (*SMM*: 72), an author much admired by Pinter, too. Pinter's observation on Kafka's work applies equally well to Amiry: 'The nightmare of that world is precisely its ordinariness. That is what is so frightening and strong.'[63] As this suggests, like Said, Amiry claims some affiliation to Jewish tradition, albeit a different one to that represented by Zionist philosophies of supremacism and annexationism. In this respect, in its quiet way it perhaps more closely resembles great war narratives like Joseph Heller's *Catch-22* or Irène Némirovsky's *Suite Française*, the unfinished and often strikingly comic epic by a Russian Jewish *émigrée* about the early days of the Nazi Occupation of France. If Némirovsky depicts some Germans and collaborators, at least, in a rounded, even positive way, Amiry has equally large sympathies. The nuanced representation of 'enemies' like Captain Rafi and Rami supports her thesis that this later Occupation has 'ruined the spirits of *both* Israelis and Palestinians' (*SMM*: 11; my emphasis). That Némirovsky's masterpiece remained uncompleted because of her transfer to Auschwitz, however, is a chilling reminder of the vulnerability of such generosity to *realpolitik* and of the wilful carelessness of human life which Occupation and deportation inevitably involves.

Conclusion

These examples of Palestinian life-writing clearly have objectives which in part severely complicate traditional conceptions of autobiography as a primarily literary mode. As the controversy over the truth claims of *Out of Place* suggests, the sub-genre has potentially powerful political resonances. Given the ever-deteriorating situation of Palestinians, economically, politically and in terms of the most basic human rights, both Palestinian life-writing and its study have a particular urgency, constituting what Sidonie Smith calls, in another context, a 'revolutionary gesture against amnesia'.[64] If this gesture is performed in relation to Palestine as a collective entity, however, it also confirms Hertha Wong's caution against assuming that foundational and singularising myths of community always over-determine individual autobiographical subjectivity in non-mainstream versions of the genre[65] (compare Chapter 2). While Palestinian life-writing echoes Robert Fraser's argument that the more oppressed a people, the more difficult it is to abstract the individual life from group history,[66] it also emphasises the individual as much as the collective, as if to counter the anonymising (and dehumanising) perception in Zionist discourse and much of the western media of Palestinians en masse as faceless, whether in the guise of 'terrorists' or victims. The contrast between Said's embrace of the classical conventions of autobiography and Amiry's of the contingent forms of diary, email and journal points to the broad range of sub-forms across which Palestinian life-writing operates. These also include memoir (for example, Ghada Karmi and Karl Sabbagh), *testimonio* (Leila Khaled, 'Souad') and 'poetic' autobiography (Mourid Barghouti). Such diversity also symbolises the variety of Palestinian identities constructed therein, not only in terms of religious confession and gender, but also of class, political affiliation and (dis)location. Equally, across its range, the sub-genre emphasises the performative construction of different and new Palestinian identities as much as the recuperation and preservation of common and older ones.

Extrapolating from the example of Palestinian life-writing, the larger sub-field of postcolonial life-writing to which it belongs is clearly concerned – like its contemporary western women's and minoritarian equivalents – with discursive forms of cultural politics. In Fanonian terms, it gives voice and agency to the colonised to advance the project of release from the burden of 'crushing objecthood'. However, these are often secondary to more obviously material forms of politics less commonly addressed in western women's life-writing, at least since the time of the Suffragettes. This instrumental use of autobiographical forms for concrete political objectives is evident right back to the precursor forms of the sub-genre. For example, Equiano's text is designed to mobilise its readers against the slave trade, as Prince's is against slavery itself. This emphasis is equally marked throughout the colonial period.[67] Thus, Majeed draws explicit links between performative acts of Self-representation in Indian nationalist autobiography and its demands for emancipation from British rule. The pattern persists even in the era of technical decolonisation. Thus, Longley observes of Aboriginal women's writing that it is often 'passionately polemical in its impulses',[68] as the discussion of Morgan in Chapter 1 confirms. Indeed, as suggested in the Introduction to my text, from the time of Commonwealth Studies, postcolonial life-writing has often been seen as a branch of 'protest writing'[69] rather than literature 'proper'.

Nonetheless, it is important to recognise that both the politics of postcolonial life-writing and its effectiveness are contested. In the first place, some postcolonial life-writers, notably – in the context of this monograph – V.S. Naipaul, disavow decolonisation politics. Even amongst authors who are leaders of nationalist struggles, there is sometimes a disavowal of the idea that their autobiographical texts are in any way representative. As seen in Chapter 2, Nehru, for example, disavows any claim to the representativity of *An Autobiography*. As has also been seen, Lim's political investments might be considered reactionary, even colonial-identified, at least in respect of Palestine. Such ambiguities haunt postcolonial life-writing from its precursor forms. Thus, Yolanda Pierce accuses Equiano of using the conventions of captivity narrative in a conservative way, to embrace uncritically the values of his captors, notably the ideology of 'the self-made man'.[70] As Chapter 1 demonstrated, Narogin levels similar charges against contemporary writers like Morgan. Indeed Whitlock warns that recent testimonial life-writing from the non-western world can not only give voice to the marginalised but also be co-opted as propaganda to support the West's current neo-colonial adventures. For example, she analyses the way that Afghan women's memoirs have sometimes been used to legitimise western intervention in that country, demonstrating that 'a cynical and highly politicized manipulation of life story is more than incidental to the war on terror'.[71] Equally, Huggan warns that western publishing houses can exploit postcolonial life-writing just as surely as other forms of postcolonial literature, marketing as an exotic commodity, thereby strengthening the reach and prestige of a globalised, neo-colonial economy rather than posing any serious challenge to it.[72] Nonetheless, as Huggan also acknowledges, producers (and, one might add, consumers, even publishers) of such work can also play the market against itself,[73] allowing marginalised or subjugated voices 'to speak of a future' where their aspirations for recognition, even liberation into full human and political rights, will eventually be realised.

It is perhaps fitting to end this text with a chapter about postcolonial life-writing's concern with concrete and compelling issues of political as well as personal emancipation and independence. In this preoccupation, the sub-genre once more demonstrates its own relative autonomy from its western analogues, as it has done, sometimes unevenly, in relation to the four thematics of subjectivity and two major aspects of style discussed in Chapters 1–6. Mary Seacole, in any objective sense one of the least empowered figures studied in this text, nonetheless speaks for postcolonial life-writers, of both genders, before and since, when she asserts that 'unless I am allowed to tell the story of my life *in my own way*, I cannot tell it at all'.[74] As is characteristic of post-colonial writing as a whole, part of seizing the initiative to tell her own story involves 'speaking truth to power' in the name of a better, more just world. Insofar as such texts do so, and to the degree that it also speaks of and to collective identifications of varying kinds, it supports the call made in *Black Skin* for the urgent development of a more inclusive and extensive conception of 'the human' than has been typically constructed in the western Enlightenment. Indeed, in final rebuttal of Gusdorf, one might conclude that whereas canonical autobiography may have articulated perspectives which have been of good use in 'western man's' systematic colonisation of the rest of the world, so postcolonial life-writing may prove equally useful in teaching the West a more credible and creditable conception of its place in the contemporary world.

Notes

Introduction

1 I use this latter term as shorthand for 'autobiographies and biographies'. I use 'life-writing' to describe work which is autobiographical without necessarily observing the classical rules of the genre, as is often the case in the Self-narration of western women and postcolonial subjects (see further below). Perceived important differences between autobiographical writing by (western) men and women have led some feminist critics to promote new terminologies to describe the latter. Thus in 1984, Domna Stanton coined the term 'autogynography'. See 'Autogynography: Is the Subject Different?' in Stanton (ed.) *The Female Autograph* (New York: New York Literary Forum, 1984): 5–22. In 1994, Leigh Gilmore offered 'autobiographics' to describe not only differences in the ways that women write their life-experiences but the techniques necessary to properly appreciate such work. See Gilmore, *Autobiographics: A Feminist Theory of Women's Self-Representation* (Ithaca, NY: Cornell University Press, 1994). The following year, Jeanne Perreault proposed 'autography' as a further alternative. See *Writing Selves: Contemporary Feminist Autography* (Minneapolis: University of Minnesota Press, 1995). Such initiatives underwrite my preference for the term 'postcolonial life-writing' rather than, following earlier postcolonial critics, 'post(-)colonial autobiography' (see below). The gendering of terms like 'autogynography' in any case precludes their adaptation to postcolonial life-writing by men. By 'postcolonial' in relation to life-writing, I mean work which recognises the impact of colonialism (especially its European forms), including its precursor and successor formations, in the constitution of the auto/biographical subjectivity of the colonised and their antecedents/descendants.
2 James Olney, *Tell Me Africa: An Approach to African Literature* (Princeton, NJ: Princeton University Press, 1973): 26.
3 www.huffingtonpost.com/2008/01/31/boy-soldier-defends-his-b_n_84195.html.
4 See Margaretta Jolly, ed., *The Encyclopedia of Life-Writing: Autobiographical and Biographical Forms* (London: Routledge, 2001).
5 Sidonie Smith and Julia Watson, *Reading Autobiography: A Guide for Interpreting Life Narratives* (Minnesota: University of Minnesota Press, 2001): 113ff.
6 Georg Misch, *A History of Autobiography in Antiquity*, trans. E.W. Dickes (1907; Westport, CT: Greenwood Press, 1973), vol. 1: 6.
7 Ibid.: 18.
8 Georges Gusdorf, 'Conditions and Limits of Autobiography', in James Olney (ed.) *Autobiography: Essays Theoretical and Critical* (Princeton, NJ: Princeton University Press, 1980): 29.
9 Roy Pascal, *Design and Truth in Autobiography* (Cambridge, MA: Harvard University Press, 1960): 22. Compare 180.
10 Gusdorf, 'Conditions': 29.

11 M.K. Gandhi, *An Autobiography: or The Story of My Experiments with Truth*, trans. Mahadev Desai (1927–29; London: Penguin, 1982): 14.

12 James Olney, 'Autobiography and the Cultural Moment: A Thematic, Historical, and Bibliographical Introduction', in Olney, *Autobiography*: 8.

13 Richard N. Coe, *When the Grass Was Taller: Autobiography and the Experience of Childhood* (New Haven, CT: Yale University Press, 1984): 40. I'm grateful to Sarah O'Mahoney for drawing Coe to my attention.

14 See, for example, R.C.P. Sinha, *The Indian Autobiographies in English* (New Delhi: S. Chand, 1978).

15 Doireann MacDermott (ed.) *Autobiographical and Biographical Writing in the Commonwealth* (Sabadell, Spain: AUSA, 1984). MacDermott usefully raises the issue of the poetics of 'Commonwealth' life-writing but does not get beyond preliminary remarks about language, community and politics, issues which my text will address in detail. I also survey a greater geo-cultural range than the Commonwealth and analyse works translated into English.

16 See, for example, John Colmer, *Australian Autobiography: The Personal Quest* (Melbourne: Oxford University Press, 1989); Sandra Pouchet Paquet, *Caribbean Autobiography: Cultural Identity and Self-Representation* (Madison, WI: University of Wisconsin Press, 2002); Debra Kelly, *Autobiography and Independence: Selfhood and Creativity in North African Postcolonial Writing in French* (Liverpool: Liverpool University Press, 2005).

17 Alfred Hornung and Ernstpeter Ruhe, eds, *Postcolonialism & Autobiography: Michelle Cliff, David Dabydeen, Opal Palmer Adisa* and *Postcolonialisme & Autobiographie: Albert Memmi, Assia Djebar, Daniel Maximin* (Atlanta, GA: Rodopi, 1998). The historical and geographical remit of these volumes is narrower than mine. It is disappointing that no real comparisons are drawn *between* rather than *within* the Caribbean and *Maghreb*. Perhaps most problematic is the editors' conception of postcolonial life-writing as a sub-set of postmodernism. See their 'Preface' to *Postcolonialism*: 1. To the extent that the latter can be understood as a distinctive discourse of the West (in Fredric Jameson's famous formulation, it is 'the cultural logic of [an American-centred] late capitalism'), this threatens to relegate 'postcolonial autobiography' to a renewed relation of dependency on the dominant centres of cultural power.

18 Françoise Lionnet, *Autobiographical Voices: Race, Gender, Self-Portraiture* (Ithaca, NY: Cornell University Press, 1989); Lionnet, *Postcolonial Representation: Women, Literature, Identity* (Ithaca, NY: Cornell University Press, 1995). These texts consider neither male postcolonial life-writers, nor antecedents to contemporary postcolonial life-writing, with the exception of a rich but problematic essay on Augustine in the former volume.

19 Gillian Whitlock, *The Intimate Empire: Reading Women's Autobiography* (London: Cassell, 2000).

20 Javed Majeed, *Autobiography, Travel and Postnational Identity: Gandhi, Nehru and Iqbal* (Basingstoke: Palgrave, 2007); Philip Holden, *Autobiography and Decolonization: Modernity, Masculinity and the Nation State* (Madison, WI: University of Wisconsin Press, 2008).

21 Gillian Whitlock, *Soft Weapons: Autobiography in Transit* (Chicago: University of Chicago Press, 2007).

22 David Huddart, *Postcolonial Theory and Autobiography* (London: Routledge, 2007). Constraints of space unfortunately forbid discussion of shorter pieces on postcolonial auto/biography for the moment.

23 Misch, *History*, vol. 1: 4.

24 Olney, 'Autobiography': 4. Compare William Spengemann, *The Forms of Autobiography* (New Haven, CT: Yale University Press, 1980): xii. Perhaps the most influential contemporary definition of autobiography, Philippe Lejeune's 'autobiographical pact', is primarily a theory of reader/author relations. See 'The Autobiographical Contract' [more widely translated as 'Pact']', trans. R. Carter, in Tzvetan Todorov (ed.) *French Literary Theory Today: A Reader* (Cambridge: Cambridge University Press, 1982): 192–222.

25 See Paul de Man, 'Autobiography as De-Facement' (1979) in Trevor Lynn Broughton, ed., *Autobiography: Critical Concepts in Literary and Cultural Studies* (London: Routledge,

2007), vol. 1: 264–74; compare Michael Sprinker, 'Fictions of the Self: the End of Autobiography', in Olney, *Autobiography*: 321–42.

26 The classic post-structuralist treatment of genre is Jacques Derrida's 'The Law of Genre', trans. Avital Ronelle, *Critical Inquiry*, 7 (1980): 55–81.

27 See Robert Fraser, *Lifting the Sentence: A Poetics of Postcolonial Fiction* (Manchester: Manchester University Press, 2000); and Rajeev Patke, *Postcolonial Poetry in English* (Oxford: Oxford University Press, 2006).

28 See Stanton, 'Autogynography': 7; compare Bella Brodzki and Celeste Schenck, 'Introduction', in Brodzki and Schenck (eds) *Life-Lines: Theorizing Women's Autobiography* (Ithaca, NY: Cornell University Press, 1988): 12.

29 Kelly, *Autobiography*: 34.

30 Ibid.: 47–8.

31 For an overview of debates on these two issues, see Ania Loomba, *Colonialism/Postcolonialism* (London: Routledge, 1998) and Reina Lewis and Sara Mills, eds., *Feminist Postcolonial Theory: A Reader* (London: Routledge, 2003). Some postcolonial women lifewriters, including Buchi Emecheta and Nawal El Saadawi (see Chapter 3), criticise western feminism's supposed focus on sexual and individual freedoms in isolation from larger political issues. See Paquet, *Caribbean*: 179; Barbara Harlow, 'From the Women's Prison: Third World Women's Narratives of Prison', in Smith and Watson, *Women*: 456; and Julia Watson, 'Unspeakable Differences: The Politics of Gender in Lesbian and Heterosexual Women's Autobiographies', in Smith and Watson, *Women*: 398–9. This supports Whitlock's warning in *The Intimate Empire* against any too hasty embrace of models of 'a transhistorical female experience' (2000: 3).

32 Such work sometimes ignores the fact that colonial women autobiographers often 'Other' the non-western subject (female as well as male) to the same degree as their masculine equivalents. See, for example, Abdulrazak Gurnah, 'Settler Writing in Kenya: "Nomenclature is an uncertain science in these wild parts"', in Howard Booth and Nigel Rigby (eds) *Modernism and Empire* (Manchester: Manchester University Press, 2000): 275–92. Such patterns challenge aspects of the strategic argument about 'intimacy' in colonial and postcolonial women's life-writing elaborated in Whitlock's *Intimate Empire*.

33 Janet V. Gunn, 'A Politics of Experience: Leila Khaled's *My People Shall Live: The Autobiography of a Revolutionary*', in Sidonie Smith and Julia Watson, eds., *De/Colonizing the Subject: The Politics of Gender in Women's Autobiography* (Minneapolis: University of Minnesota Press, 1992): 77.

34 Smith and Watson, *Reading*: 3.

35 See Margot Badran, 'Expressing Feminism and Nationalism in Autobiography: the Memoirs of an Egyptian Educator', in Smith and Watson, *De/Colonizing*: 270–93.

36 On this distinction, see Deniz Kandiyoti, 'Identity and its Discontents: Women and the Nation', *Millennium: Journal of International Studies*, 20(3) (1991): 429–43.

37 I'm drawing on the argument of 'Three Women's Texts and a Critique of Imperialism', where Spivak makes a more general argument about the emergence of the western feminist subject at the expense of the colonised. See H.L. Gates, *'Race', Writing, and Difference* (London: University of Chicago Press, 1986): 262–80.

38 Linda Warley, 'Locating the Subject of Post-colonial Autobiography', *Kunapipi*, 15(1) (1993): 23.

39 See Sidonie Smith, *A Poetics of Women's Autobiography: Marginality and the Fiction of Self-Representation* (Bloomington, IN: Indiana University Press, 1987): 15, 17.

40 Misch finds abundant autobiographical writing in ancient Assyria and Babylon. See *History*, vol. 1. Richard Bowring traces the long history of women's autobiographical writing in the East in 'The Female Hand in Heian Japan: A First Reading', in Stanton, *Female*: 55–62. Equally, Badran argues that: 'Recording one's life story is a centuries-old practice in Egypt and elsewhere in the Arab and Islamic worlds.' See 'Expressing': 274. Compare Hertha D. Sweet Wong, 'Plains Indian Names and "the Autobiographical

Act"', in Kathleen Ashley, Leigh Gilmore and Gerald Peters, eds, *Autobiography and Postmodernism* (Amherst, MA: University of Massachusetts Press, 1994): 212–39; and Kristin Brustad *et al.*, 'The Fallacy of Western Origins', in Broughton, *Autobiography*, vol. 3: 375–93. In more recent reflections on his famous essay, Gusdorf disarmingly admits he was then uninterested in 'distant antecedents and foreign lands'. See *Les Écritures de Moi: Lignes de Vie* (Paris: Odile Jacob, 1991): 16 (my translation). However, this entails no retraction of his original arguments; ibid.: 48.

41 Laura Marcus, *Auto/biographical Discourses: Theory, Criticism, Practice* (Manchester: Manchester University Press, 1994): 220.

42 For an overview of such influences, see Sidonie Smith and Julia Watson, 'Introduction: Situating Subjectivity in Women's Autobiographical Practices', in Smith and Watson (eds) *Women, Autobiography, Theory: A Reader* (Madison, WI: University of Wisconsin Press, 1998): 3–52. The arguments of French feminism that biology influences the psychosexual constitution of men and women have been less sympathetically received. See Sidonie Smith's account of Cixous in *Subjectivity, Identity, and the Body: Women's Autobiographical Practices in the Twentieth Century* (Bloomington, IN: Indiana University Press, 1993): 163ff. Since 'postcolonial' is only ever a *cultural* rather than a biological category, no essentialist explanation of the differences in its conception of autobiographical Selfhood is tenable.

43 Paul Smith, *Discerning the Subject* (Minneapolis: University of Minnesota Press, 1988): 104. Compare Misch, *History*, vol. 1: 7. The idea of auto/biographical unity of Selfhood has been severely complicated by the advent of postmodernist thinking. See Chapter 1.

44 Sidonie Smith, *Subjectivity*: 155. Counter-positions to this argument and those relating to other thematics of subjectivity will be discussed in Chapters 1–3.

45 Gilmore, *Autobiographics*: xiii.

46 Shirley Neuman, '"An Appearance Walking in a Forest the Sexes Burn": Autobiography and the Construction of the Feminine Body', in Ashley *et al.*, *Autobiography*: 293.

47 Hélène Cixous, 'The Laugh of the Medusa' (1975), trans. K. and P. Cohen, in Elaine Marks and Isabelle de Courtivron (eds) *New French Feminisms* (Brighton: Harvester, 1980): 250.

48 See Smith and Watson, *Reading Autobiography*: 61–3.

49 Misch, *History*, vol. 1: 19.

50 Paquet, *Caribbean*: 8.

51 Wole Soyinka, *Myth, Literature and the African World* (Cambridge: Cambridge University Press, 1995): 34.

52 I take this concept from Dipesh Chakrabarty's relativisation of western historiography in *Provincializing Europe: Postcolonial Thought and Historical Difference* (London: Princeton University Press, 2000).

53 Soyinka, *Myth*: 34–6.

54 Frantz Fanon, *Black Skin/White Masks*, trans. C.L. Markmann ([1952] London: Pluto, 1986): 152.

55 Ashis Nandy, *The Intimate Enemy* (1983) in *Exiled at Home* (New Delhi: Oxford University Press, 1998): 55 (my emphasis).

56 Gayatri Spivak, 'The Political Economy of Women as Seen by a Literary Critic'; in Elizabeth Weed (ed.) *Coming to Terms: Feminism, Theory, Politics* (New York: Routledge, 1989): 227. On the postcolonial critique of western psychoanalysis, see Mrinalini Greedharry, *Postcolonial Theory and Psychoanalysis* (Basingstoke: Palgrave, 2008).

57 See, for example, Paul Edwards and Rosalind Shaw, 'The Invisible Chi in Equiano's *Interesting Narrative*', *Journal of Religion in Africa*, 19(2) (1989): 146–56. (See also Chapter 1.)

58 Shirley Geok-Lin Lim, 'Terms of Empowerment in Kamala Das's *My Story*', in Smith and Watson, *De/Colonizing*: 346–69.

59 See, for example, Linda Anderson's discussion of Carolyn Steedman's *Landscape for a Good Woman* (1986) in *Autobiography* (London: Routledge, 2001): 110ff.

60 Bill Ashcroft, Gareth Griffiths, and Helen Tiffin, *The Empire Writes Back: Theory and Practice in Post-colonial Literatures* (London: Routledge, 1989): 8–9.
61 Misch, *History*, vol. 1: 4–5.
62 Lejeune, 'Autobiographical': 192.
63 Ibid.
64 Shari Benstock, 'Introduction', in *The Private Self: Theory and Practice of Women's Autobiographical Writings* (London: University of North Carolina Press, 1988): 2.
65 Hegel is perhaps the most notorious example of this tendency. For a superb discussion of his (mis)construction of Africa, see Caroline Rooney, *African Literature, Animism and Politics* (London: Routledge, 2001): 154ff.
66 For a useful discussion of this concept, see Toril Moi, *Sexual/Textual Politics* (London: Routledge, 1985): 113ff.
67 Julia Swindells, 'Conclusion: Autobiography and the Politics of "The Personal"', in Swindells (ed.) *The Uses of Autobiography* (London: Taylor and Francis, 1995): 205.
68 MacDermott, *Autobiographical*: 10, 26.
69 Regenia Gagnier, 'The Literary Standard, Working-Class Autobiography, and Gender', in Smith and Watson, *Women*: 264; compare Germaine Brée, 'Foreword' to Brodzki and Schenck, *Life-Lines*: ix.
70 Strangely, Huddart does not discuss this most obviously autobiographical theoretical text in his analysis of the role of autobiography within postcolonial theory.
71 C.L. Innes, *The Cambridge Introduction to Postcolonial Literatures in English* (Cambridge: Cambridge University Press, 2007): 56. While recognising that *Black Skin* is an 'often autobiographical manifesto', Innes does not explore its poetics in any depth.
72 Anjali Prabhu, 'Narration in Frantz Fanon's *Peau noire, masques blancs*: Some Reconsiderations', *Research in African Literatures*, 37(4) (2006): 189.
73 Ngugi wa Thiongo, 'The Language of African Literature' (1986), in Patrick Williams and Laura Chrisman (eds) *Colonial Discourse and Post-Colonial Theory: A Reader* (Hemel Hempstead: Harvester Wheatsheaf, 1993): 441.
74 A quite different problem arises in relation to texts translated from non-European languages. Nawal El Saadawi (see Chapter 3) observes that 30–40 per cent of any novel is lost in translation. See Jennifer Cohen, '"But Have Some Art With You": An Interview with Nawal El Saadawi', *Literature and Medicine*, 14(1): (1995): 63.
75 Sinha, *Indian*: v. Compare G.N. Devy, 'Romantic, Post-Romantic and Neo-Romantic Autobiography in Indian English Literature', in MacDermott, *Autobiographical*: 63–4; and Nirad Chaudhuri, *The Autobiography of an Unknown Indian* (1951; London: Picador, 1991): 393.
76 Mulk Raj Anand, *Autobiography*, Part One; *Story of a Childhood under the Raj: Pilpali Sahab* (New Delhi: Arnold-Heinemann, 1985), n.p.
77 V.S. Naipaul, 'Indian Autobiographies' (1965), in *Literary Occasions: Essays* (London: Picador, 2003): 143.

1 Centred and decentred Selves

1 Smith, *Subjectivity*: 8; compare Gilmore, *Autobiographics*: 185.
2 Misch, *History*: 7.
3 Gusdorf, 'Conditions': 35, 38.
4 The argument that autobiographical Selfhood, of either gender, is sovereign, centred and unified may seem counter-intuitive. For one thing, Auto/biography Studies has long explored the split between the narrated and narrating 'I' of autobiography (as have writers like Rousseau). In the wake of postmodernism, moreover, humanist notions of the unified Self may seem untenable. The unconscious, the workings of ideology and the constitution of the Subject by/in language are variously held to undermine the conception of the unitary Self consolidated in the Enlightenment. Postmodernism therefore clearly poses a challenge to arguments that dispersed

subjectivity may characterise women's life-writing (and, by implication, its postcolonial analogues). See Paul Smith, *Discerning*, Marcus, *Auto/biographical* (Chapter 5) and Anderson, *Autobiography* (Chapter 2). Nonetheless, as Karl Weintraub asserts, one must beware of anachronism, or at least employ a double optic in addressing auto-biography which does not frame itself within the terms of such theorisations of the Subject. He argues that the critic's task 'is to come to an understanding of the self-conception an Augustine, for example, had of himself, and not whether he "correctly" (to be judged by some modern theory) understood himself'. See Weintraub, 'Auto-biography and Historical Consciousness' (1979) in Broughton, *Autobiography*, vol. 1: 249. Such thinking conserves a place for intentionality (and agency) in auto/biographical writing which is clearly embraced by most life-writers. In any case, Mary Evans argues that for all the impact of postmodernism within the academy, belief in the 'integrated individual' remains strong: '[The] social expectation – increasingly enforced ... is that we are a "knowable" person [*sic*], a person with a coherent emotional *curriculum vitae*.' See Evans, *Missing Persons: The Impossibility of Auto/biography* (London: Routledge, 1999): 23.

5 Spengemann, *Forms*: 132.
6 Evans, *Missing*: 83. Compare Gilmore, *Autobiographics*: 185–6; and Betty Bergland, 'Postmodernism and the Autobiographical Subject: Reconstructing the "Other"', in Ashley *et al.*, *Autobiography*: 181.
7 Smith, *Subjectivity*: 155.
8 Brodzki and Schenck, 'Introduction': 6.
9 Lee Quinby, 'The Subject of Memoirs: *The Woman Warrior*'s Technology of Ideographic Selfhood' (1976), in Smith and Watson, *De/Colonizing*: 299; compare Lourdes Torres, 'The Construction of the Self in U.S. Latina Autobiographies' (1994), in Smith and Watson, *Women*: 283, 285.
10 Lionnet, *Autobiographical*: 16.
11 Linda Hutcheon, 'Circling the Downspout of Empire' (1989), in Bill Ashcroft, Gareth Grifiths and Helen Tiffin (eds) *The Post-Colonial Studies Reader* (London: Routledge, 1995): 130–1.
12 Gilmore, *Autobiographics*: 75. Compare Smith, *Subjectivity*: 155–6; Perreault, *Writing*: 8–9; Whitlock, *Intimate*: 5.
13 bell hooks, 'Postmodern Blackness' (1991), in Williams and Chrisman, *Colonial*: 425. Compare Torres, 'Construction': 277; and Wong, 'Plains Indian Names and "the Autobiographical Act"', in Ashley *et al.*, *Autobiography*: 212.
14 Kateryna Longley, 'Autobiographical Story Telling by Australian Aboriginal Women', in Smith and Watson, *De/Colonizing*: 371.
15 John Thieme, 'Appropriating Ancestral Heirlooms: The Quest for Tradition in Derek Walcott's *Another Life*', in MacDermott, *Autobiographical*: 215.
16 Paquet, *Caribbean*: 234.
17 Fanon, *Black*: 112, 119.
18 Ibid.: 136.
19 Ibid.: 63.
20 Sally Morgan, *My Place* (London: Virago, [1987] 2001): 106; hereafter cited as *MP* in the text.
21 Eric Michaels, 'Para-ethnography', *Art and Text*, 30 (1988): 50; compare Subhash Jair-eth, 'The "I" in Sally Morgan's *My Place*: Writing of a Monologised Self', *Westerly*, 40 (3) (1995): 69–78.
22 Mudrooroo Narogin, *Writing from the Fringe: A Study of Modern Aboriginal Literature* (Mel-bourne: Hyland, 1990): 149. He modifies this criticism on 162–3.
23 Carolyn Bliss, 'The Mythology of Family: Three Texts of Popular Culture', *New Lit-eratures Review*, 18 (1989): 65.
24 Russell West, 'Uncovering Collective Crimes: Sally Morgan's *My Place* as Australian Indigenous Detective Narrative', in Dorothea Fischer-Hornung and Monika Mueller,

eds, *Sleuthing Ethnicity: The Detective in Multiethnic Crime Fiction* (London: Associated Universities Press, 2003): 281.

25 Anne Brewster, *Reading Aboriginal Women's Autobiography* (Sydney: Sydney University Press, 1996): 4.

26 See, for example, Penny van Toorn, 'Indigenous Texts and Narratives', in Elizabeth Webby (ed.) *The Cambridge Companion to Australian Literature* (Cambridge: Cambridge University Press, 2000): 36.

27 Bliss, 'Mythology': 65.

28 Elvira Pulitano, '"One More Story to Tell": Diasporic Articulations in Sally Morgan's *My Place*', in Sheila Collingwood-Whittick (ed.) *The Pain of Unbelonging: Alienation and Identity in Australasian Literature* (Amsterdam: Rodopi, 2007): 52.

29 See Penny van Toorn, 'Indigenous Australian Life Writing: Tactics and Transformations', in Bain Attwood and Fiona Magowan (eds) *Telling Stories: Indigenous History and Memory in Australia and New Zealand* (Wellington, New Zealand: Bridget Williams, 2001): 4–5.

30 Joyce Zonana, '"I was cryin', all the people were cryin', my mother was cryin'"': Aboriginality and Maternity in Sally Morgan's *My Place*', in Elizabeth Brown-Guillory, *Women of Color: Mother–Daughter Relationships in 20th-Century Literature* (Austin, TX: University of Texas Press, 1996): 65.

31 Sheila Collingwood-Whittick, 'Sally Morgan's *My Place*: Exposing the (Ab)original "Text" Behind Whitefellas' History', *Commonwealth Essays and Studies*, 25(1) (2002): 43.

32 West, 'Uncovering': 280–99 *passim*.

33 Graham Huggan, *Australian Literature: Postcolonialism, Racism, Transnationalism* (Oxford: Oxford University Press, 2007): 101.

34 The veracity of Equiano's account of his early life has been disputed since the publication of the *Interesting Narrative*. For an excellent overview of this debate, see Anthony Carrigan, '"Negotiating Personal Identity and Cultural Memory" in Olaudah Equiano's *Interesting Narrative*', *Wasafiri*, 48 (Summer, 2006): 42–7.

35 Tanya Caldwell, '"Talking Too Much English": Languages of Economy and Politics in Equiano's *The Interesting Narrative*', *Early American Literature*, 34(3) (1999): 264.

36 Olaudah Equiano, *The Interesting Narrative and Other Writings*, ed. Vincent Carretta (London: Penguin, [1789] 1995): 69. Hereafter cited as *IN* in the text.

37 Jesús Benito and Ana Manzanas, 'The (De-)Construction of the "Other" in *The Interesting Narrative of the Life of Olaudah Equiano*', in Maria Diedrich, H.L. Gates and Carl Pedersen (eds) *Black Imagination and the Middle Passage* (New York: Oxford University Press, 1999): 53.

38 While Equiano's stance has been criticised, as Geraldine Murphy laconically observes, 'it is hard to disagree with his judgement … that purchasing British commodities was preferable to being one.' See 'Olaudah Equiano, Accidental Tourist', *Eighteenth-Century Studies*, 27(4) (1994): 561. Initially, at least, Equiano's entrepreneurship is designed to gather the wherewithal to purchase his freedom.

39 Caldwell, '"Talking"': 265.

40 Bunyan is also an inter-text in Buchi Emecheta, *Head Above Water* (Oxford: Heinemann, [1986] 1994): 15, C.L.R. James and Brendan Behan (see Chapter 2).

41 Adam Potkay, 'Olaudah Equiano and the Art of Spiritual Autobiography', *Eighteenth-Century Studies*, 27(4) (1994): 677, 92.

42 Potkay specifically endorses Caldwell's argument in 'History, Oratory, and God in Equiano's *Interesting Narrative*', *Eighteenth-Century Studies*, 34(4) (2001): 609.

43 Murphy, 'Olaudah': 553.

44 Benito and Manzanas, '(De-)Construction': 53.

45 Michael Wiley argues that, given recent historical examples of white cannibalism, Equiano's fears are real. 'Consuming Africa: Geography and Identity in Olaudah Equiano's *Interesting Narrative*', *Studies in Romanticism*, 44(2) (2005): 173–5.

46 Caldwell, '"Talking"': 273.

47 Susan Marren, 'Between Slavery and Freedom: The Transgressive Self in Olaudah Equiano's Autobiography', *PMLA*, 108(1) (1993): 101.
48 Douglas Anderson, 'Division below the Surface: Olaudah Equiano's *Interesting Narrative*', *Studies in Romanticism*, 43(3) (2000): 459.
49 Ibid.
50 William Mottolese, '"Almost an Englishman": Equiano and the Colonial Gift of Language', *Bucknell Review*, 41(2) (1998): 161.
51 Robin Sabino and Jennifer Hall, 'The Path Not Taken: Cultural Identity in the Interesting Life of Olaudah Equiano', *MELUS*, 24(1) (1999): 5.
52 See also Edwards and Shaw, 'Invisible'.
53 Wilfred Samuels, 'Disguised Voice in *The Interesting Narrative of Olaudah Equiano, or Gustavus Vassa, the African*', *Black American Literature Forum*, 19(2) (1985): 66. Samuels further claims that Equiano resembles the African folk trickster Anansi (ibid.: 67).
54 Vincent Carretta, *Equiano, the African: Biography of a Self-Made Man* (London: University of Georgia Press, 2005): xviii.
55 Helen Thomas, *Romanticism and Slave Narrative: Transatlantic Testimonies* (Cambridge: Cambridge University Press, 2000): 226, 245; compare Mottolese's emphasis on Equiano's 'syncretic' identity in '"Almost"': 160.
56 In this respect I differ from Marren, who stresses Equiano's 'numerous [unresolved] contradictions and ambiguities'. See 'Between': 96.
57 Anderson, 'Division': *passim*.
58 One might argue that, especially for a reader in 1789, this duality is anticipated in the engraving of Equiano which precedes the title page, with its distinct signifiers of 'blackness' and 'whiteness'.
59 Carretta, *Equiano*: xvi.
60 Augustine, *Confessions*, trans. H. Chadwick (Oxford: Oxford University Press, 1998): 24.
61 Edward Said, *Out of Place: A Memoir* (London: Granta, 1999): 295.
62 Sindiwe Magona, *To My Children's Children: An Autobiography* (London: Women's Press, 1991): 6.
63 Majeed, *Autobiography*: 3 and *passim*.
64 Whitlock, *Soft*: 10.
65 L.S. Senghor, 'Negritude: A Humanism of the Twentieth Century' (1965), in Williams and Chrisman, *Colonial Discourse*: 30–1.
66 Smith, *Discerning*: 153.
67 Whitlock, *Intimate*: 6.
68 Similar refinement of Lionnet's theory of *'logiques métisses'* in *Postcolonial* (15ff) is also required.
69 Perreault, *Writing*: 9.
70 Edouard Glissant, *Poetics of Relation*, trans. Betsy Wing (1990; Ann Arbor, MI: University of Michigan Press, 1997): 14.
71 Salman Rushdie, *Imaginary Homelands: Essays and Criticism 1981–1991* (London: Granta, 1992): 15.

2 Relational Selves

1 Gilmore, *Autobiographics*: 127. Compare Evans, *Missing*: 83; Smith, *Subjectivity*: 19.
2 Misch, *History*, vol. 1: 9 (my emphasis).
3 Gusdorf, 'Conditions': 29. See also Smith's analysis of Francis Hart in *Poetics*: 12; and Gilmore's of Weintraub in *Autobiographics*: 127.
4 The argument that male autobiographical Selfhood is essentially non-relational seems counter-intuitive. It is a truism of psychoanalytic theory that, irrespective of gender, individuation and personality development take place in the context of family and social relationships. The 'linguistic turn' in post-structuralism has asserted that the Self only comes into existence when it is narrativised within a system of language which is

not the property of the individual. See Paul Smith, *Discerning*, Marcus, *Auto/biographical* (Chapter 5) and Anderson, *Autobiography* (Chapter 2). In any case, it is difficult to think of a male-authored example of the genre which contains *no* account of relations with 'Others', whether God, family, colleagues or friends (and enemies) – or, more commonly, a combination of these. Equally, the fact that autobiography is generally designed to be consumed by others inevitably implies some commitment to principles of relationality. Further, to the extent that such autobiographers become canonical, this is partly a consequence of their representative and, therefore, relational qualities. Arguably, however, in canonical autobiography 'relationality' is generally less concretely immediate in comparison with women's writing. In Augustine's *Confessions*, the most significant relationship is the highly abstract one with God. Montaigne has happily retreated from the world to the privacy of a library, where 'relationality' is conceived in the primarily textual terms of an engagement with the great minds of the past. For Rousseau, the great admirer of Robinson Crusoe, family has less importance still, as suggested by the subsidiary role assigned to Thérèse and the notorious abandonment of his children to the public charge. Curiously for such an otherwise politically engaged man, there is almost nothing in Barthes's autobiography on the social implications of his affective life (aside from his mother) or sexuality, let alone analysis of how relations in these spheres shaped his personality. Space constraints preclude analysis of other questions concerning reader relations, specifically the way that life-writing's meanings might change according to the kind of readers who consume it, where and when it is consumed.

5 Olney, 'Autobiography': 17.
6 Brodzki and Schenck, 'Introduction': 8.
7 Mary Mason, 'The Other Voice: Autobiographies of Women Writers' (1980), in Smith and Watson, *Women*: 321.
8 Perreault, *Writing*: 2; compare Maroula Joannou, '"She Who Would Be Politically Free Herself Must Strike the Blow": Suffragette Autobiography and Suffragette Militancy', in Swindells, *Uses*: 31–44.
9 Torres, 'Construction': 278.
10 Doris Sommer, '"Not Just a Personal Story": Women's *Testimonios* and the Plural Self', in Brodzki and Schenck, *Life-Lines*: 130. Compare Lionnet, *Autobiographical*: 36; *Postcolonial*: 26, 39.
11 Longley, 'Autobiographical': 375.
12 Olney, 'Autobiography': 18.
13 Carole Boyce Davies, 'Collaboration and the Ordering Imperative in Life Story Production', in Smith and Watson, *De/Colonizing*: 7.
14 Gagnier, 'Literary': 264.
15 Cited in Paquet, *Caribbean*: 17.
16 Shirley Geok-Lin Lim, 'Semiotics, Experience, and the Material Self: An Inquiry into the Subject of the Contemporary Asian American Woman Writer', in Smith and Watson, *Women*: 445–6.
17 See Glissant, *Poetics*.
18 Fanon, *Black*: 110.
19 In the French original, Fanon uses terms like 'le noir' and 'le blanc' as both generic and gendered terms.
20 Ibid.: 213.
21 C.L.R. James, *Beyond a Boundary* (London: Serpent's Tail, [1963] 1994): 160. Hereafter cited as *BaB* in the text.
22 Anna Grimshaw, 'Introduction: C.L.R. James: A Revolutionary Vision for the Twentieth Century', in Grimshaw (ed.) *The C.L.R. James Reader* (Oxford: Blackwell, 1992): 19.
23 Ibid.: 13; compare Paul Buhle, *C.L.R. James: The Artist as Revolutionary* (London: Verso, 1988): 42.
24 Farrukh Dhondy, *C.L.R. James* (London: Weidenfeld and Nicolson, 2001): x.

25 To Constance Webb, n.d. (1944) in Grimshaw, *C.L.R. James Reader*: 162.

26 Ibid.: 152.

27 Even if James's Marxism/Trotskyism can be taken as a symptom of 'assimilation', in itself a problematic argument, James's relationship with both was contestatory, notably on the grounds of their inattention to race as a category of identity and of their hostility to popular culture. Similar arguments might be made about James's nationalism. Rather than being simply 'a derivative discourse' (see Partha Chatterjee, *Nationalism and the Colonial World: A Derivative Discourse?* [London: Zed, 1986]), it has distinctively Caribbean inflections in the same way as the West Indian style of cricket.

28 Buhle, *C.L.R. James*: 7.

29 Grimshaw, 'Introduction': 14.

30 Brett St Louis, *Rethinking Race, Politics, and Poetics: C.L.R. James's Critique of Modernity* (London: Routledge, 2007): 161.

31 C.L.R. James, *Cricket*, ed. Anna Grimshaw (London: Allison and Busby, 1986): 218.

32 Ato Quayson, 'Caribbean Configurations: Characterological Types and the Frames of Hybridity', *Interventions: International Journal of Postcolonial Studies*, 1(3) (1999): 340; compare Anthony Bogues, *Caliban's Freedom: The Early Political Thought of C.L.R. James* (London: Pluto, 1997): 24.

33 Aldon Nielsen, *C.L.R. James: A Critical Introduction* (Jackson: University of Mississippi Press, 1997): 182.

34 Grimshaw, 'Introduction': 12.

35 St Louis, *Rethinking*: 3.

36 Grant Farred, '"Victorian with a Rebel Seed": C.L.R. James, Postcolonial Intellectual', *Social Text*, 38 (1994): 30.

37 C.L.R. James, 'Whitman and Melville', in *C.L.R. James Reader*: 209.

38 Brendan Behan, *Borstal Boy* (London: Arrow, [1958] 1990): 121. Hereafter *BB* in the text.

39 There is some debate over the target of Behan's mission and whether it was officially sanctioned. See Ted E. Boyle, *Brendan Behan* (New York: Twayne, 1969): 37ff.

40 Kipling is mentioned on 210 in more neutral terms, reflecting Behan's changing attitude towards England.

41 E.H. Mikhail, ed., *The Letters of Brendan Behan* (Basingstoke: Macmillan, 1992): 7.

42 Rae Jeffs, *Brendan Behan: Man and Showman* (London: Corgi, [1966] 1968): 16.

43 Behan describes North Dublin as 'the last outpost of toughness' in *Hold Your Hour and Have Another* (London: Hutchinson, 1963): 149; however, *BB* is not above using class stereotypes to position Behan as 'better' than some of his antagonists. See, for example, pp. 221, 242, 258, 359. For a socialist, moreover, he is curiously affirmative of the semi-feudal society in Borstal. In some ways that part of his narrative resembles the nostalgic public-schooldays genre.

44 Colbert Kearney, *The Writings of Brendan Behan* (Dublin: Gill and Macmillan, 1977): 85.

45 Homosexuality was not legalised in Eire until 1993. The banning of *Borstal Boy* there for many years can be understood partly in terms of Behan's sympathetic depiction of the homosocial carceral worlds through which he moves.

46 Peter René Gerdes suggests that: 'In proportion to its population Ireland has produced more prison literature than any other country.' See *The Major Works of Brendan Behan* (Frankfurt: Peter Lang, 1973): 93.

47 Ulick O'Connor, however, accused Behan of a propensity to '"play Paddy to the Saxon"'. See John Brannigan, *Brendan Behan: Cultural Nationalism and the Revisionist Writer* (Dublin: Four Courts Press, 2002): 44. It is difficult for a contemporary English reader to tell how much of Behan's language is invented. However, Kearney argues that Behan was 'an arranger of existing language rather than an inventor'; *Writings*: 102.

48 Behan later wrote that by the time he left Borstal he had 'an almost English accent'. See *Confessions*: 13.

49 Kearney, *Writings*: 101. Compare Brannigan, *Brendan*: 144ff.

50 By contrast, Margaret Sheridan links Behan's cursing to the example of the Citizen and Private Carr in Joyce's *Ulysses*. See E.H. Mikhail, ed., *The Art of Brendan Behan* (London: Vision, 1979): 87.

51 Brannigan, *Brendan*: 129.

52 Compare some canonical western autobiography (Edmund Gosse, James Mill, for example).

53 V.S. Naipaul, *Letters Between a Father and Son* (London: Little, Brown, 1999).

54 See Gagnier, 'Literary', for a discussion of the complex and uneven articulation of class and gender identities in western women's life-writing.

55 Cited in Perreault, *Writing*: 197.

56 Hertha D. Sweet Wong, 'First-Person Plural: Subjectivity and Community in Native American Women's Autobiography', in Smith and Watson, *Women*: 170; compare Quinby, 'Subject': 297, 299.

57 Lionnet, *Postcolonial*: 22.

58 Devy, 'Romantic': 65.

59 Olney, 'Autobiography': 13. Compare *Tell*: 26.

60 Jawaharlal Nehru, *An Autobiography: With Musings on Recent Events in India* (Bombay: Allied Publishers, [1936] 1962): 596.

61 V.S. Naipaul, *A Way in the World: A Sequence* (London: Minerva: 1994): 18, 16.

62 See Kobena Mercer, 'Black Art and the Burden of Representation', *Third Text*, 10 (Spring) 1990: 61–78.

63 Robert Fraser, 'Dimensions of Personality: Elements of the Autobiographical Mode', in MacDermott, *Autobiographical*: 86.

3 Embodied Selves

1 Sidonie Smith, 'Identity's Body', in Ashley *et al.*, *Autobiography*: 266; compare Shirley Neuman, 'Autobiography, Bodies, Manhood', in Smith and Watson, *Women*: 416. Such claims may seem surprising, even in relation to the canonical western tradition, not least because such autobiographers are often preoccupied by the relationship of the genre to the (literal) death of the Subject. See Marcus, *Auto/biographical*: 208ff. Further, Augustine's struggle against the flesh is a major theme up to his conversion. Montaigne's 'melancholy' seems inexplicable without reference to the 'stone' which plagued his everyday life. Rousseau's encounters with the bodies of others, notably the masturbating 'Moor', and the malformed nipple of Zulietta, are decisive in his psychosexual development. See Rousseau, *Confessions*, trans. A Scholar (Oxford: Oxford University Press, 2000): 65ff, 311ff. For Barthes, the body is crucial in undoing the binarism characteristic of western thinking. Anticipating Judith Butler, he conceives of the Body as a site on which social relations are inscribed: 'The social division occurs within my body: my body itself is social.' See Roland Barthes, *Roland BARTHES by Roland Barthes*, trans. R. Howard (1975; New York: Farrar, Straus and Giroux, 1977): 124. Nonetheless, the western canon certainly appears to prioritise other aspects of autobiographical Selfhood. For Augustine, the Body is something which must be transcended to achieve spiritual self-realisation. In Montaigne, (the failure of) the Body is something to be stoically endured if it is not to distract from his intellectual engagement with the great minds in his library. For Rousseau, bodily desire is especially dangerous insofar as it takes him 'almost beyond the grasp of reason' and threatens to prevent him from remaining 'whole for [him]self'. See Rousseau, *Confessions*: 106, 191. Meanwhile, as Paul Smith notes, 'the nature and construction of the sexed "subject" [are] a consideration almost entirely absent from Barthes's work' (Paul Smith, *Discerning the Subject*, Minneapolis: University of Minnesota Press, 1988: xxxii). Instead, as with earlier canonical texts, the focus is on the development of the writer's mind.

2 Gilmore, *Autobiographics*: 14, 84.

3 Neuman, 'Autobiography': 415.

4 Misch, *History*: 8, 13 (my emphasis).
5 Gusdorf, 'Conditions': 38 (my emphasis), 44.
6 Mason, 'Other': 321. Compare Gilmore, *Autobiographics*: 84.
7 Gilmore, *Autobiographics*: 84.
8 Fedwa Malti-Douglas, *Men, Women and God(s): Nawal El Saadawi and Arab Feminist Poetics* (Berkeley, CA: University of California Press, 1995): 28.
9 Smith, 'Identity's Body': 271.
10 Lim, 'Semiotics': 449; compare Nancy Mairs, 'The Way In', in Smith and Watson, *Women*: 471; and Smith, *Subjectivity*: 23.
11 John Beverley, 'The Margin at the Center: on *Testimonio* (Testimonial Narrative)', in Smith and Watson, *De/Colonizing*: 109.
12 Paquet, *Caribbean*: 41.
13 Neuman, '"An Appearance"': 294; compare Smith, *Subjectivity*: 12, 16–17.
14 Conversely, Watson suggests that for some postcolonial life-writers, notably Buchi Emecheta, western feminism's emphasis on the sexual dimensions of embodiment is something to be wary of. See 'Unspeakable': 398–9. See also the discussion of El Saadawi below.
15 Fanon, *Black*: 111, 138.
16 Ibid.: 126–7.
17 M.K. Gandhi, *An Autobiography: or The Story of My Experiments with Truth*, trans. Mahadev Desai (London: Penguin, [1927–29] 1982): 406. Hereafter cited in the text as *AA*.
18 K. Chellappan, 'The Discovery of India and the Self in Three Autobiographies', in H.H. Anniah Gowda (ed.) *The Colonial and the Neo-Colonial Encounters in Commonwealth Literature* (Mysore: University of Mysore, 1983): 96; compare N. Radhakrishnan, 'Foreword', in K.D. Gangrade, *Gandhi's Autobiography: Moral Lessons* (New Delhi: Gandhi Smriti and Darshan Samith, 1998): ix.
19 Jeffrey Meyers, 'Indian Autobiography: Gandhi and Chaudhuri', in Carol Ramelb (ed.) *Biography East and West: Selected Conference Papers* (Honolulu: University of Hawaii, 1989): 113.
20 Joseph Alter, *Gandhi's Body: Sex, Diet, and the Politics of Nationalism* (Philadelphia, PA: University of Pennsylvania Press, 2000): 18.
21 See, for example, Erik Erikson, *Life History and the Historical Moment* (New York: Norton, 1975): 124 ff.
22 Indentured labour in South Africa and the tithe system in the indigo industry in Champeran are prime instances of the exploitation of the bodies of the colonised, as labour power.
23 Parama Roy, 'Meat-Eating, Masculinity, and Renunciation in India: A Gandhian Grammar of Diet', *Gender and History*, 14(1) (2002): 63.
24 The socialised dimensions of individual bodies are particularly well reflected in this conflict over 'ownership' of Gandhi's body.
25 Contrast Gandhi's early 'failures' with prostitutes (as traumatic as Rousseau's) in which he 'felt as though my manhood had been injured' (*AA*: 37).
26 Quoted in Bikhu Parekh, *Colonialism, Tradition and Reform: An Analysis of Gandhi's Political Discourse* (London: Sage, 1989): 199.
27 See Robert J.C. Young, *Postcolonialism: An Historical Introduction* (Oxford: Blackwell, 2001): 323.
28 David Arnold argues that South African prisons taught Gandhi the importance of the suffering body as political spectacle/symbol. See 'The Self and The Cell: Indian Prison Narratives as Life Histories', in David Arnold and Stuart Blackburn (eds) *Telling Lives in India: Biography, Autobiography, and Life History* (Delhi: Permanent Black, 2004): 37.
29 Julie Codell, 'Excursive Discursive in Gandhi's *Autobiography*: Undressing and Redressing the Transnational Self', in David Amigoni (ed.) *Life Writing and Victorian Culture* (Aldershot: Ashgate, 2006): 137.
30 Alter, *Gandhi's Body*: 43.

31 For discussions of *An Autobiography* as an experimental hybrid of eastern and western traditions in terms of both its thematics of Selfhood and form, see Majeed, *Autobiography*: 217ff; Parekh, *Colonialism*: 251ff; and Vijay Mishra, 'Defining the Self in Indian Literary and Filmic Texts', in Wimal Dissanayake (ed.) *Narratives of Agency: Self-Making in China, India, and Japan* (London: University of Minnesota Press, 1996): 117–50.

32 Nawal El Saadawi, *A Daughter of Isis: The Autobiography of Nawal El Saadawi*, trans. Sherif Hetata (1999; London: Zed, 2002): 223. Cited hereafter in this chapter as *DI*.

33 Cohen, '"But Have Some Art"': 71.

34 I follow El Saadawi in using this term for a practice sometimes described as 'clitoridectomy' or 'female genital mutilation'.

35 According to Rita Stephen, 92 per cent of Egyptian women continue to undergo circumcision. See 'Arab Women Writing Their Sexuality', *Hawwa: Journal of Women of the Middle East and the Islamic World*, 4(2–3) (2006): 170.

36 Compare Badran, 'Expressing': 276.

37 D.H. Melhem rightly argues that for El Saadawi 'postcolonial means neo-colonial'. See 'Nawal El Saadawi's "Daughter of Isis": Life and Times via the Plenitude of Her Writings', *Aljadid: A Review and Record of Arab Culture and Arts*, 5.29 (1999): 12.

38 Cohen, '"But Have Some Art"': 69.

39 Fedwa Malti-Douglas, 'Writing Nawal El Saadawi', in Diane Elam and Robyn Wiegman (eds) *Feminism Beside Itself* (London: Routledge, 1995): 284. Amal Amireh partly blames western appropriations of El Saadawi for her negative reputation in the Arab world: 'The socialist feminist is rewritten as a liberal individualist and the anti-imperialist as a native informant. This framing often discredits El Saadawi with her Arab audiences.' See 'Framing Nawal El Saadawi: Arab Feminism in a Transnational World', *Signs*, 26(1) (2000): 228.

40 Cohen, '"But Have Some Art"': 65.

41 Amireh, 'Framing': 220.

42 Malti-Douglas, 'Writing Nawal El Saadawi': 290. See also Cohen, '"But Have Some Art"': 67.

43 Fanon, *Black*: 232.

44 The portrait's significance as a corporeal representation extends further. First, it serves partly to authenticate the claim that it is 'written by himself', in the manner of a photograph, thereby countering any supposition that what follows has been invented for strategic purposes by a white abolitionist. It also affirms his education and truthfulness (he is holding a Bible, which associates his text with 'Holy Writ') and his respectability (he is dressed as a member of the British middle classes).

45 Neuman, '"Appearance"': 294.

46 Seacole, *Wonderful Adventures*: 5.

47 See, for example, Jenny Sharpe, *Allegories of Empire: The Figure of Woman in the Colonial Text* (Minnesota: University of Minnesota Press, 1993).

48 Equiano, *Interesting*: 38.

49 Claude McKay, *A Long Way from Home* (London: Pluto, [1937] 1985): 88, 76.

50 While McKay's bisexuality complicates this argument, it does not undermine it.

51 Smith, 'Identity's Body': 288.

52 Fanon, *Black*: 109–14; McKay, *Long*: 183; Emecheta, *Head*: 169–70; compare 29.

4 Located Selves

1 On the Body as 'place', see, for example, Linda McDowell, *Gender, Identity and Place: Understanding Feminist Geographies* (Cambridge: Polity, 1999): 34. Compare Wendy Harcourt and Arturo Escobar, *Women and the Politics of Place* (Bloomfield, CT: Kumarian Press, 2005): 2.

2 McDowell, *Gender*: 4. Mona Domosh and Joni Seager argue that 'places' are 'spaces that have been invested with meaning'. See *Putting Women in their Place: Feminist Geographers Make Sense of the World* (London: Guilford, 2001): xxii.

3 Smith, 'Identity's Body': 267 (my emphasis).

4 Neuman, 'Autobiography': 415 (my emphasis).

5 On the very rare occasions to the contrary, for example, Lionnet's discussion of Augustine, such analysis has usually been undertaken from a minoritarian/postcolonial perspective. See *Autobiographical*: 19ff.

6 Mairs, 'Way': 471; compare Smith, *Subjectivity*: 23.

7 Susan Stanford Friedman, *Mappings: Feminism and the Cultural Geographies of Encounter* (Princeton, NJ: Princeton University Press, 1998): 19.

8 Brodzki and Schenck, 'Introduction': 14.

9 Bella Brodzki, 'Mothering, Displacement, and Language in the Autobiographies of Nathalie Sarraute and Christa Wolf', in Brodzki and Schenck, *Life-Lines*: 243–4.

10 Benstock, 'Introduction': 1. Compare Smith and Watson's *Reading*. Taking their cue from Audre Lorde's claim that 'our place was the very house of difference' (ibid.: 37), the authors explore the 'sites of storytelling' (ibid.: 58) primarily in terms of institutional contexts of production and consumption.

11 Felicity Nussbaum, 'Eighteenth-Century Women's Autobiographical Commonplaces', in Benstock, *Private*: 150.

12 See Edward Said, *Orientalism* (London: Peregrine, [1978] 1991): 20.

13 To some degree, the absence of such a focus within mainstream Auto/biography Studies can be attributed to the apparently marginal importance which canonical autobiographers themselves accord the issues involved. Augustine makes something of his urgent desire to return to Africa once his mother Monica dies, and of her desire to be buried there. Montaigne occasionally alerts the reader to his specific regional identity, for example, in his comments on the distance of Bordeaux from Paris and the peculiar dialect of his region. Rousseau, too, sometimes discusses his roots in Geneva and is desperate to return there when he begins to suffer persecution. And, like Montaigne, Barthes draws attention to his attachment to his natal culture in Aquitaine. However, to different degrees, all four figures disclaim the importance of their particular geocultural roots and current locations compared to other dimensions of subjectivity. On his return to Africa, Augustine constructs himself as the spokesman of the Catholic (i.e. 'universal') Church in explicit opposition to the regional Christianities of North Africa. Montaigne positions himself primarily in relation to an equally 'universal' classical culture, a mode of self-identification reinforced by being brought up a Latin speaker. As he is chased from pillar to post, Rousseau abjures his citizenship rights and prefers to wander the earth like Cain. For Barthes, the world of 'text' into which he dissolves himself has no particular geographical locus or affiliation.

14 Gusdorf, 'Conditions': 32.

15 See Anderson, *Autobiography*: 4.

16 Spengemann, *Forms*: 192ff. Olney is a partial exception to this pattern. However, he is prone to generalisation, even essentialism, which discounts the vast geo-cultural variations even within Africa. See *Tell*: 26 and 'Autobiography': 14–17.

17 Smith and Watson, *Reading*: 57.

18 Ibid.: 58.

19 Cited in Innes, *Cambridge*: 72.

20 Warley, 'Locating': 23; compare Whitlock, *Soft*: 10. Such issues have been more commonly explored in postcolonial *fiction*. See, for instance, Lionnet, *Autobiographical* and Lionnet, *Postcolonial*; and Rosemary Marangoly George, *The Politics of Home: Postcolonial Relocations and Twentieth-Century Fiction* (Cambridge: Cambridge University Press, 1996).

21 See Benny Morris, *The Birth of the Palestinian Refugee Problem, 1947–1949* (Cambridge: Cambridge University Press, 1987) and Ilan Pappé, *The Ethnic Cleansing of Palestine* (Oxford: Oneworld, 2006).

22 http://news.bbc.co.uk/1/hi/world/middle_east/6339835.stm.

23 Fanon, *Black*: 88 (my emphasis).

24 Ibid.: 16 (compare 25), 230.

25 Ibid.: 151–2, 223.
26 Wole Soyinka, *Aké: The Years of Childhood* (1981; New York: Vintage, 1983): 149. Hereafter cited as *A* in the text.
27 Tim Cribb, 'African Autobiography and the Idea of the Nation', in Bruce Bennett, Susan Cowan, Jacqueline Lo, Satendra Nadan and Jennifer Webb (eds) *Resistance and Reconciliation: Writing in the Commonwealth* (Canberra: ACLALS, 2003): 64.
28 Soyinka, in Jo Gulledge, ed., 'Seminar on *Aké* with Wole Soyinka', *The Southern Review*, 23(3) (1987): 511.
29 Mpalive-Hangson Msiska, *Wole Soyinka* (Plymouth: Northcote House, 1998): 82.
30 Derek Wright, *Wole Soyinka Revisited* (New York: Twayne, 1993): 141.
31 Biodun Jeyifo, *Wole Soyinka: Politics, Poetics and Postcolonialism* (Cambridge: Cambridge University Press, 2004): 192; Ato Quayson, 'Wole Soyinka and Autobiography as Political Unconscious', *Journal of Commonwealth Literature*, 31(2) (1996): 21.
32 See, for example, David Harvey, *The Condition of Postmodernity: An Enquiry into the Origins of Social Change* (Oxford: Blackwell, 1990).
33 James Gibbs, *Wole Soyinka* (Basingstoke: Macmillan, 1986): 14.
34 Fraser, 'Dimensions': 85.
35 Gulledge, 'Seminar': 512.
36 Wright, *Wole*: 12.
37 Mpalive-Hangson Msiska, *Postcolonial Identity in Wole Soyinka* (Amsterdam: Rodopi, 2007): xxxi.
38 Louis James, 'Wole Soyinka's *Aké*: Autobiography and the Limits of Experience', in MacDermott, *Autobiographical*: 114.
39 Shirley Geok-Lin Lim, *Among the White Moon Faces: Memoirs of an Asian American Woman* (1996; Singapore: Times Editions/Marshall Cavendish, 2004): 35. Hereafter cited in this chapter as *AWMF*.
40 See Pauline Newton, *Transcultural Women of Late Twentieth-Century U.S. American Literature* (Aldershot: Ashgate, 2005): 107; compare Eleanor Ty, *The Politics of the Visible in Asian American Narrative* (London: University of Toronto Press, 2004): 91.
41 See Ngugi's account of his secondary education in 'The Language of African Literature'.
42 Shirley Geok-Lin Lim, 'The Im/Possibility of Life-Writing in Two Languages', in Isabelle de Courtivron (ed.) *Lives in Translation: Bilingual Writers on Identity and Creativity* (Basingstoke: Palgrave, 2003): 44.
43 Mohammed Quayum, 'Shirley Geok-Lin Lim: An Interview', *MELUS*, 28(4) (2003): 85.
44 Compare Sara Suleri's conception of her writing as a 'home' in *Meatless Days: A Memoir* (1989; London: Flamingo, 1991): 173. See also Chapter 6.
45 Jeffrey Partridge, *Beyond Literary Chinatown* (London: University of Washington Press, 2007): 104; compare Ty, *Politics*: 96.
46 Nehru, *Autobiography*: 596.
47 McKay, *Long*: 150.
48 Glissant, *Poetics*: 12, 33.
49 Said, *Out of Place*: 294.
50 Glissant, *Poetics*: 18.
51 Paquet, *Caribbean*: 260.

5 Working the borders of genre in postcolonial life-writing

1 See Caren Kaplan, 'Resisting Autobiography: Out-law Genres and Transnational Feminist Subjects', in Smith and Watson, *De/Colonizing*: 117.
2 See Marcus, *Auto/biographical*: Chapter 6; compare Gilmore, 'The Mark of Autobiography: Postmodernism, Autobiography, and Genre', in Ashley *et al.*, *Autobiography*: 5; and Anderson, *Autobiography*: 7–17.
3 Misch, *History*: 7.
4 Gusdorf, 'Conditions': 35; compare Pascal, *Design*: 22–3.

5　Gusdorf, 'Conditions': 35.

6　Olney, 'Autobiography': 25. Olney himself partially dissents from this argument.

7　Gusdorf, 'Conditions': 43, 41. Again, Gusdorf partially dissents from this view.

8　Estelle Jelinek, 'Introduction: Women's Autobiography and the Male Tradition', in Jelinek (ed.) *Women's Autobiography: Essays in Criticism* (Bloomington, IN: Indiana University Press, 1980): 17.

9　Ibid.; compare Smith, *Poetics*: 17.

10　Liz Stanley, *The Auto/biographical I: The Theory and Practice of Feminist Auto/biography* (Manchester: Manchester University Press, 1992): 13.

11　See, for example, Marcus, *Auto/biographical*: 7–8, 229–69; compare Swindells, 'Introduction', in Swindells, *Uses*: 9.

12　Smith, *Poetics*: 59. Compare Benstock, 'Introduction': 2.

13　Gilmore, *Autobiographics*: 96; compare Smith, *Poetics*: 53–4.

14　The first letter will be capitalised when referring to texts which narrativise history (lower case), the latter being understood as the experiences and events which constitute the past.

15　Torres, 'Construction': 277.

16　Lionnet, *Autobiographical*: 4; Lionnet, *Postcolonial*: 23.

17　Fanon, *Black*: 14, 60. The opening page exemplifies this fragmentary tendency even at the micrological level.

18　Cited in Coe, *When*: 3 and 5; compare MacDermott, *Autobiographical*: 8–10.

19　Misch, *History*: 11; compare Gusdorf, 'Conditions': 42; and Gilmore, *Limits*: 9.

20　Pascal, *Design*; compare Gusdorf, 'Conditions': 43 and Evans, *Missing*: 16, 24.

21　Spengemann, *Forms*: xii.

22　As Eakin comments, one can conflate these genres only 'by wilfully ignoring the autobiographer's explicit posture as autobiographer in the text'. See *Fictions*: 4.

23　Spengemann, *Forms*: xii; compare Eakin, *Fictions*: 3, 36.

24　de Man, 'Autobiography': 266. But one should distinguish between 'immanent' and willed slippage between the two, otherwise the writer is denied any agency.

25　Evans, *Missing*: 1; compare Bergland, 'Postmodernism': 134; and Smith, 'Performativity, Autobiographical Practice, Resistance', in Smith and Watson, *Women*: 108.

26　Gusdorf, 'Conditions': 43.

27　Misch argues that 'lies' in autobiography paradoxically reveal truths about the 'spirit' of the writer which it is the prime preoccupation of the genre to express. See *History*: 9. Compare Gusdorf, 'Conditions': 47; and Jean Starobinski, 'The Style of Autobiography', in Olney, *Autobiography*: 75.

28　Lejeune, 'Autobiographical': 192.

29　See Anderson, *Autobiography*: 132–3.

30　On Menchú and Beah, see www.wikipedia.org/wiki/Rigoberta_Menchu%C3%BA; and http://www.huffingtonpost.com/2008/01/31/boy-soldier-defends-his-b_n_84195.html.

31　It might seem contentious to claim Naipaul as a Caribbean life-writer. However, I do so because the two texts under consideration focus strongly on his formation there.

32　Paquet, *Caribbean*: 3.

33　See also the discussion of James in Chapter 2.

34　Thieme, 'Appropriating': 215–21.

35　V.S. Naipaul, *Finding the Centre: Two Narratives* (Harmondsworth: Penguin, [1984] 1985): 70. Henceforth cited in the text as *FC*.

36　V.S. Naipaul, *A Way in the World: A Sequence* (London: Minerva, 1994): 70. Henceforth cited in the text as *WW*.

37　Compare Naipaul, *Reading and Writing: A Personal Account* (New York: New York Review of Books Inc., 2000): 7, 10, 13.

38　Symptomatically, Naipaul relates early uncertainties with first-person narrative to his position as a 'colonial' (*FC*: 11).

39 Stephanie Jones, 'The Politics and Poetics of Diaspora in V.S. Naipaul's *A Way in the World*', *Journal of Commonwealth Literature*, 35(1) (2000): 87.

40 de Man, 'Autobiography': 266. If either of Naipaul's sub-titles aims to impose aesthetic unity, it is doubtful whether they succeed. For example, the concept of sequence as temporal ordering is contradicted by the fact that the second 'autobiographical' section precedes the first in historical time.

41 See Marcus, *Auto/biographical*: 144–5; compare Gilmore, *Autobiographics*: 11, 185.

42 See Lionnet, 'Of Mangoes and Maroons: Language, History, and the Multicultural Subject of Michelle Cliff's *Abeng*', in Smith and Watson, *De/Colonizing*: 321–45. Gilmore, *Autobiographics*: 100ff and *Limits*: 99ff.

43 See Moore-Gilbert, *Hanif Kureishi* (Manchester: Manchester University Press, 2001): 171–9.

44 Suleri, *Meatless Days: A Memoir* (London: Flamingo, [1989] 1991): 156.

45 Misch, *History*: 2.

46 Gusdorf, 'Conditions': 35, 36.

47 Weintraub, 'Autobiography': 249.

48 Marcus, *Auto/biographical*: 181.

49 Misch, *History*: 15; compare x.

50 Gusdorf, 'Conditions': 36; Weintraub, 'Autobiography': 239.

51 Olney, 'Autobiography': 20.

52 Misch, *History*: 2.

53 Gandhi, *Autobiography*: 258; compare Nehru's insistence that the reader who mistakes his autobiography for 'a survey of recent Indian history [may] lead him to attach a wider importance to it than it deserves'; *Autobiography*: xii.

54 Swindells, 'Introduction': 9.

55 Jerry White, 'Beyond Autobiography', in Raphael Samuel (ed.) *People's History and Socialist Theory* (London: Routledge and Kegan Paul, 1981): 35–6.

56 See, for example, Joan Scott, 'Feminism's History', in Sue Morgan (ed.) *The Feminist History Reader* (London: Routledge, 2006): 388ff. A parallel move towards an explicitly 'postcolonial historiography' began at the same time as feminist historiography. See Arnold Temu and Bonaventure Swai, *Historians and Africanist History: A Critique: Postcolonial Historiography Examined* (London: Zed, 1981); Alessandro Triulzi, 'Decolonising African History', in Samuel, *People's*: 286–319; and the work of the Indian 'Subaltern Studies' group.

57 Sue Morgan, 'Introduction: Writing Feminist History: Theoretical Debates and Critical Practices', in Morgan, *Feminist*: 1.

58 Ibid.: 8.

59 Ibid.: 3. In strong contrast to White, Raphael Samuel urges colleagues to 'learn from life histories, whether in the form of oral history or written autobiography'. See 'People's History', in Samuel, *People's*: xxxii.

60 Morgan, 'Introduction': 31.

61 See, for example, Joannou, 'She': 36.

62 Like Hegel's Africa, Marx's rural India is outside historical time. See Said, *Orientalism*: 153–6. Nirad Chaudhuri provides strong counter-evidence in his stress on the communal History of rural India. See *Autobiography*: 15, for example. Henceforth cited as *AUI* in the text. Compare Ganeswar Mishra, 'How Does an Indian Village Speak?: A Study of the Form of Prafulla Mohanti's *My Village, My Life*', in MacDermott, *Autobiographical*: 157–62. Conversely, Claude McKay complains of comparable deficiencies in recent twentieth-century western History. Reading H.G. Wells's *Outline of History* (1920), he records being 'shocked' by the lack of attention to Africa and Africans in this supposed 'world History'. See McKay, *Long*: 121–4.

63 Anne Goldman, 'Autobiography, Ethnography, and History: a Model for Reading', in Smith and Watson, *Women*: 295.

64 See, for example, Lionnet, *Postcolonial*: 22.

65 Longley, 'Autobiographical': 372 (my emphasis).
66 Compare Weintraub's account of Gibbon's *Autobiography* in 'Autobiography': 248.
67 To this degree, Chaudhuri's text, like Gibbon's, is also an 'auto*biblio*graphy'. Ibid.: 244.
68 See Samuel, *People's*: xxvi.
69 Edward Gibbon, *Autobiography*, ed. M.M. Reese (London: Routledge and Kegan Paul, [1796] 1970): 1.
70 Ruvani Ranasinha, *South Asian Writers in Twentieth-Century Britain: Culture in Translation* (Oxford: Clarendon 2007): 74; compare 71–2.
71 See Chatterjee, *Nationalism*.
72 Naipaul, 'Indian': 143.
73 James, *Beyond*: n.p.; Mary Seacole, *The Wonderful Adventures of Mrs Seacole in Many Lands*, ed. Sarah Salih (1857; London: Penguin, 2005): 128. Henceforth cited as *WA* in the text.
74 McKay, *Long*: 124.
75 In contrast to Marcus, Swindells and Anderson, who are silent on the issue, Smith and Watson do consider travel-writing in relation to auto/biography. See *Reading*: 90–5, 99–105. However, the Subjects discussed are almost all white western males and the larger implications of the conjunction for the generic identity of auto/biography are not.
76 See, for example, Gusdorf, 'Conditions': 28; Spengemann, *Forms*: 171. One might consider that this offers an obvious opportunity to open up Auto/biography Studies from a gendered perspective.
77 Patrick Holland and Graham Huggan, *Tourists with Typewriters: Critical Reflections on Contemporary Travel Writing* (1998; Ann Arbor, MI: University of Michigan Press, 2000): 12. They argue that *contemporary* travel writing is partly distinguished by mockery of this desire, as part of a more general tendency to ironical self-reflexiveness in the genre. In this respect, as in others, Seacole anticipates some of the 'comic techniques of contemporary travel writing' as well as the 'relative lack of introspection' (ibid.: 17) of the Chatwinian model.
78 Ibid.: 17. Other parallels between the two genres include the fact that both are plagued by issues of truth claims (each has been prone to spectacular hoaxes) and problems of definition so acute that they are sometimes considered to be in terminal crisis.
79 Ibid.
80 Vincent Carretta, 'Olaudah Equiano: African British Abolitionist and Founder of the African American Slave Narrative', in Audrey Fisch (ed.) *The Cambridge Companion to the African American Slave Narrative* (Cambridge: Cambridge University Press, 2007): 47.
81 Majeed provides a masterly analysis of the relations between travel and identity-formation in relation to Gandhi and Nehru in *Autobiography*.
82 Compare Equiano's prefatory material. This device is not unprecedented, even in canonical autobiography (see Rousseau's *Confessions*, for example), reinforcing the habitual truth claims made by its practitioners and their equally conventional disclaimers of vanity as a motivation for writing.
83 Compare Seacole's suppression of any account of the 'other lands' she visits en route from the Crimea at the end of the text (*WA*: 187).
84 *WA* counts as autobiography according to Naipaul's definition of the genre as 'a story of a life or deeds done' (*FC*: 9); and as travel-writing by virtue of its emphasis on 'adventure' and 'the manners and customs' of at least some of the peoples encountered. To some extent, it also conforms to the 'trials and tribulations' model of spiritual autobiography.
85 Sara Salih, 'Introduction', to Seacole, *Wonderful*: xv–l.
86 Ibid.: xviii.
87 Pratt, *Imperial Eyes*: 168–9.
88 Said's critique of the genre in *Orientalism* has been echoed in many subsequent analyses. See, for example, Nicholas Thomas, *Colonialism's Culture: Anthropology, Travel and Government* (Cambridge: Polity, 1994).

89 Salih, 'Introduction': xxix.
90 Holland and Huggan, *Tourists*: 14.
91 Pratt, *Imperial Eyes*: 7.
92 Devy, 'Romantic' 65.
93 Aside from Pratt, See also Sara Mills, *Discourses of Difference: An Analysis of Women's Travel Writing and Colonialism* (London: Routledge, 1991).

6 Non-western narrative resources in postcolonial life-writing

1 See, for example, Ashcroft *et al.*, *Empire*: 179ff; compare Elleke Boehmer, *Colonial and Postcolonial Literature* (Oxford: Oxford University Press, 1995): 187ff; Dennis Walder, *Postcolonial Literatures in English: History, Language, Theory* (Oxford: Blackwell, 1998): 116ff.
2 See, for example, Virginia Woolf, *A Room of One's Own* (1928) and Cixous, 'Laugh'.
3 Majeed, *Autobiography*: 217; Pilar Casamada, 'The *Autobiography* of Mahatma Gandhi', in MacDermott, *Autobiographical*: 45–8.
4 Devy, 'Romantic': 67.
5 Lim, 'Terms': 362.
6 Mishra, 'How Does': 160.
7 Devy, 'Romantic': 64.
8 Cited in Philomena Mariani, ed., *Critical Fictions: The Politics of Imaginative Writing* (Seattle: Bay Press, 1991): 227.
9 Bharati Mukherjee, 'A Four-Hundred-Year-Old Woman', in Mariani, *Critical*: 24.
10 Salman Rushdie, 'Introduction', in Salman Rushdie and Elizabeth West (eds) *The Vintage Book of Indian Writing* (London: Vintage, 1997): xii.
11 Ibid.: x.
12 Devy himself estimates that even in 1971, nearly two million Indians had English as their first language, with a vastly larger number speaking it as a second language. See *In Another Tongue: Essays on Indian English Literature* (New York: Peter Lang, 1993): 99.
13 Rushdie, *Imaginary Homelands*: 17.
14 Ibid.
15 Chinua Achebe, 'The African Writer and the English Language' (1965), in Achebe, *Morning Yet on Creation Day: Essays* (London: Heinemann, 1977): 61.
16 Whitlock, *Soft*: 4ff.
17 Fanon, *Black*: 18.
18 Ibid.: 38.
19 Ibid.: 31–2.
20 Ibid.: 35.
21 Ibid.: 26, 164.
22 Francis Jeanson, 'Préface' and 'Reconnaissance de Fanon', in Fanon, *Peau Noire, Masques Blancs,* ed. F. Jeanson (Paris: Seuil, 1965): 234, 12 (my translations).
23 Fanon, *Black*: 153.
24 Ibid.: 174, 9. The oral qualities of *Black Skin* are enhanced by Fanon's method of composition, which involved dictating to Josie Dublé while 'he strode up and down the room like an actor declaiming his lines'. See David Macey, *Frantz Fanon: A Life* (London: Granta, 2000): 134.
25 Djebar, *Women of Algiers in their Apartment*, trans. Marjolijn de Jager (1982; London: University Press of Virginia, 1992): 172. Hereafter *WoA* in this chapter. Compare Djebar, *Ces voix qui m'assiègent ... en marge de ma francophonie* (Paris: Albin Michel, 1999): 181 (all subsequent translations mine). For more on how this interdiction affects women writers from the *Maghreb*, see Badran, 'Expressing': 276–7.
26 Compare Sara Suleri's experience, discussed in the next section. When she wanted to act, her Pakistani Muslim father insisted she use a stage name to prevent her real one being 'sullied'. See Sara Suleri Goodyear, *Boys Will Be Boys: A Daughter's Elegy* (Chicago: University of Chicago Press, 2003): 99. Henceforth cited as *B* in the text.

27 Mireille Calle-Gruber, *Assia Djebar* (Paris: adpf, 2006): 17.
28 Djebar, *Ces voix*: 112.
29 Calle-Gruber, *Assia*: 18 (my translation).
30 Compare Djebar, *Ces voix*: 35–6.
31 Assia Djebar, *So Vast the Prison*, trans. Betsy Wing (1995; London: Seven Stories Press, 1999): 206. Compare Suleri's relationship with Urdu and English. See *Boys*: 69.
32 Djebar, *Ces voix*: 177. Compare Suleri's description of Punjabi as 'a singularly male language'; *Boys*: 69.
33 Assia Djebar, *Fantasia: An Algerian Cavalcade*, trans. Dorothy S. Blair (Portsmouth, NH: Heinemann, [1985] 1993): 202. Hereafter cited as *F* in the text.
34 Anne Donadey, 'The Multilingual Strategies of Postcolonial Literature: Assia Djebar's Algerian Palimpsest', *World Literature Today*, 74(1) (2000): 27; Djebar, *Ces voix*: 29.
35 Mildred Mortimer, 'Entretien avec Assia Djebar, Ecrivain Algérien', *Research in African Literatures*, 28(2) (1992): 203.
36 For readings of Augustine as 'postcolonial', see Lionnet, *Autobiographical*: 19ff; and my 'The *Confessions* of Saint Augustine: Roots and Routes of Postcolonial Life-Writing', *A/B: Auto/Biography Studies*, 20(2) (2005): 155–69.
37 Compare Naipaul's use of this device in *A Way in the World*.
38 Reproduced on p. 242 of the text.
39 Djebar, *So Vast*: 72.
40 The best account of Djebar's use of the conventions of *nouba* in this film is Réda Bensmaïa, *Experimental Nations: Or, the Invention of the Maghreb* (Princeton, NJ: Princeton University Press, 2003).
41 Tony Langlois, 'Algeria', in Stanley Sadie (ed.) *The New Grove Dictionary of Music and Musicians*, 2nd edn, London: Macmillan, 2001, vol. 1: 369.
42 Ibid.: 369.
43 Bensmaïa, *Experimental*: 185; compare Salah el Mahdi, *La Musique Arabe* (Paris: Alphonse Leduc, 1972): 11.
44 They had still not been fully resolved in *La Nouba*, although Djebar describes it with symptomatic complexity as 'a "diary" of myself and my relations' (*Ces voix*: 100). For example – despite obvious parallels with Djebar – the principal protagonist is called Lila.
45 Langlois, 'Algeria': 371.
46 el Mahdi, *Musique*: 12.
47 Jane Hiddleston, *Assia Djebar: Out of Algeria* (Liverpool: Liverpool University Press, 2006): 69.
48 These parallels operate at the level of theme as well as form. (Indeed, some of the same women whose testimony is recuperated in *La Nouba* reappear in the later work.)
49 Christopher Field, '*Fantasia*', in Sadie, *New Grove Dictionary*, vol. 8: 545.
50 Ibid.: 555.
51 Ibid.: 546.
52 Ibid.: 555.
53 Hadi Bougherara, *Voyage Sentimental en Musique Arabo-Andalouse* (Paris: EDIF, 2002): 114; Mahmoud Guettat, *La Musique classique du Maghreb* (Paris: Sindbad, 1980): 305 (both translations mine).
54 el Mahdi, *Musique Arabe*: 11–12.
55 See Langlois, 'Algeria': *passim*.
56 Eugène Fromentin, *Une Année dans Le Sahel*, ed. L. Morel (1858; Oxford: Clarendon, 1911): 199 (all translations mine).
57 Dorothy Blair, 'Introduction', to Djebar, *Fantasia*: (n.p.).
58 Fromentin offers another example of such transfer. The word for money among the Hadjouts is *douro* (*Une Année*: 190). This is either an abbreviated adaptation of the *louis d'or*, a French coin of the time, or – more likely – the Spanish coin of that name, pointing to long-standing economic/cultural flows between Europe and the *maghreb*.

59 Ibid.: 186–7.
60 Ibid.: 187.
61 Ibid.: 196.
62 Djebar, *Ces voix*: 136.
63 Guettat, *Musique*: 188, 304.
64 Valérie Orlando identifies some striking parallels between his text and *Fantasia* at the level of form as well as theme. See '*Preface*: History/Story', in Fromentin, *Between Sea and Sahara: An Algerian Journal*, trans. Blake Robinson (Athens, OH: Ohio University Press, 1999): ix–xiii.
65 Donadey, 'Multilingual': 30ff.
66 Djebar, *Ces voix*: 51.
67 Lejeune is cited twice in an essay of 1986 in *Ces voix*: 121, 123.
68 Although Suleri married in 1993, I'll call her by the name which appears on *Meatless Days*, on which this section focuses. Suleri's father Zia had intended to write an auto-biography entitled *Boys Will Be Boys*. See Suleri, *Meatless Days: A Memoir* (London: Flamingo, [1989] 1991): 127, 183. Henceforth cited as *MD* in this chapter.
69 Sara Suleri Goodyear, *Boys Will Be Boys: A Daughter's Elegy* (Chicago: University of Chicago Press, 2003): 14.
70 As the daughter of a Welsh mother and Pakistani father, Suleri allegorises some conceptions of postcolonial 'hybridity'. But note her comment that 'I was never born a colonized person and do not really know the elation that he [Zia] felt when he hoisted up the Pakistani flag in London' (*B*: 120).
71 The 'miniatures' on display in the museum in 1976, the year Suleri left for the US, are catalogued in *Miniature Paintings on Display in the Lahore Museum: Mughal and Rajasthani Schools* (Lahore: Lahore Museum, 1976).
72 See, for example, Plate 26 in Som Prakash Verma, *Painting the Mughal Experience* (New Delhi: Oxford University Press, 2005). Compare 77–80.
73 Ibid.: 10.
74 Reproduced between pages 9 and 10 of *Miniature Paintings* and dated to the early eighteenth century.
75 Verma, *Painting*: 5.
76 Milo Beach, *Mughal and Rajput Painting, The New Cambridge History of India*, 1.3 (Cambridge: Cambridge University Press, 1992): 16.
77 Ibid.: 18.
78 Verma, *Painting*: 6–7.
79 D.J. Matthews and Christopher Shackle, 'Introduction', in D.J. Matthews and C. Shackle (eds) *An Anthology of Classical Urdu Love Lyrics: Texts and Translations* (Oxford: Oxford University Press, 1972): 1. Note Suleri's discussion of the 'couplet', or *sher*, on *B*: 69. Suleri herself wrote poetry from an early age, several examples being quoted in *Boys*. *MD* could be described as a series of love-poems to Suleri's family.
80 Ralph Russell and Khurshidad Islam, 'Ghalib: Life and Letters', in Ralph Russell (ed.) *The Oxford India Ghalib: Life, Letters and Ghazals* (New Delhi: Oxford University Press, 2003): 115. Several Mughal emperors also wrote memoirs. Babur's are mentioned on *B*: 44. This non-western tradition of auto/biographical writing may constitute another prompt for Suleri. Space constraints preclude me from pursuing this here.
81 *B*: 114. Note, too, the Yeats epigraph on *B*: 113. Ghālib's own children died in infancy, though he adopted two.
82 See *B*: 18; compare Ralph Russell, 'Introduction: Ghalib: A Self-Portrait', in Russell, *Oxford India*: 6.
83 Aijaz Ahmad, 'Introduction', in Ahmad (ed.) *Ghazals of Ghālib: Versions from the Urdu* (1971; Delhi: Oxford University Press, 1994): viii.
84 Ibid.: vii.
85 Russell, 'Introduction': 15.
86 Ahmad, 'Introduction': x. Compare Matthews and Shackle, 'Introduction': 10.

87 Ralph Russell, 'Getting to Know Ghalib', in Russell, ed., *Oxford India*: 288.

88 Ahmad, 'Introduction': xvii.

89 Ibid.: xvi.

90 Russell, 'Getting': 287.

91 Email from Sara Suleri, 8 April 2008.

92 Ahmad, 'Introduction': xxv.

93 Ibid. Compare Beach's stress on 'emotional understatement' in Mughal 'miniatures'; *Mughal*: 57.

94 Russell, 'Getting': 289.

95 Ahmad, 'Introduction': xxxi, xvi; Matthews and Shackle, 'Introduction': 7, 32.

96 Ahmad, 'Introduction': xv.

97 Matthews and Shackle, 'Introduction': 6.

98 Verma, *Painting*: 10.

99 Russell, 'Getting': 291.

100 Beach, *Mughal*: 95.

101 Compare Suleri's 'Woman Skin Deep: Feminism and the Postcolonial Condition', *Critical Inquiry*, 18(4) (1992): 756–69.

102 Comparable with the 'impurity' of the *nouba*, both Mughal painting and the *ghazal* can be understood as a hybrid of foreign (Persian) and Indian 'languages' with the former also being increasingly influenced by European art. See Verma, *Painting*: 57. Compare Beach, *Mughal*: xxxi; Ahmad, 'Introduction': xv.

103 Suleri has followed the same career path, currently working in the English department at Yale.

104 Jane Austen, *Letters to Her Sister Cassandra and Others*, ed. R.W. Chapman (Oxford: Clarendon, 1932), vol. 2: 469.

105 Ahmad, 'Introduction': vii; compare xxiv.

106 Lejeune, 'Autobiographical': 192; Spengemann, *Forms*: 171, xiv–xvi; compare the highly poetic language of Fanon's *Black Skin*. Fanon wrote to Jeanson that: 'I search, when I write about such things, to touch my reader affectively ... that is to say, his irrational side, almost bodily.' See *Peau*: 12.

107 Compare the phrase 'we Indians' in *MD*: 152.

108 Mary Prince, *The History of Mary Prince*, ed. Sara Salih (1831; London: Penguin, 2000): 3.

109 Ibid.: 10, 18–19 respectively.

110 However, one should not see orality as exclusively the property of postcolonial life-writing, for which reason it has not been discussed within the space constraints here.

111 Lionnet, 'Of Mangoes': 324.

112 Mukherjee, 'Four-Hundred': 27.

113 On the 'fresco' as an indigenous cultural form, see Beach, *Mughal*: 2, 89. Suleri's allusions to this 'public' form (*MD*: 172–3) seem significant in the context of her exposure of family 'secrets', as well as herself. See the clues offered on *MD*: 173. On Allende's use of *muralismo*, see *Paula*, trans. Margaret Peden (London: Flamingo, [1994] 1996): 23. Compare her image of the quilt to figure memory on 297 and 308. Allende claims affiliation to postcolonialism through her 'tot of Araucan or Mapuche Indian' blood (ibid.: 14).

114 Fanon, *Black*: 18; compare Thieme, 'Appropriating': 216.

115 Ibid.: 153.

116 Ibid.: 36.

117 This may explain the comparative rarity of postcolonial life-writing written entirely in Creole. Rare exceptions include Arnold Apple's *Son of Guyana* (1973) and Sistren Collective's *Lionheart Gal: Life Stories of Jamaican Women* (1986).

118 Rushdie, *Imaginary Homelands*: 17.

119 C.L. Innes, *A History of Black and Asian Writing in Britain 1700–2000* (Cambridge: Cambridge University Press, 2002): 131.

7 Political Self-representation in postcolonial life-writing

1 Misch, *History*: x, 15.
2 Gusdorf, 'Conditions': 28, 36 (my emphasis).
3 Spengemann, *Forms*: xiv–xvi.
4 Sau-ling Cynthia Wong, 'Immigrant Autobiography: Some Questions of Definition and Approach', in Smith and Watson, *Women*: 309. Compare Regenia Gagnier's argument about the 'functional' nature of much working-class writing as a factor in its exclusion from the canon; 'Literary': 264. By contrast, Devy claims that the focus on the individual in classical autobiography is intrinsically inimical to the concerns of less privileged sectors of Indian society. See 'Romantic': 65.
5 Evans, *Missing*: 138; compare Gilmore, *Limits*: 13.
6 Swindells, 'Conclusion': 205.
7 Whitlock, *Soft*: 10.
8 Smith, *Subjectivity*: 154.
9 Gilmore, 'Mark': 6; compare Gillian Whitlock, 'Introduction: Disobedient Subjects', in *Autographs: Contemporary Australian Autobiography* (St Lucia, Queensland: University of Queensland Press, 1996): ix.
10 Gilmore, *Autobiographics*: 3, 5; compare Gilmore, 'Mark': 12.
11 Smith: *Subjectivity*: 159.
12 Joannou, '"She"': 31–44.
13 Smith, *Subjectivity*: 157, 162.
14 See, for example, Wong, 'Immigrant': 309; Longley, 'Autobiographical': 372; Lionnet, 'Of Mangoes': 321.
15 Fanon, *Black*: 109.
16 Ibid.: 219; compare 224.
17 Ibid.: 226.
18 See, for example, *My Name is Rachel Corrie: The Writings of Rachel Corrie*, ed. by Alan Rickman and Katharine Viner (London: Royal Court, 2005); *The Shooting of Thomas Hurndall*, dir. Rowan Joffe (C4, 2008).
19 For a flavour of these regimes of abuse, consult the websites of Israeli Human Rights Organisations such as *B'tselem* and ICAHD.
20 See Eyal Weizman, *Hollow Land: Israel's Architecture of Occupation* (London: Verso, 2007). This wall was authorised by Israeli Prime Minister Ariel Sharon in 2002 to physically separate Israel from West Bank Palestinians, nominally to protect Israelis against the suicide bombings provoked by the frustrations of Occupation. It has, of course, conveniently been used to appropriate substantial tracts of prime Palestinian agricultural land and the water resources supporting it, thereby cutting off many communities from their livelihood. Construction proceeds apace, despite the judgement of the International Court of Justice in 2004 that it violates international law insofar as it is built on Palestinian rather than Israeli land.
21 This Convention was specifically designed to prevent the recurrence of tactics of population transfer employed by the Nazis. So desperate has Israel been to pursue its territorial ambitions by creating 'facts on the ground', that it has even imported impoverished Peruvian Indians (hastily 'converted' to Judaism) to swell the number of illegal settlers in Palestine. See Neri Livneh, 'How 90 Peruvians became the latest Jewish settlers', *The Guardian*, 7 August 2002: www.guardian.co.uk/israel/comment/0,10551,770315,00.html.
22 See, for example, Aijaz Ahmad, *In Theory: Classes, Nations, Literatures* (London: Verso, 1992): 18, 32; Thomas, *Colonialism's*: 17, 27; Neil Lazarus, *Nationalism and Cultural Practice in the Postcolonial World* (Cambridge: Cambridge University Press, 1999): 136–7.
23 See Abdirahman Hussein's judicious critique in *Edward Said: Criticism and Society* (London: Verso, 2002): 229ff of my failure to give sufficient weight to the Palestinian dimensions and orientations of Said's thinking in my *Postcolonial Theory: Contexts, Practices, Politics* (1997).

24 Donna Divine, '"Difficult Journey – Mountainous Journey", the Memoirs of Fadwa Tuqan', in Stanton, *Female*: 187–204.
25 Gunn, 'Politics'; Whitlock, *Soft*: 123–30.
26 Fanon, *Black*: 91.
27 Ibid.: 188.
28 See Chapter 2, Section 4 of the UN Charter at http://www.un.org/aboutun/charter/. Israel is not, of course, the only State in modern times to have breached this article.
29 Fanon, *Black*: 195.
30 Lim, *Among*: 195–6.
31 Ibid.: 196.
32 Ibid.
33 Ibid.: 246.
34 See my 'Postcolonialism and "the Figure of the Jew": Caryl Phillips and Zadie Smith', in James Acheson (ed.) *The Contemporary British Novel* (Edinburgh: Edinburgh University Press 2005): 108–17.
35 Email to me, 25 Sept. 2008.
36 Ghada Karmi, *In Search of Fatima: A Palestinian Story* (London: Verso, 2002): 210. I'm grateful to Sophia Brown for drawing this passage to my attention.
37 Edward Said, 'Between Worlds', in Said, *Reflections on Exile and Other Literary and Cultural Essays* (London: Granta, 2000): 566.
38 Said, *Out of Place* (London: Granta, [1999] 2000): 132. Hereafter cited parenthetically in the text as *OP*.
39 Cited in Judith Butler, *Precarious Lives: The Power of Mourning and Violence* (London: Verso, 2004): 10.
40 Tobias Döring, 'Edward Said and the Fiction of Autobiography', *Wasafiri*, 21(2) (2006): 74. One similarity with Conrad that Döring's excellent account overlooks is that Said also describes his text as a 'personal record'. See *Out of Place*: xv.
41 Edward Said, *Joseph Conrad and the Fiction of Autobiography* (Cambridge, MA: Harvard University Press, 1966): 4.
42 Anonymous, 'Said's Memoir Takes its Place Amid Attempts to Discredit', *Aljadid: A Review and Record of Arab Culture and Arts*, 5(29) (1999): 6.
43 Said, 'Between': 568.
44 Bryan Turner, 'Edward Said and the Exilic Ethic: On Being Out of Place', *Theory, Culture & Society*, 17(6) (2000): 127.
45 Alon Confino, 'Intellectuals and the Lure of Exile: Home and Exile in the Autobiographies of Edward Said and George Steiner', *The Hedgehog Review: Critical Reflections on Contemporary Culture*, 7(3) (2005): 26–7.
46 See Weiner, '"My Beautiful Old House" and other Fabrications by Edward Said', *Commentary*, 108(2) (1999): 23–31. As Alon Confino laconically remarks, 'This essay tells us more about Weiner and his like than about Said.' See 'Remembering Talbiyah: On Edward Said's *Out of Place*', *Israel Studies*, 5.2 (2000): 190. Nadia Gindi (who makes an appearance as one of Said's childhood friends in *OP*) provides a devastating account of Weiner's 'research methods' in 'On the Margins of a Memoir: a Personal Reading of Said's *Out of Place*', *Alif: Journal of Comparative Poetics*, 20(1) (2000): 294–5.
47 Weiner's piece was published weeks before *Out of Place* (doubtless as a 'spoiler'). See www.meforum.org/article/191.
48 Edward Alexander, 'Professor of Terror', *Commentary*, 88(2) (1989): 49–50.
49 Said, 'Introduction', *Reflections*: xxv.
50 Said, *Reflections on Exile*: 173.
51 Ibid.: 175.
52 Döring, 'Edward': 75.
53 Turner, 'Edward': 126; Confino, 'Intellectuals': 26.
54 Suad Amiry, *Sharon and My Mother-in-Law: Ramallah Diaries* (2003–4; London: Granta, 2005): ix. Cited hereafter as *SMM*.

55 In 2006, Israel unilaterally withdrew its Occupation forces and illegal settlers from Gaza (while quietly grabbing a much larger acreage of the West Bank in 'compensation' – to little protest from the West (see Chris McGreal, 'Israel Redraws the Roadmap, Building Quietly and Quickly', *The Guardian*, 18 October 2005: 17). Gaza has been left an anomalous territory without real autonomy. Despite holding democratic elections, the 'international community' has failed to support the wishes of the people of Gaza to determine their own political future (or to make Israel abide by numerous UN resolutions, beginning with 194 in 1948, the sanctity of which were also widely urged by Bush and Blair to justify their aggression against Iraq in 2003). Having offered so little support to Arafat's secular Palestine Liberation Organisation, the West expresses hypocritical outrage that disappointed Gazans turned instead to Islamic *Hamas*.

56 For detailed discussions of the strategy of dispersal of Palestinians pursued by Zionist terror gangs and *Haganah* regulars alike in 1947–48, see Morris, *Birth* and Pappé, *Ethnic Cleansing*.

57 See, for example, Gusdorf, 'Conditions': 35, 42.

58 *Sharon*'s citation of Shehadeh's *Strangers in the House* (2002) is significant, since it, too, is a personal memoir (by a Ramallah-based human rights lawyer), the title of which invokes not only the Israeli takeover of Palestine but Shehadeh's personal conflict with his father.

59 Mernessi is the author of a celebrated memoir, *Dreams of Trespass* (1995).

60 For example, the bolan Heights in Syira on the tombstones of many of the fundamentalists associated with Sharon's mentor, former Prime Minister Menahem Begin, is engraved a map comprising Mandate Palestine *and* Transjordan (modern Jordan), on which is superimposed a hand clutching a rifle. These included Eitan Livni, father of the current *Kadima* leader Tzipi Livni (who launched the devestating war on Gaza in December 2008 to shore up crumbling electoral support), and commander of the Irgun at the time of the terror bombing of the King David Hotel in July 1946 which indiscriminately slaughtered Jews, Arabs and British alike. See Leonard Doyle, 'Israeli "ruler-in waiting" Plans to Starve Hamas' (2006): www.independent.co.uk/news/world/middle-east/israeli-rulerinwaiting-plans-to-starve-hamas-468293.html.

61 See Nur Masalha, ed., *Catastrophe Remembered: Palestine, Israel and the Internal Refugees* (London: Zed, 2005).

62 Cited in Michael Billingham, *The Life and Work of Harold Pinter* (London: Faber, 1996): 129.

63 Mel Gussow, *Conversations with Pinter* (London: Nick Hern, 1994): 88.

64 Smith, *Subjectivity*: 182.

65 Wong, 'First-Person': 172.

66 Fraser, 'Dimensions': 86.

67 One shouldn't overlook more private motives for the instrumentalisation of (post)colonial life-writing. Prince's *History* and Seacole's *Wonderful Adventures* are in part specifically aimed at improving their authors' financial circumstances.

68 Longley, 'Autobiographical': 372.

69 MacDermott, 'Introduction': 10.

70 Yolanda Pierce, 'Redeeming Bondage: The Captivity Narrative and the Spiritual Autobiography in the African American Slave Narrative Tradition', in Fisch, *Cambridge*: 83.

71 Whitlock, *Soft*: 3.

72 Huggan, *Australian Literature*: *passim*.

73 Ibid.: 176.

74 Seacole, *Wonderful*: 128.

Select bibliography

Achebe, Chinua (1965) 'The African Writer and the English Language', in C. Achebe, *Morning Yet on Creation Day: Essays*, London: Heinemann, 1977: 55–62.

Ahmad, Aijaz (1992) *In Theory: Classes, Nations, Literatures*, London: Verso.

——([1971] 1994) 'Introduction', in A. Ahmad (ed.) *Ghazals of Ghālib: Versions from the Urdu*, Delhi: Oxford University Press: vii–xxviii.

Allende, Isabel (1996) *Paula*, trans. Margaret Peden, London: Flamingo.

Alter, Joseph (2000) *Gandhi's Body: Sex, Diet, and the Politics of Nationalism*, Philadelphia, PA: University of Pennsylvania Press.

Amireh, Amal (2000): 'Framing Nawal El Saadawi: Arab Feminism in a Transnational World', *Signs*, 26(1): 215–49.

Amiry, Suad (2003–4) *Sharon and My Mother-in-Law: Ramallah Diaries*, London: Granta.

Anand, Mulk Raj (1985) *Autobiography*, Part One; *Story of a Childhood under the Raj: Pilpali Sahab*, New Delhi: Arnold-Heinemann.

Anderson, Douglas (2000) 'Division below the Surface: Olaudah Equiano's *Interesting Narrative*', *Studies in Romanticism*, 43(3): 439–60.

Anderson, Linda (2001) *Autobiography*, London: Routledge.

Anonymous (1999) 'Said's Memoir Takes its Place Amid Attempts to Discredit', *Aljadid: A Review and Record of Arab Culture and Arts*, 5(29): 6, 21.

Arnold, David (2004) 'The Self and The Cell: Indian Prison Narratives as Life Histories', in David Arnold and Stuart Blackburn (eds) *Telling Lives in India: Biography, Autobiography, and Life History*, Delhi: Permanent Black: 29–53.

Ashcroft, Bill, Griffiths, Gareth and Tiffin, Helen (1989) *The Empire Writes Back: Theory and Practice in Post-colonial Literatures*, London: Routledge.

Ashley, Kathleen, Gilmore, Leigh and Peters, Gerald (eds) (1994) *Autobiography and Post-modernism*, Amherst MA: University of Massachusetts Press.

Austen, Jane (1932) *Letters to Her Sister Cassandra and Others*, ed. R.W. Chapman, Oxford: Clarendon, vol. 2.

Badran, Margot (1992) 'Expressing Feminism and Nationalism in Autobiography: the Memoirs of an Egyptian Educator', in Smith and Watson, *De/Colonizing the Subject*: 270–93.

Barthes, R. (1977) *Roland BARTHES by Roland Barthes*, trans. R. Howard, New York: Farrar, Straus and Giroux.

Beach, Milo (1992) *Mughal and Rajput Painting, The New Cambridge History of India*, 1.3, Cambridge: Cambridge University Press.

Behan, Brendan ([1958] 1990) *Borstal Boy*, London: Arrow.

—— (1963) *Hold Your Hour and Have Another*, London: Hutchinson.

—— (1965)*Confessions of an Irish Rebel*, London: Arena.

Benito, Jesús and Manzanas, Ana (1999) 'The (De-)Construction of the "Other" in *The Interesting Narrative of the Life of Olaudah Equiano*', in Maria Diedrich, H.L. Gates and Carl Pedersen (eds) *Black Imagination and the Middle Passage*, New York: Oxford University Press: 47–56.

Bensmaïa, Réda (2003).. *Experimental Nations: Or, the Invention of the Maghreb*, Princeton, NJ: Princeton University Press.

Benstock, Shari (1988a) 'Introduction', in Benstock, *The Private Self*: 1–6.

—— (ed.) (1988b) *The Private Self: Theory and Practice of Women's Autobiographical Writings*, London: University of North Carolina Press.

Bergland, Betty (1994) 'Postmodernism and the Autobiographical Subject: Reconstructing the "Other"', in Ashley *et al.*, *Autobiography and Postmodernism*: 130–66.

Beverley, John (1992) 'The Margin at the Center: on *Testimonio* (Testimonial Narrative)', in Smith and Watson, *De/Colonizing*: 91–114.

Bliss, Carolyn (1989) 'The Mythology of Family: Three Texts of Popular Culture', *New Literatures Review*, 18: 60–72.

Boehmer, Elleke (1995) *Colonial and Postcolonial Literature*, Oxford: Oxford University Press.

Bogues, Anthony (1997) *Caliban's Freedom: The Early Political Thought of C.L.R. James*, London: Pluto.

Bougherara, Hadi (2002) *Voyage Sentimental en Musique Arabo-Andalouse*, Paris: EDIF.

Boyle, Ted E. (1969) *Brendan Behan*, New York: Twayne.

Brannigan, John (2002) *Brendan Behan: Cultural Nationalism and the Revisionist Writer*, Dublin: Four Courts Press.

Brée, Germaine (1988) 'Foreword', in Brodzki and Schenck, *Life-Lines*: ix–xii.

Brewster, Anne (1996) *Reading Aboriginal Women's Autobiography*, Sydney: Sydney University Press.

Brodzki, Bella (1988) 'Mothering, Displacement, and Language in the Autobiographies of Nathalie Sarraute and Christa Wolf', in Brodzki and Schenck, *Life-Lines*: 243–59.

Brodzki, Bella and Schenck, Celeste (1988a) 'Introduction', in Brodzki and Schenck, *Life-Lines*: 1–15.

—— (eds) (1988b) *Life-Lines: Theorizing Women's Autobiography*, Ithaca, NY: Cornell University Press.

Broughton, Trevor Lynn (ed.) (2007) *Autobiography: Critical Concepts in Literary and Cultural Studies*, 4 vols, London: Routledge.

Buhle, Paul (1988) *C.L.R. James: The Artist as Revolutionary*, London: Verso.

Caldwell, Tanya (1999) '"Talking Too Much English": Languages of Economy and Politics in Equiano's *The Interesting Narrative*', *Early American Literature*, 34(3): 263–82.

Calle-Gruber, Mireille (2006) *Assia Djebar*, Paris: adpf.

Carretta, Vincent (2005) *Equiano, the African: Biography of a Self-Made Man*, London: University of Georgia Press.

—— (2007) 'Olaudah Equiano: African British Abolitionist and Founder of the African American Slave Narrative', in Fisch, *Cambridge*: 44–64.

Carrigan, Anthony (2006) '"Negotiating Personal Identity and Cultural Memory" in Olaudah Equiano's *Interesting Narrative*', *Wasafiri*, 48(Summer): 42–7.

Chatterjee, Partha (1986) *Nationalism and the Colonial World: A Derivative Discourse?* London: Zed.

Chaudhuri, Nirad ([1951] 1991) *The Autobiography of an Unknown Indian*, London: Picador.

Chellappan, K. (1983) 'The Discovery of India and the Self in Three Autobiographies', in H.H. Anniah Gowda (ed.) *The Colonial and the Neo-Colonial Encounters in Commonwealth Literature*, Mysore: University of Mysore: 95–106.

Cixous, Hélène (1980) 'The Laugh of the Medusa', trans. K. and P. Cohen, in Elaine Marks and Isabelle de Courtivron (eds) *New French Feminisms*, Brighton: Harvester: 245–64.

Coe, Richard N. (1984) *When the Grass Was Taller: Autobiography and the Experience of Childhood*, New Haven, CT: Yale University Press.

Cohen, Jennifer (1995) '"But Have Some Art With You": An Interview with Nawal El Saadawi', *Literature and Medicine*, 14(1): 53–71.

Collingwood-Whittick, Sheila (2002) 'Sally Morgan's *My Place*: Exposing the (Ab)original "Text" Behind Whitefellas' History', *Commonwealth Essays and Studies*, 25(1): 41–58.

Confino, Alon (2000) 'Remembering Talbiyah: On Edward Said's *Out of Place*', *Israel Studies*, 5(2): 182–98.

——— (2005) 'Intellectuals and the Lure of Exile: Home and Exile in the Autobiographies of Edward Said and George Steiner', *The Hedgehog Review: Critical Reflections on Contemporary Culture*, 7(3): 20–8.

Cribb, Tim (2003) 'African Autobiography and the Idea of the Nation', in Bruce Bennett, Susan Cowan, Jacqueline Lo, Satendra Nadan and Jennifer Webb (eds) *Resistance and Reconciliation: Writing in the Commonwealth*, Canberra: ACLALS: 63–73.

Davies, Carole Boyce (1992) 'Collaboration and the Ordering Imperative in Life Story Production', in Smith and Watson, *De/Colonizing*: 3–19.

de Man, Paul (1979) 'Autobiography as De-Facement', in Broughton (ed.) *Autobiography*, vol. 1: 264–74.

Devy, G.N. (1984) 'Romantic, Post-Romantic and Neo-Romantic Autobiography in Indian English Literature', in MacDermott, *Autobiographical*: 63–7.

——— (1993) *In Another Tongue: Essays on Indian English Literature*, New York: Peter Lang.

Dhondy, Farrukh (2001) *C.L.R. James*, London: Weidenfeld and Nicolson.

Divine, Donna (1984) '"Difficult Journey – Mountainous Journey", the Memoirs of Fadwa Tuqan', in Stanton, *Female*: 187–204.

Djebar, Assia ([1982] 1992) *Women of Algiers in their Apartment*, trans. Marjolijn de Jager, London: University Press of Virginia.

——— (1985) *Fantasia: An Algerian Cavalcade*, trans and intro. Dorothy S. Blair, Portsmouth, NH: Heinemann.

——— (1995) *So Vast the Prison*, trans. Betsy Wing, London: Seven Stories Press.

——— (1999) *Ces voix qui m'assiègent ... en marge de ma francophonie*, Paris: Albin Michel.

Donadey, Anne (2000) 'The Multilingual Strategies of Postcolonial Literature: Assia Djebar's Algerian Palimpsest', *World Literature Today*, 74(1): 27–36.

Döring, Tobias (2006) 'Edward Said and the Fiction of Autobiography', *Wasafiri*, 21(2): 71–8.

Eakin, John Paul (1985) *Fictions of Autobiography: Studies in the Art of Self-Invention*, Princeton, NJ: Princeton University Press.

Edwards, Paul and Shaw, Rosalind (1989) 'The Invisible Chi in Equiano's *Interesting Narrative*', *Journal of Religion in Africa*, 19(2): 146–56.

El Saadawi, Nawal (1999) *A Daughter of Isis: The Autobiography of Nawal El Saadawi*, trans. Sherif Hetata, London: Zed.

Emecheta, Buchi ([1986] 1994) *Head Above Water*, Oxford: Heinemann.

Equiano, Olaudah ([1789] 1995) *The Interesting Narrative and Other Writings*, ed. Vincent Carretta, London: Penguin.

Erikson, Erik (1975) *Life History and the Historical Moment*, New York: Norton.

Evans, Mary (1999) *Missing Persons: The Impossibility of Auto/biography*, London: Routledge.

Fanon, Frantz ([1952] 1986) *Black Skin/White Masks*, trans. C.L. Markmann, London: Pluto.

——— (1965) *Peau Noire, Masques Blancs*, ed. F. Jeanson, Paris: Seuil.

Farred, Grant (1994) '"Victorian with a Rebel Seed": C.L.R. James, Postcolonial Intellectual', *Social Text*, 38: 21–38.

Field, Christopher (2001) '*Fantasia*', in S. Sadie (eds) *The New Grove Dictionary of Music and Musicians*, London: Macmillan, vol. 8: 545–58.

Fisch, Audrey (ed.) (2007) *The Cambridge Companion to the African American Slave Narrative*, Cambridge: Cambridge University Press.

Fraser, Robert (1984) 'Dimensions of Personality: Elements of the Autobiographical Mode', in MacDermott, *Autobiographical*: 83–7.

Fromentin, Eugène ([1858] 1911) *Une Année dans Le Sahel*, ed. L. Morel, Oxford: Clarendon.

Gagnier, Regenia (1992) 'The Literary Standard, Working-Class Autobiography, and Gender', in Smith and Watson, *Women:* 264–75.

Gandhi, M.K. ([1927–29] 1982) *An Autobiography or The Story of My Experiments with Truth*, trans. Mahadev Desai, London: Penguin.

Gerdes, Peter René (1973) *The Major Works of Brendan Behan*, Frankfurt: Peter Lang.

Gibbon, Edward ([1796] 1970) *Autobiography*, ed. M.M. Reese, London: Routledge and Kegan Paul.

Gibbs, James (1986) *Wole Soyinka*, Basingstoke: Macmillan.

Gilmore, Leigh (1994a) *Autobiographics: A Feminist Theory of Women's Self-Representation*, Ithaca, NY: Cornell University Press.

—— (1994b) 'The Mark of Autobiography: Postmodernism, Autobiography, and Genre', in Ashley *et al.*, *Autobiography and Postmodernism*: 3–20.

—— (2001) *The Limits of Autobiography: Trauma and Testimony*, Ithaca, NY: Cornell University Press.

Gindi, Nadia (2000) 'On the Margins of a Memoir: a Personal Reading of Said's *Out of Place*', *Alif: Journal of Comparative Poetics*, 20(1): 284–98.

Glissant, Edouard ([1990] 1997) *Poetics of Relation*, trans. Betsy Wing, Ann Arbor, MI: University of Michigan Press.

Goldman, Anne (1992) 'Autobiography, Ethnography, and History: A Model for Reading', in Smith and Watson, *Women*: 288–98.

Goodyear, Sara Suleri (2003) *Boys Will Be Boys: A Daughter's Elegy*, Chicago: University of Chicago Press.

Grimshaw, Anna (1992a) 'Introduction: C.L.R. James: A Revolutionary Vision for the Twentieth Century', in Grimshaw, *The C.L.R. James Reader*: 1–22.

—— (ed.) (1992b) *The C.L.R. James Reader*, Oxford: Blackwell.

Guettat, Mahmoud (1980) *La Musique classique du Maghreb*, Paris: Sindbad.

Gulledge, Jo (ed.) (1987) 'Seminar on *Aké* with Wole Soyinka', *The Southern Review*, 23(3): 511–26.

Gunn, Janet V. (1992) 'A Politics of Experience: Leila Khaled's *My People Shall Live: The Autobiography of a Revolutionary*', in Smith and Watson, eds, *De/Colonizing*: 65–80.

Gusdorf, Georges (1980) 'Conditions and Limits of Autobiography', in Olney, *Autobiography*: 28–48.

—— (1991) *Les Écritures de Moi: Lignes de Vie*, Paris: Odile Jacob.

Harcourt, Wendy and Escobar, Arturo (2005) *Women and the Politics of Place*, Bloomfield, CT: Kumarian Press.

Harlow, Barbara (1992) 'From the Women's Prison: Third World Women's Narratives of Prison', in Smith and Watson, *Women*: 453–66.

Hiddleston, Jane (2006) *Assia Djebar: Out of Algeria*, Liverpool: Liverpool University Press.

Holden, Philip (2008) *Autobiography and Decolonization: Modernity, Masculinity and the Nation State*, Madison, WI: University of Wisconsin Press.

Holland, Patrick and Huggan, Graham (1998) *Tourists with Typewriters: Critical Reflections on Contemporary Travel Writing*, Ann Arbor, MI: University of Michigan Press.

hooks, bell (1991) 'Postmodern Blackness', in P. Williams and L. Chrisman, *Colonial*: 421–7.

Hornung, Alfred and Ruhe, Ernstpeter (eds) (1998a) *Postcolonialism & Autobiography: Michelle Cliff, David Dabydeen, Opal Palmer Adisa*, Atlanta, GA: Rodopi.

—— (1998b) *Postcolonialisme & Autobiographie: Albert Memmi, Assia Djebar, Daniel Maximin*, Atlanta, GA: Rodopi.

Huddart, David (2007) *Postcolonial Theory and Autobiography*, London: Routledge.

Huggan, Graham (2007) *Australian Literature: Postcolonialism, Racism, Transnationalism*, Oxford: Oxford University Press.

Hussein, Abdirahman (2002) *Edward Said: Criticism and Society*, London: Verso.

Hutcheon, Linda ([1989] 1995) 'Circling the Downspout of Empire', in Bill Ashcroft, Gareth Griffiths and Helen Tiffin (eds) *The Post-Colonial Studies Reader*, London: Routledge: 130–5.

Innes, C.L. (2002) *A History of Black and Asian Writing in Britain 1700–2000*, Cambridge: Cambridge University Press.

—— (2007) *The Cambridge Introduction to Postcolonial Literatures in English*, Cambridge: Cambridge University Press.

Jaireth, Subhash (1995) 'The "I" in Sally Morgan's *My Place*: Writing of a Monologised Self', *Westerly*, 40(3): 69–78.

James, C.L.R. ([1963] 1994) *Beyond a Boundary*, London: Serpent's Tail.

—— (1986) *Cricket*, ed. Anna Grimshaw, London: Allison and Busby.

—— (1992a) 'Popular Art and the Cultural Tradition', in Ana Grimshaw, *The C.L.R. James Reader*: 247–54.

—— (1992b) 'Whitman and Melville', in Ana Grimshaw, *The C.L.R. James Reader*: 202–19.

James, Louis (1984) 'Wole Soyinka's *Aké*: Autobiography and the Limits of Experience', in MacDermott, *Autobiographical*: 113–16.

Jeffs, Rae ([1966] 1968) *Brendan Behan: Man and Showman*, London: Corgi.

Jelinek, Estelle (1980) 'Introduction: Women's Autobiography and the Male Tradition', in E. Jelinek (ed.) *Women's Autobiography: Essays in Criticism*, Bloomington, IN: Indiana University Press: 1–20.

Jeyifo, Biodun (2004) *Wole Soyinka: Politics, Poetics and Postcolonialism*, Cambridge: Cambridge University Press.

Joannou, Maroula (1995) '"She Who Would Be Politically Free Herself Must Strike the Blow": Suffragette Autobiography and Suffragette Militancy', in Swindells, *The Uses of Autobiography*: 31–44.

Jolly, Margaretta (ed.) (2001) *The Encyclopedia of Life-Writing: Autobiographical and Biographical Forms*, London: Routledge.

Jones, Stephanie (2000) 'The Politics and Poetics of Diaspora in V.S. Naipaul's *A Way in the World*', *Journal of Commonwealth Literature*, 35(1): 87–98.

Kaplan, Caren (1992) 'Resisting Autobiography: Out-law Genres and Transnational Feminist Subjects', in Smith and Watson, *De/Colonizing*: 115–38.

Karmi, Ghada (2002) *In Search of Fatima: A Palestinian Story*, London: Verso.

Kearney, Colbert (1977) *The Writings of Brendan Behan*, Dublin: Gill and Macmillan.

Kelly, Debra (2005) *Autobiography and Independence: Selfhood and Creativity in North African Postcolonial Writing in French*, Liverpool: Liverpool University Press.

Langlois, Tony (2001) 'Algeria', in Stanley Sadie (ed.) *The New Grove Dictionary of Music and Musicians*, 2nd edn, London: Macmillan, vol. 1: 368–72.

Lazarus, Neil (1999) *Nationalism and Cultural Practice in the Postcolonial World*, Cambridge: Cambridge University Press.

Lejeune, Philippe (1982) 'The Autobiographical Contract', trans. R. Carter, in Tzvetan Todorov (ed.) *French Literary Theory Today: A Reader*, Cambridge: Cambridge University Press: 192–222.

Lim, Shirley Geok-Lin (1992a) 'Semiotics, Experience, and the Material Self: An Inquiry into the Subject of the Contemporary Asian American Woman Writer', in Smith and Watson, *Women*: 441–52.

—— (1992b) 'Terms of Empowerment in Kamala Das's *My Story*', in Smith and Watson, *De/Colonizing*: 346–69.

—— ([1996] 2004) *Among the White Moon Faces: Memoirs of an Asian American Woman*, Singapore: Times Editions/Marshall Cavendish.

—— (2003) 'The Im/Possibility of Life-Writing in Two Languages', in Isabelle de Courtivron (ed.) *Lives in Translation: Bilingual Writers on Identity and Creativity*, Basingstoke: Palgrave: 39–47.

Lionnet, Françoise (1989) *Autobiographical Voices: Race, Gender, Self-Portraiture*, Ithaca, NY: Cornell University Press.

—— (1992) 'Of Mangoes and Maroons: Language, History, and the Multicultural Subject of Michelle Cliff's *Abeng*', in Smith and Watson, *De/Colonizing*: 321–45.

—— (1995) *Postcolonial Representations: Women, Literature, Identity*, Ithaca, NY: Cornell University Press.

Longley, Kateryna (1992) 'Autobiographical Story Telling by Australian Aboriginal Women', in Smith and Watson, *De/Colonizing*: 370–84.

MacDermott, Doireann (ed.) (1984) *Autobiographical and Biographical Writing in the Commonwealth*, Sabadell, Spain: AUSA.

McDowell, Linda (1999) *Gender, Identity and Place: Understanding Feminist Geographies*, Cambridge: Polity.

Macey, David (2000) *Frantz Fanon: A Life*, London: Granta.

McKay, Claude ([1937] 1985) *A Long Way from Home*, London: Pluto.

Magona, Sindiwe (1991) *To My Children's Children: An Autobiography*, London: Women's Press.

Mahdi, Salah el (1972) *La Musique Arabe*, Paris: Alphonse Leduc.

Mairs, Nancy (1992) 'The Way In', in Smith and Watson, *Women*: 471–3.

Majeed, Javed (2007) *Autobiography, Travel and Postnational Identity: Gandhi, Nehru and Iqbal*, Basingstoke: Palgrave.

Malti-Douglas, Fedwa (1995a) *Men, Women, and God(s): Nawal El Saadawi and Arab Feminist Poetics*, Berkeley, CA: University of California Press.

—— (1995b) 'Writing Nawal El Saadawi', in Diane Elam and Robyn Wiegman (eds) *Feminism Beside Itself*, London: Routledge: 283–96.

Marcus, Laura (1994) *Auto/biographical Discourses: Theory, Criticism, Practice*, Manchester: Manchester University Press.

Mariani, Philomena (ed.) (1991) *Critical Fictions: The Politics of Imaginative Writing*, Seattle: Bay Press.

Marren, Susan (1993) 'Between Slavery and Freedom: The Transgressive Self in Olaudah Equiano's Autobiography', *PMLA*, 108(1): 94–105.

Mason, Mary (1992) 'The Other Voice: Autobiographies of Women Writers', in Smith and Watson, *Women*: 321–4.

Matthews, D.J. and Shackle, Christopher (1972) 'Introduction', in D.J. Matthews and C. Shackle (eds) *An Anthology of Classical Urdu Love Lyrics: Texts and Translations*, Oxford: Oxford University Press: 1–16.

Melhem, D.H. (1999) 'Nawal El Saadawi's "Daughter of Isis": Life and Times via the Plenitude of Her Writings', *Aljadid: A Review and Record of Arab Culture and Arts*, 5(29): 12–13.

Meyers, Jeffrey (1989) 'Indian Autobiography: Gandhi and Chaudhuri', in Carol Ramelb (ed.) *Biography East and West: Selected Conference Papers*, Honolulu: University of Hawaii: 113–21.

Michaels, Eric (1988) 'Para-ethnography', *Art and Text*, 30: 42–51.

Mikhail, E.H. (1976) *Miniature Paintings on Display in the Lahore Museum: Mughal and Rajasthani Schools*, Lahore: Lahore Museum.

—— (ed.) (1979) *The Art of Brendan Behan*, London: Vision.

—— (ed.) (1982) *Brendan Behan: Interviews and Recollections*, London: Macmillan.

—— (ed.) (1992) *The letters of Brendan Behan*, Basingstoke: Macmillan.

Misch, Georg ([1907] 1973) *A History of Autobiography in Antiquity*, trans. E.W. Dickes, Westport, CT: Greenwood Press, vol.1.

Mishra, Ganeswar (1984) 'How Does an Indian Village Speak [*sic*]?: A Study of the Form of Prafulla Mohanti's *My Village, My Life*', in MacDermott, *Autobiographical*: 157–62.

Mishra, Vijay (1996) 'Defining the Self in Indian Literary and Filmic Texts', in Wimal Dissanayake (ed.) *Narratives of Agency: Self-Making in China, India, and Japan*, London: University of Minnesota Press: 117–50.

Moi, Toril (1985) *Sexual/Textual Politics*, London: Routledge.

Moore-Gilbert, Bart (2001) *Hanif Kureishi*, Manchester: Manchester University Press.

—— (2005) 'The *Confessions* of Saint Augustine: Roots and Routes of Postcolonial Life-Writing', *A/B: Auto/Biography Studies*, 20(2): 155–69.

Morgan, Sally ([1987] 2001) *My Place*, London: Virago.

Morgan, Sue (ed.) (2006a) *The Feminist History Reader*, London: Routledge.

—— (2006b) 'Introduction: Writing Feminist History: Theoretical Debates and Critical Practices', in Morgan, *Feminist*: 1–48.

Mortimer, Mildred (1992) 'Entretien avec Assia Djebar, Ecrivain Algérien', *Research in African Literatures*, 28(2): 197–203.

Mottolese, William (1998) '"Almost an Englishman": Equiano and the Colonial Gift of Language', *Bucknell Review*, 41(2): 160–71.

Msiska, Mpalive-Hangson (1998) *Wole Soyinka*, Plymouth: Northcote House.

—— (2007) *Postcolonial Identity in Wole Soyinka*, Amsterdam: Rodopi.

Mukherjee, Bharati (1991) 'A Four-Hundred-Year-Old Woman', in Mariani, *Critical*: 24–8.

Murphy, Geraldine (1994) 'Olaudah Equiano, Accidental Tourist', *Eighteenth-Century Studies*, 27(4): 551–68.

Naipaul, V.S. ([1965] 2003) 'Indian Autobiographies', in V.S. Naipaul, *Literary Occasions: Essays*, London: Picador: 139–45.

—— (1984) *Finding the Centre: Two Narratives*, Harmondsworth: Penguin.

—— (1994) *A Way in the World: A Sequence*, London: Minerva.

—— (2000) *Reading and Writing: A Personal Account*, New York: New York Review of Books.

Nandy, Ashis ([1983] 1998) *The Intimate Enemy*, in *Exiled at Home*, New Delhi: Oxford University Press.

Narogin, Mudrooroo (1990) *Writing from the Fringe: A Study of Modern Aboriginal Literature*, Melbourne: Hyland.

Nehru, Jawaharlal ([1936] 1962) *An Autobiography: With Musings on Recent Events in India*, Bombay: Allied Publishers.

Neuman, Shirley (1994) '"An Appearance Walking in a Forest the Sexes Burn": Autobiography and the Construction of the Feminine Body', in Ashley *et al.*, *Autobiography*: 293–315.

—— (1998) 'Autobiography, Bodies, Manhood', in Smith and Watson, *Women*: 415–24.

Newton, Pauline (2005) *Transcultural Women of Late Twentieth-Century U.S. American Literature*, Aldershot: Ashgate.

Ngugi wa Thiongo (1986) 'The Language of African Literature', in Williams and Chrisman, *Colonial*: 435–55.

Nielsen, Aldon (1997) *C.L.R. James: A Critical Introduction*, Jackson: University of Mississippi Press.

Nussbaum, Felicity (1988) 'Eighteenth-Century Women's Autobiographical Commonplaces', in Benstock, *Private*: 147–71.

Olney, James (1973) *Tell Me Africa: An Approach to African Literature*, Princeton, NJ: Princeton University Press.

—— (1980a) 'Autobiography and the Cultural Moment: A Thematic, Historical, and Bibliographical Introduction', in Olney, *Autobiography*: 3–27.

—— (ed.) (1980b) *Autobiography: Essays Theoretical and Critical*, Princeton, NJ: Princeton University Press.

Orlando, Valérie (1999) '*Preface*: History / Story', in Fromentin, *Between Sea and Sahara: An Algerian Journal*, trans. Blake Robinson, Athens, OH: Ohio University Press: ix–xiii.

Paquet, Sandra Pouchet (2002) *Caribbean Autobiography: Cultural Identity and Self-Representation*, Madison, WI: University of Wisconsin Press.

Parekh, Bikhu (1989) *Colonialism, Tradition and Reform: An Analysis of Gandhi's Political Discourse*, London: Sage.

Partridge, Jeffrey (2007) *Beyond Literary Chinatown*, London: University of Washington Press.

Pascal, Roy (1960) *Design and Truth in Autobiography*, Cambridge, MA: Harvard University Press.

Perreault, Jeanne (1995) *Writing Selves: Contemporary Feminist Autography*, Minneapolis: University of Minnesota Press.

Pierce, Yolanda (2007) 'Redeeming Bondage: The Captivity Narrative and the Spiritual Autobiography in the African American Slave Narrative Tradition', in Fisch, *Cambridge*: 83–98.

Potkay, Adam (1994) 'Olaudah Equiano and the Art of Spiritual Autobiography', *Eighteenth-Century Studies*, 27(4): 677–92.

—— (2001) 'History, Oratory, and God in Equiano's *Interesting Narrative*', *Eighteenth-Century Studies*, 34(4): 601–14.

Prabhu, Anjali 2006) 'Narration in Frantz Fanon's *Peau noire, masques blancs*: Some Reconsiderations', *Research in African Literatures*, 37(4): 189–210.

Pratt, Mary Louise (1991) *Imperial Eyes: Travel Writing and Transculturation*, London: Routledge.

Prince, Mary ([1831] 2000) *The History of Mary Prince*, ed. Sara Salih, London: Penguin.

Pulitano, Elvira (2007) '"One More Story to Tell": Diasporic Articulations in Sally Morgan's *My Place*', in Sheila Collingwood-Whittick (ed.) *The Pain of Unbelonging: Alienation and Identity in Australasian Literature*, Amsterdam: Rodopi: 37–55.

Quayson, Ato (1996) 'Wole Soyinka and Autobiography as Political Unconscious', *Journal of Commonwealth Literature*, 31(2): 19–32.

—— (1999) 'Caribbean Configurations: Characterological Types and the Frames of Hybridity', *Interventions: International Journal of Postcolonial Studies*, 1(3): 331–44.

Quayum, Mohammed (2003) 'Shirley Geok-Lin Lim: An Interview', *MELUS*, 28(4): 83–100.

Quinby, Lee ([1976] 1992) 'The Subject of Memoirs: *The Woman Warrior*'s Technology of Ideographic Selfhood', in Smith and Watson, *De/Colonizing*: 297–320.

Radhakrishnan, N. (1998) 'Foreword', in K.D. Gangrade, *Gandhi's Autobiography: Moral Lessons*, New Delhi: Gandhi Smriti and Darshan Samith: ix–xvii.

Ranasinha, Ruvani (2007) *South Asian Writers in Twentieth-Century Britain: Culture in Translation*, Oxford: Clarendon.

Rooney, Caroline (2001) *African Literature, Animism and Politics*, London: Routledge.

Rousseau, Jean-Jacques (2000) *Confessions*, trans. A Scholar, Oxford: Oxford University Press.

Roy, Parama (2002) 'Meat-Eating, Masculinity, and Renunciation in India: A Gandhian Grammar of Diet', *Gender and History*, 14(1): 62–91.

Rushdie, Salman (1992) *Imaginary Homelands: Essays and Criticism 1981–1991*, London: Granta.

——(1997) 'Introduction', in S. Rushdie and Elizabeth West (eds) *The Vintage Book of Indian Writing*, London: Vintage: ix–xxiii.

Russell, Ralph (2003a) 'Getting to Know Ghalib', in Russell, *Oxford India Ghalib*: 283–324.

—— (2003b) 'Introduction: Ghalib: A Self-Portrait', in Russell, *Oxford India Ghalib*: 1–25.

—— (ed.) (2003c) *The Oxford India Ghalib: Life, Letters and Ghazals*, New Delhi: Oxford University Press.

Russell, Ralph and Islam, Khurshidad (2003) 'Ghalib: Life and Letters', in Russell, *Oxford India Ghalib*: 229–61.

Sabino, Robin and Hall, Jennifer (1999) 'The Path Not Taken: Cultural Identity in the Interesting Life of Olaudah Equiano', *MELUS*, 24(1): 5–19.

Said, Edward (1966) *Joseph Conrad and the Fiction of Autobiography*, Cambridge, MA: Harvard University Press.

——([1978] 1991) *Orientalism*, London: Peregrine.

—— (1999) *Out of Place*, London: Granta.

—— (2000a) *Reflections on Exile and Other Literary and Cultural Essays*, London: Granta.

—— (2000b) 'Introduction', in Said, *Reflections*: xi–xxxv.

—— (2000c) 'Between Worlds', in Said, *Reflections*: 554–68.

Salih, Sara (2005) 'Introduction', in M. Seacole, *Wonderful Adventures*: xv–l.

Samuel, Raphael (ed.) (1981a) *People's History and Socialist Theory*, London: Routledge and Kegan Paul.

—— (1981b) 'Introduction: People's History', in Samuel, *People's History and Socialist Theory*: xiv–xxxix.

Samuels, Wilfred (1985) 'Disguised Voice in *The Interesting Narrative of Olaudah Equiano, or Gustavus Vassa, the African*', *Black American Literature Forum*, 19(2): 64–9.

Scott, Joan (2006) 'Feminism's History', in Morgan, *Feminist*: 388–98.

Seacole, Mary ([1857] 2005) *The Wonderful Adventures of Mrs Seacole in Many Lands*, ed. Sara Salih, London: Penguin.

Senghor, L.S. (1965) 'Negritude: A Humanism of the Twentieth Century', in P. Williams and L. Chrisman, *Colonial Discourse*: 27–35.

Sinha, R.C.P. (1978) *The Indian Autobiographies in English*, New Delhi: S. Chand.

Smith, Paul (1988) *Discerning the Subject*, Minneapolis: University of Minnesota Press.

Smith, Sidonie (1987) *A Poetics of Women's Autobiography: Marginality and the Fiction of Self-Representation*, Bloomington, IN: Indiana University Press.

—— (1993) *Subjectivity, Identity, and the Body: Women's Autobiographical Practices in the Twentieth Century*, Bloomington, IN: Indiana University Press.

—— (1994) 'Identity's Body', in Ashley *et al.*, *Autobiography*: 226–92.

—— (1998) 'Performativity, Autobiographical Practice, Resistance', in Smith and Watson, *Women*: 108–15.

Smith, Sidonie and Watson, Julia (eds) (1992) *De/Colonizing the Subject: The Politics of Gender in Women's Autobiography*, Minneapolis: University of Minnesota Press.

—— (1998a) 'Introduction: Situating Subjectivity in Women's Autobiographical Practices', in Smith and Watson, *Women*: 3–52.

—— (eds) (1998b) *Women, Autobiography, Theory: A Reader*, Madison, WI: University of Wisconsin Press.

—— (2001) *Reading Autobiography: A Guide for Interpreting Life Narratives*, Minneapolis: University of Minnesota Press.

Sommer, Doris (1988) '"Not Just a Personal Story": Women's *Testimonios* and the Plural Self', in Brodzki and Schenck, *Life-Lines*: 107–30.

Soyinka, Wole ([1981] 1983) *Aké: The Years of Childhood*, New York: Vintage.

—— (1995) *Myth, Literature and the African World*, Cambridge: Cambridge University Press.

Spengemann, William (1980) *The Forms of Autobiography*, New Haven, CT: Yale University Press.

Spivak, Gayatri (1986) 'Three Women's Texts and a Critique of Imperialism', in H.L. Gates (ed.) *Race, Writing, and Difference*, Chicago: University of Chicago Press: 262–80.

—— (1989) 'The Political Economy of Women as Seen by a Literary Critic', in Elizabeth Weed (ed.) *Coming to Terms: Feminism, Theory, Politics*, New York: Routledge: 218–29.

Sprinker, Michael (1980) 'Fictions of the Self: the End of Autobiography', in Olney, *Autobiography*: 321–42.

St Louis, Brett (2007) *Rethinking Race, Politics, and Poetics: C.L.R. James's Critique of Modernity*, London: Routledge.

Stanley, Liz (1992) *The Auto/biographical I: The Theory and Practice of Feminist Auto/biography*, Manchester: Manchester University Press.

Stanton, Domna (1984a) 'Autogynography: Is the Subject Different?' in Stanton, *Female*: 5–24.

—— (ed.) (1984b) *The Female Autograph*, New York: New York Literary Forum.

Starobinski, Jean (1980) 'The Style of Autobiography', in Olney, *Autobiography*: 73–83.

Stephen, Rita (2006) 'Arab Women Writing Their Sexuality', *Hawwa: Journal of Women of the Middle East and the Islamic World*, 4(2–3): 151–80.

Suleri, Sara ([1989] 1991) *Meatless Days: A Memoir*, London: Flamingo.

Swindells, Julia (ed.) (1995a) *The Uses of Autobiography*. London: Taylor and Francis.

—— (1995b) 'Conclusion: Autobiography and the Politics of "The Personal"', in Swindells, *Uses*: 205–14.

—— (1995c) 'Introduction', in Swindells, *Uses*: 1–12.

Thieme, John (1984) 'Appropriating Ancestral Heirlooms: The Quest for Tradition in Derek Walcott's *Another Life*', in MacDermott, *Autobiographical*: 215–21.

Thomas, Helen (2000) *Romanticism and Slave Narrative: Transatlantic Testimonies*, Cambridge: Cambridge University Press.

Thomas, Nicholas (1994) *Colonialism's Culture: Anthropology, Travel and Government*, Cambridge: Polity.

Torres, Lourdes (1998) 'The Construction of the Self in U.S. Latina Autobiographies', in Smith and Watson, *Women*: 276–87.

Turner, Bryan (2000) 'Edward Said and the Exilic Ethic: On Being Out of Place', *Theory, Culture & Society*, 17(6): 125–9.

Ty, Eleanor (2004) *The Politics of the Visible in Asian American Narrative*, London: University of Toronto Press.

van Toorn, Penny (2000) 'Indigenous Texts and Narratives', in Elizabeth Webby (ed.) *The Cambridge Companion to Australian Literature*, Cambridge: Cambridge University Press: 19–49.

—— (2001) 'Indigenous Australian Life Writing: Tactics and Transformations', in Bain Attwood and Fiona Magowan (eds) *Telling Stories: Indigenous History and Memory in Australia and New Zealand*, Wellington, New Zealand: Bridget Williams: 1–20.

Verma, Som Prakash (2005) *Painting the Mughal Experience*, New Delhi: Oxford University Press.

Walder, Dennis (1998) *Postcolonial Literatures in English: History, Language, Theory*, Oxford: Blackwell.

Warley, Linda (1993) 'Locating the Subject of Post-colonial Autobiography', *Kunapipi*, 15 (1): 23–31.

Watson, Julia (1998) 'Unspeakable Differences: The Politics of Gender in Lesbian and Heterosexual Women's Autobiographies', in Smith and Watson, *Women*: 393–402.

Weiner, Justus Reid (1999) '"My Beautiful Old House" and Other Fabrications by Edward Said', *Commentary*, 108(2): 23–31.

Weintraub, Karl (1979) 'Autobiography and Historical Consciousness', in Broughton, *Autobiography*, vol. 1: 237–63.

West, Russell (2003) 'Uncovering Collective Crimes: Sally Morgan's *My Place* as Australian Indigenous Detective Narrative', in Dorothea Fischer-Hornung and Monika Mueller (eds) *Sleuthing Ethnicity: The Detective in Multiethnic Crime Fiction*, London: Associated Universities Press: 280–99.

White, Jerry (1981) 'Beyond Autobiography', in Samuel, *People's*: 33–42.

Whitlock, Gillian (1996) 'Introduction: Disobedient Subjects', in *Autographs: Contemporary Australian Autobiography*, St Lucia, Queensland: University of Queensland Press: ix–xxx.

—— (2000) *The Intimate Empire: Reading Women's Autobiography*, London: Cassell.

—— (2007) *Soft Weapons: Autobiography in Transit*, Chicago: University of Chicago Press.

Wiley, Michael (2005) 'Consuming Africa: Geography and Identity in Olaudah Equiano's *Interesting Narrative*', *Studies in Romanticism*, 44(2): 165–79.

Williams, Patrick and Chrisman, Laura (eds) (1993) *Colonial Discourse and Post-Colonial Theory: A Reader*, Hemel Hempstead: Harvester Wheatsheaf.

Wokler, Robert (1995) *Rousseau*, Oxford: Oxford University Press.

Wong, Hertha D. Sweet (1994) 'Plains Indian Names and "the Autobiographical Act"', in Ashley *et al.*, *Autobiography*: 212–39.

—— (1998) 'First-Person Plural: Subjectivity and Community in Native American Women's Autobiography', in Smith and Watson, *Women*: 168–78.

Wong, Sau-ling Cynthia (1998) 'Immigrant Autobiography: Some Questions of Definition and Approach', in Smith and Watson, *Women*: 299–315.

Wright, Derek (1993) *Wole Soyinka Revisited*, New York: Twayne.

Young, Robert J.C. (2001) *Postcolonialism: An Historical Introduction*, Oxford: Blackwell.

Zonana, Joyce (1996) '"I was cryin', all the people were cryin', my mother was cryin"': Aboriginality and Maternity' in Sally Morgan's *My Place*', in Elizabeth Brown-Guillory, *Women of Color: Mother–Daughter Relationships in 20th-Century Literature*, Austin, TX: University of Texas Press: 57–73.

Index